There it is again

Don Watson

There it is again

Don Watson

VINTAGE BOOKS
Australia

A Vintage Australia book
Published by Penguin Random House Australia Pty Ltd
Level 3, 100 Pacific Highway, North Sydney NSW 2060
www.penguin.com.au

First published by Vintage Australia in 2017

Addresses for the Penguin Random House group of companies can be found at global.penguinrandomhouse.com/offices.

National Library of Australia
Cataloguing-in-Publication entry

Watson, Don, 1949– author
There it is again: selected non-fiction / Don Watson

ISBN 978 0 14378 700 6 (paperback)

Watson, Don, 1949–
Essays
World politics
Australia – Politics and government
Australia – Social conditions
Australia – Social life and customs

Cover image and design by Sandy Cull, gogoGingko
Typeset in 11/16.5 Palatino LT by Midland Typesetters, Australia
Printed in Australia by Griffin Press, an accredited ISO AS/NZS 14001:2004 Environmental Management System printer

Penguin Random House Australia uses papers that are natural, renewable and recyclable products and made from wood grown in sustainable forests. The logging and manufacturing processes are expected to conform to the environmental regulations of the country of origin.

Contents

'The basis of optimism is sheer terror'
– Oscar Wilde

Rabbit Syndrome

John Updike's Rabbit quartet is on one reading a denunciation of American society as merciless and foetid as anything written about Rome or Babylon. It began in 1960 with *Rabbit Run*. Harry 'Rabbit' Angstrom, high-school basketball hero, flees one night from his pregnant 'poor dumb mutt' of a wife, Janice, his two-year-old son and their home in Brewer, Pennsylvania. He drives the dreadful highways to West Virginia; from nowhere to nowhere. But he can't quite do it, so he goes back; back to Brewer, and his old basketball coach, the egregious Tothero who introduces him to the prostitute Ruth. Ruth turns out to be just about the only person of any moral density in the whole saga (unless it is Thelma, an unloved friend's wife who loves Harry, who is dying of lupus, whom he sodomises on request, of whom he says to her husband at her funeral, 'she was a fantastic lay'.) Alas, Rabbit leaves Ruth, rising from her bed in the middle of the night when the minister (with whom he regularly plays golf) rings to tell him that Janice is in labour. Fourteen years later Janice leaves Harry for a Greek car salesman, and Harry sets up house with their son, Nelson, and an eighteen-year-old junkie whose body he shares with Skeeter, a messianic Negro. He runs the gamut of seventies decadence and Reaganite reaction. He reads, almost exclusively, *Consumer Reports*, and its verdicts form the staple of his conversation. He is a man of almost incredible crassness. His sexual obsession is inexhaustible and highly tuned. Nothing else comes close to exercising his imagination like the merest suggestion of nipples or pussy. He stops thinking of female possibility only when survival instincts compel some other thought – to sell a Toyota, watch television, eat salted peanuts or improve his golf swing. (Rabbit has a little in common with Homer Simpson.) Or to indulge in some second-hand patriotism – Pop, if you like, to the Mom of his pudenda fantasies. Rabbit is a Christian, Updike makes a point of telling us early in the first book.

But we get the feeling that Rabbit has some greatness in him. His instincts are sure, even if his thinking is not. Life and death might frighten him, but no earthly being does. His love of the female body, while obsessive, is unrestrained and marvellous in the detail of observation. He glories in it. From these reflections and others about Toyota Corollas and salted peanuts we are left in no doubt that he is both sentient and conscious. And Rabbit has an occasional intimation about death and the human condition that defies his platitudinous myopia and brainlessness and puts him well clear of the lower primates. Just now it is startling to discover in the mind of the one character the observation that, 'all in all', America just has to be the 'happiest . . . country the world has ever seen', and the thought he has at the start of the final volume that the plane arriving with his hopeless son on board portends his own demise. Open-heart surgery and angioplasty can't save Rabbit: he eats himself to death, dying on a suburban basketball court in his mid-fifties, trying to recapture youth's glories 40 pounds above a healthy weight. He could go no other way, unless it was on the golf course, or in the middle of that other addiction of the American male, a blow job.

The Rabbit books may be read in various ways – for example, as a ruthless dissection of the male psyche (Rabbit is outrageous but never less than familiar); as a satire on the human condition or modern American life; as an unsentimental but ultimately forgiving domestic portrait; as an elegy for the soul of America, torn between God and Nature, a sort of visceral proof that American commerce was, as Perry Miller said, 'conceived in the bed of religion'. Updike steps into the 'woeful putrefaction' the old Puritan preachers saw at the centre of New England life, but not to judge as they did, only to describe or to laugh or to join the general melancholy. He does not need to judge, it is enough that he sees. He sees the hollowness at the centre, the door closed to possibility. 'Your life has no reflective content,' Jill, Rabbit's eighteen-year-old lay, tells him. 'It's all instinct and when your instinct lets you down, you have nothing to trust. That's what makes you cynical. Cynicism is tired pragmatism. Pragmatism suited a certain moment here, the frontier moment, it did the work very wastefully and ruthlessly but it did it.' But it's no longer useful. 'You carry an old God with you, and an angry old patriotism,' she says. Jill burns to death in Rabbit's house while he stands outside and watches with his disintegrating twelve-year-old.

Ruth, the abandoned lover, is more direct – she calls him 'Mr Death himself. You're not just nothing, you're worse than nothing.' So Rabbit, 'a typical good-hearted, imperialist racist', his body a decaying vessel poisoned by fast food and wasted potential, his imagination dimmed by prejudice and television, running on ignorance and fear, smears with shit those few things which are pure, Ruth says, and echoes the emptiness Updike sees at the core of America.

Naturally Rabbit has been equated with Uncle Sam himself. He is coarse, philistine and provincial; he is alienated from the land, religion and history, from his children, his imagination and his potential. Like a real rabbit he lives by his appetites for sex and food, and like a real American he tries to fill the remaining space with golf, daiquiris and dreams of a house with a sunken living room: the small objects to which, if the pursuit of happiness is to mean anything and a democracy is to work, the soul clings. 'One does not see anything until one sees its beauty,' Oscar Wilde said. Poor Rabbit sees beauty only in ass or a three-pointer – and money which he associates with ass in any case. He reunites with his wife for the convenience of her father's money and a job at his Toyota agency. Taking advantage of a surge in gold prices after the Russian invasion of Afghanistan, he buys bullion, spreads it on the matrimonial bed and he and the mutt rut like rabbits in it. It's the unexamined life – worse the un*imagined* life – taken to its highest point. So it was inevitable that the Rabbit quartet would be called 'a powerful critique of America'.

It is not, of course, a critique we have to accept, any more than we are obliged to take George W. Bush as representative of the American mind. The truth could lie anywhere between the President and Gore Vidal and other perennially disenchanted American souls. Foreign critics of the United States should not kid themselves: no scorn of theirs will match what Americans say about themselves. 'If you find so much that is unworthy of reverence in the United States, then why do you live here?' H. L. Mencken asked himself. 'Why do men go to zoos?' he replied.

Nowhere else are the words 'free' and 'freedom' so pervasive. Their anthem proclaims the land of the free, and no patriotic American speech fails to mention it. And in many ways, no doubt, it is a remarkably free country. Australians make much less of the idea, taking it more for granted, perhaps because Britain for so long seemed to guarantee it. The absence of the word from our public rhetoric and popular writing, relative to America at least, may also be due in part to a first half-century when a significant proportion of the population was *not* free. Upon their emancipation, convicts in Australia calculated that it was not in their interests to draw attention to the past by singing songs of freedom, unlike black Americans who were in no position to hide the fact that they had once been slaves. Like 'The Star Spangled Banner', 'Advance Australia Fair' declares that we are free, but the observation is granted no more status than the one in the next line that the country is an island. The Americans, of course, are less 'girt by sea', but, even if they were girt entirely, it is doubtful they would feel constrained to say so in their national anthem.

It is without doubt the strangest country when it comes to politics. For all their unequivocal professions of love, the idea of freedom seems to produce in Americans a good deal of fear. In the citadel of freedom, the child of the enlightenment, the word 'liberal' now carries the same meaning as its opposite. Desperate to avoid branding, candidates for office weave and dart and burrow in all directions, for to be identified as a 'liberal' today is rather like being tagged 'communist' a generation ago. In 1996 Lewis Lapham, the liberal editor of *Harper's*, noted the publication of a book by Robert H. Bork, a Yale Law

Professor nominated by Ronald Reagan for the Supreme Court and in 1996 a regular guest on the major American talk shows. The book, called *Slouching towards Gomorrah*, was a jeremiad from one who, in his own words, 'detests modern liberalism and all its works'. For modern liberalism, read multiculturalists, radical feminists, homosexual activists, black extremists, intellectual 'nihilists' and various other categories of people consumed by hatred and 'contempt for American society'. This diatribe sounds familiar to our own ears, of course, accustomed as they now are to the abuse of 'elites', special interest groups, black armband historians, pushy blacks and chattering classes. But it is much more pungent in its American context, where it comes with slavering endorsements from the Christian Coalition and various influential right-wingers. *Slouching towards Gomorrah* quickly hit the bestseller lists. Lapham noted its resemblance to medieval millenarian tracts, with its lists of modern 'liberals' as the equivalents of tenth-century associates of Satan. Most remarkable was Bork's wish to jettison the enlightenment in which the republic was created and recreate the United States as a Puritan theocracy.

The book was published in the same week as the Taliban seized control of most of Afghanistan, an irony that Lapham did not fail to note. He doubted if the Taliban had read Bork, yet even without him, 'they seemed to know how to go about the great task of putting an end to the nonsense of liberty and equality'.

We need not accept such acerbic views of America. We can agree with any of the more favourable assessments: that it is the best society yet achieved in an imperfect world, through to the one revived in recent times casting America as the repository of Good in the war against Evil – from Homer Simpson to Ned Flanders next door if you will. Of course, just the other day those now most fervently casting it as Good were the ones saying it was sunk in Evil, and for the same people the city of the twin towers was the proof of it. New York was Gomorrah on the Hudson. But who are we to talk if American politics is full of contradictions? We vilify people fleeing from the tyranny we are fighting. Whether we think America is essentially good or positively bad does not matter in the end: it is very likely both – it contains multitudes, as Walt Whitman said of himself. What matters is that Australia exhibits negative traits of culture and personality very like those we and others see exhibited in the United States.

Perhaps Rabbit is a metaphor that Updike never intended: a distant metaphor for the soul of Australia, the country which, like Rabbit, recoils in fear from the insight that its life is its own and no one else's, and changes the angle to accommodate its fear. The country that tries but cannot leave the safety of an unsatisfying union (not the British, not the Americans) and abandons anything more challenging even when it knows that fulfilment lies there. Whose imagination works only in fits and starts, flutters into life under the impulse of certain stimuli and then settles back into the familiar and second-hand. That, if recent indications can be trusted, is losing the capacity that Rabbit wonders at in women – the 'strange way they have . . . of really caring about somebody beyond themselves'. The country that declares itself the luckiest and best on earth and listens avidly to shock jocks abusing anyone who suggests otherwise while all the time telling us how bad it is; whose appetite for crap is bottomless; that talks high principles but values pragmatism and practises unqualified self-interest; substitutes platitudes for wisdom; suffers the same Protestant curse but without the fires of hell to warm it. That seeks shelter beneath those American bombers and just now shows every sign that it will find its definition there: huddling rabbit-like, never venturing too far from the burrow.

Quarterly Essay, 2001

The Public Language

English is an accommodating language. What with the Normans, the colonies, the Industrial Revolution, the information revolution, the New English Bible, globalism, multiculturalism, it grows from umpteen roots and is forever changing – or 'going pear-shaped' to use the current expression. There are also the Americans who went out on their own somewhat – and, according to Dr Johnson, infected English with a 'tract of corruption'. They created their own rhetorical tradition and made English, like much else they contacted including entire peoples, peculiarly reflections of themselves. 'England and America are two countries separated by a common language,' George Bernard Shaw is supposed to have said. And when we hear George W. Bush and Tony Blair we know how accurate that observation was.

But the long view suggests it is best not to worry too much. We might as well admonish Shakespeare for adding hundreds of new words when he found the language could not support his literary ambitions. Appalled by the 'decay' of English Johnson compiled a dictionary that he hoped might make words 'permanent like the things they denote'. His dictionary was marvellous but his hope was vain.

Pronunciation and meaning have shifted as often as the words themselves. In the last quarter of the 18th century, just as New South Wales was founded, Britain's new wealthy decided they could put a social gap between themselves and those on whom they sat by establishing new rules of pronunciation and vocabulary. To choose one from hundreds of other consequences of this enterprise, *vermin* became the word by which rats and other unwholesome creatures would be known in England (and Sydney). Across the Atlantic, the good folks having recently decided they didn't hold with English ways, they stuck with *varmints* – and *varmints* they have hunted to this day.

As a child Samuel Lysons was taught, like all the Lysons before him, to mute the 'h' in *humble, hospital* and *herbs*. But in the 1860s in *The Vulgar Tongue* he complained that now he was expected to pronounce the 'h' in these words and mute it in others where for centuries it had been audible. You can hardly blame him for grizzling: or Henry Parkes and others of his generation who never figured out the formula for 'h's.

Samuel Johnson's curmudgeonly descendants still lurk in the letters page of our newspapers, waiting to smite any author of a split infinitive or unfamiliar word or phrase. This year, in a couple of letters clogged with rage, I was savaged for using the words *methodology* and *historiography* – though in keeping with Johnson's dictum they denoted accurately what I meant and, with almost three centuries' residence in English dictionaries between them, have a reasonable claim to permanence. The pedants should be writing to the ABC to tell them not to say the Prime Minister 'has refuted allegations'. But even when they're right these people miss the point. We could spend every waking hour fuming about the misused words, misplaced apostrophes, misquoted homilies and epithets. This week I heard a politician say that he liked 'to get up the goat' of his opponent. Flying home I heard the same usage satirised in an episode of *Kath and Kim*. Who knows who came first? Many Australians under 40 speak with the same rising inflection we hear in our soap operas. It excruciates the rest of us who learned from our forebears only the laconic descending mumble, and the new style is worse for being joined to Americanisms. A majority of the young prefer *butt* to *bum*, and more and more kick *ass* instead of *arse*. Children and teenagers tell me that the supermarket is *on* Smith Street when I have always thought it was *in* it. If I object they say there's no need to holler at them. They ask like the Americans, 'Are you done?' when they want to know if I have finished my tea. I wait nervously for the day when a granddaughter takes my glass and tells me she doesn't hold with drinking. But it is important to try not to care too much.

Education will be useful but it won't hold back the tide. Imitation is much the stronger element for the very good reason illustrated by the parrot, that imitation is linked to survival.

Imagine you are a parrot in the White House, or within earshot – and who is not? We have to cope with this:

> And if the values are good enough for our people they ought to be good enough for others, not in a way to impose because these are God-given values. These aren't United States-created values. These are values of freedom and the human condition and mothers loving their children.

The President's words are at once startling and confounding, and it's possible that the President was startled and confounded as he said them. It is as if by the imperfect power of speech he has inadvertently strayed into self-analysis and discovered all the contradictions of the American mind in the one afternoon. The Monroe Doctrine is in there in embryonic form, the traditional ambivalence about the imperial mission, the vision thing, the mother thing – and above all the thing about one indivisible republic under God. President Bush finds himself attempting to unravel a central strand in American orthodoxy – the strand of Providence, the belief that America is governed through God, and that God-given values and United States-created values are the same. And, it stands to reason, values don't come any better than this – people ought to be grateful for chrissakes.

Naturally it's the President's prose not the strand that comes apart.

Who knows what side of the American equation George W. Bush comes down on: Jeffersonian secularism or the theocratic strain. It is possible he does not know himself. John Ashcroft, his Attorney General, knows however. We need look no further than his rendition of his own song 'Let the Eagle Soar'.[1] No rational person can hear this without wondering a) how he became Attorney General; b) if we are not in even greater danger than we thought; c) why the faithful always think that singing helps; and d) if belief in God can only be maintained at fundamentalist pitch by a sort of Promethean urge to set something *against* God, by way of proving His power, or perhaps just a need for Him.

The President's reflections on matters pertaining to power offer little enlightenment or comfort – but because we do not want to be excluded and think survival depends on imitation, we can be sure that something like them will be parroted in Canberra. The question is, can we do it and keep our dignity?

'Confident action that will yield positive results,' President Bush says, 'provides a kind of slipstream into which reluctant nations and leaders can get behind and show themselves that there has been something, you know, something positive has happened toward peace.'

It must be possible to fight international terrorism and tyranny and still keep a halfway decent grip on the language. It might even be necessary.

We tried hard but dropped off along with the rest of the world – Tony Blair apart – when the President talked about an 'axis of evil'. There was first the logical problem that the three countries said to form the axis are not connected in any way that constitutes an axis; at least not as described by any of the seven definitions of *axis* in the *American Heritage Dictionary*. What the phrase has instead of anything remotely like logic or truth is a cultural ring to it, an echo of the good old days; it sounds like the sort of thing a man should go after with a gun. A varmint in other words, or rather three of them – and who can say if in some future edition of the *AHD three or more varmints randomly arranged* will not be an eighth definition of *axis*.

Perhaps that is why the axis of evil sounded splendid to conservative America and barmy to just about everyone else. Most people might accept 'evil' as apt enough when we speak about Saddam or North Korea or September 11 or the former Soviet 'empire', notwithstanding the obvious objection that it is a very select list in a very naughty world. But the axis of evil was just too American: too much like a sounding of its own depths, wherein lie witches, masked men with shotguns, evil angels and angels of the elect.[2] Words have that power.

In David Ireland's novel *The Glass Canoe*, a sociologist ponders a footballer in his local pub, and asks how an inarticulate brute whose ordinary powers of thought are barely adequate to his own survival can display on a rugby field the mental agility of a genius. How can he at full tilt anticipate in an instant not just the first reactions of his opponents but the second and the third, a whole sequence of them, and compute in that instant the strategy that will leave them looking like fools? It's a conundrum of the same order as one attributed to Orson Welles when he addressed a small audience somewhere in America: after outlining his accomplishments he is supposed to have said, 'Strange isn't it – how many of me and how few of you?' Why can Marcel Proust write a sentence of several hundred words that readers remember for the rest of their lives, yet a corporate or political leader writing of something more important than a madeleine or a pot of asparagus-scented urine finds himself immediately, as Thomas Hobbes put it, 'entangled in words, as a bird in lime-twigs; the more he struggles, the more belimed'.

Why is it, for instance, that for style, sentiment and truth, nothing our leaders have said about death in the last death-filled 18 months has approached 'It comes equally to us all, and makes us all equal when it comes?' It seems as fit now as it was when it was written 400 years ago. Why have people who claim they owe so much to him taken grandiosity from Lincoln's language, but not the power in it? Put aside the political reflections and all the other wonders of the Gettysburg Address: he says, 'The brave men, living and dead, who struggled here . . .' Read it aloud. It's the 'struggled' that strikes the nerve-ends. It's a familiar word, hackneyed in some contexts but visceral in this one. Imagine if he had said 'fought', 'clashed', 'risked their lives', 'paid the ultimate price', 'demonstrated their commitment'. Lincoln must have wanted a word to say that it was terrible, terribly human. Not a memorable word, but a word that would make the thing it denoted memorable – for, as he says a moment later, the world will not 'long remember what we say here, but it can never forget what they did here'.

All verbs have inherent force. A well-chosen one like Lincoln's can be extraordinarily powerful. We don't hear verbs much these days. They try to master or inspire us with clichés, catchphrases and commitment to everything that to their tin ears sounds great. We don't understand or even hear them properly. We don't care – partly because their words anaesthetise us, partly because like parrots we're interested mainly in the gesture and not the meaning.

Fifty years ago Orwell and Spender among others noted how the language of communism dulled the senses of its adherents and hid the lies. Spender remembered the way in which good citizens were exhorted to have 'certain socially useful qualities: industry, hatred, perhaps purity . . . in a word those which made for the utmost devotion to the cause. One did not need charity, pity, tolerance, humility, truth, personal loyalty. Now in the private sector words like 'commitment' and 'accountability' are the watchwords for staff devotion to the cause, and they have been substituted for precisely the same qualities Spender noticed missing in communism. The words vanish with the things they signify – 'wisdom', 'decency', 'civility': you will not find them in a corporate document of any kind. They're as rare as verbs. In the same way companies (and political parties) talk of their 'strategic initiatives' and 'key values' to the absolute exclusion of 'imagination', 'foresight', 'gumption', 'belief'. These words have all but gone from the language of commerce, politics and the public service.

Of course it is beyond our leaders to write like John Donne or Abraham Lincoln, and we should hope fervently that they don't try. But that is no reason not to call on the language, which is no different to saying the lessons recorded in the culture, in life. We don't because in public life the language has never been held in less regard – not in Donne's time, Johnson's, Lincoln's or George Orwell's. It withers in the dungeons of the techno-cratic mind. It has no place in the media. In politics it lacks all qualifications for the main game. Instead we get 'a commitment to ensuring the ongoing viability' of parrot droppings.

Lincoln is not the only example of a politician with a feel for language. President Grant fought in two wars, the Mexican and the Civil War. Out of the first, the US, with the imperial throttle wide open, acquired Texas. In his *Personal Memoirs* Grant condemned both the annexation and the war. The army he commanded won the Civil War for the Union. But he believed the war could have been avoided if the 'poor white trash' of the South, with no interest in slavery and nothing to gain from secession, had not been incited into fighting by that class who did have interests and felt they had 'a sort of divine right to control public affairs'. Grant was much more than soldier: his powers of reasoning and language were equally impressive. His description of the way he went about his *Memoirs* was remark-ably like Hobbes' first principle of speech – 'to transferre our Mentall Discourse, into Verbal: or the Trayne of our Thoughts, into a Trayne of Words'. Grant's trains led him to the conclusion that there would have been no secession (and no war) 'if there had been a fair and calm expression of opinion, unbiased by threats, and if the ballot of one legal voter had counted for as much as that of any other. But there was no calm discussion of the question.'

Today's war party might have a case as strong as Grant's, but perhaps we should wait until they can put it into words like his before we are persuaded.

The Bulletin, 2002

From *Recollections of a Bleeding Heart*

A political adviser is a kind of funnel and should be wide at one end and narrow at the other. The wide end is to take in information from every imaginable source, the narrow end to fit snugly in the Prime Minister's ear. The wide end is permanently open to the media, the public service, the polls, other ministers and their staff, the caucus, the party secretariat and the rank and file, wives and friends, eccentrics, critics, lobbies, political geniuses and idiots alike. The narrow end discharges the decoction when it is all boiled down – one droplet at a time for preference, so he can quietly absorb it. It is a sure sign of the novice that he sprays his advice all over the place. Inside the funnel, of course, there must be a filter.

Presumably no two Prime Ministers' offices are the same, but vary according to the personalities which inhabit them, particularly the personality of the Prime Minister. Ours always had a large if not defining element of chaos about it: 'organised chaos' or 'creative chaos', Don Russell used to call it, but often it was just chaos or even 'hopeless chaos'. I imagine offices also vary according to the nature and the state of the government. Paul Keating's government was almost always under siege or on the verge of it; and for better or worse, Paul Keating defined how the government travelled. From where I sat he *was* the government – or sometimes *we* were. It was not that anyone thought the PMO had an absolute monopoly on wisdom. In fact much that was attempted or done was driven by or drawn down from the perceptions and advice of people outside. But it remains true that the leader has to lead and can't if he listens to every voice he hears. It is also true that those who complained most loudly that Keating and his office did not listen to outsiders were least often seen and never heard and their complaints came second-hand.

We were cut off, without question. It was like a clam opening and closing according to some unseen stimulus – aggression, fear, the need to breathe. Working in a burrow made tunnel vision almost a condition of the job. It did not mean, necessarily, that you did not hear or see what was going on outside; rather that your focus had to be intense. It was less than an ideal state for everyone, inside or outside. When it was over I wondered if it had been a form of madness. But I don't know if there was any choice. Whatever we imagine ourselves to be, advisers – and this I became – are effectively in service, like footmen, bodyguards, astrologers and jesters, and they can serve no one else or any other cause or interest. It simply will not work any other way.

After a while you didn't have to look to know what was going on. You could sense urgency, panic, elation without turning your head or moving from your chair. Your brain became connected to that corridor and the corridor was connected to other brains and the sounds of voices, doors opening and closing, padding feet and other intangible signals told you the temper of the place without interruption to your work. Silence was welcome, though there never was true silence. The computers buzzed, the phones rang incessantly and a clutch of personal assistants answered them. The PAs were assembled at a point where the burrow opened out, before turning past pigeonholes and on into the media office. Day and night, amid myriad other essential tasks, they typed away and took phone calls from everyone in the country who had a whinge. It was a clearing house for the culture of complaint. Some of the callers were cranks and some were visionaries and many of them were regulars. The Hewett brothers, Hal and Don, who had grapes and avocados in Sunraysia, were visionaries but rang so regularly they were sometimes mistaken for cranks. The most persistent or annoying of these callers the PAs put on 'hands free' and continued typing while offering a polite word every now and then, and you could hear the voices of the lonely, the furious and the inspired rattling away when you passed.

After a year or so I settled in a room adjacent to the big bend in the burrow where it swept around towards the PM's front doors. This billabong-like position combined a small disadvantage with a large advantage. The disadvantage was that people often gathered noisily outside, as flotsam does in river bends. It was, however, the only office which allowed me to keep a watch on the PM's doors and an ear on the principal adviser's. It was the place nearest to the pulse. Not that I needed to know everything, but something about the job made *wanting* to know inescapable. It was important to know roughly his whereabouts, his company and his mood. I knew either by their voices or by the sound of the door being closed so their voices could not be heard. I knew who the principal adviser was talking to and when the PM had entered by the new door which connected their offices. I knew by the movement of

Mark Ryan and Greg Turnbull when something was breaking or threatening with the media. After a while I didn't have to listen to hear it, any more than I had to listen for the sound of the shredder through the wall after Question Time. You would hear him on the TV monitor moving that further questions be put on the notice paper, and five minutes later the thing would whirr away as he shredded his notes. I can still hear it now.

Time was punctuated by TV stings and reality defined by what the news said reality had been in the preceding hour, or day or week, and what, as a consequence of this, it was likely to be in the foreseeable future. Between real and recorded time there was never more than a thin transparent membrane. It might feel like an illusion one moment, the next like hyper-reality – and why wouldn't it feel like that in a place where truth was processed? We waded through information: none of it, excepting that in our collective memory, with a provenance of more than a week. It came as newspapers, whole or in clippings from all over the country; from the NMLS (the National Media Liaison Service, known as 'animals') daily media summaries of what the shock-jocks, talkback callers and political gurus were saying. It came from people who never stopped phoning or faxing. It came from the press gallery which our media advisers regularly roved to see what the journalists thought the story was, and if it was the wrong story they pointed them towards the right one and hoped it made a difference to the news. Every day began and ended with the news, and weeks ended with the Saturday columns, especially Ramsey's in *The Sydney Morning Herald*. Many half-days were ruled at either end by news, many hours began one way and ended another with the news. Time existed for the news. The news decided the shape of your day – what you would think, how you would feel, what you would do.

It was addictive and exhausting: addictive because it was the fastest gratification to be had – what you say at 10.45 is news at 11; or even better it obliges your enemies at 11.15 to say something other than what they intended to say, perhaps something you didn't want said. It was exhausting because you lost as often as you won and the gratification of success was about as sustaining as a jelly bean. And yet this was LIFE.

Daily life in the PMO was a truth contest. All day long truth was asserted, denied, demolished, reasserted. And there wasn't a book in the place.

2002

Oscar and the ALP

Oscar Wilde never had much clout in Australian politics. Paul Keating had a soft spot for him, but many of his old colleagues would think this typically contrary of their former leader, and consistent with his wilful lack of interest in team games and the American Civil War. It is true that Wilde was a bit of a dandy and as unsuited to the Australian political climate as he was to Reading Gaol. Yet so long as he is not taken literally (seriously, yes, but *never* literally), there are rousing thoughts in Wilde for people who imagine more humane and honourable societies.

Labor will resist of course. Australian Labor was born pragmatic and 'sans doctrines'. No theorists, including Marx, ever got a grip on it. Likewise revolutionaries and martyrs, foreign or domestic: Labor never fell for them. If the term 'socialist' ever described the party, it always meant different things to different parts of it. 'Democratic socialist' or 'social democratic' have been picked up from time to time, but soon put down again; probably because they smell of Europe, doctrine and theorising. They are all there, or have been at different times; but all of them combined have had probably less influence than the orthodoxies of Jesus Christ and J. M. Keynes.

Labor's deepest instincts are gradualist and its affections patriotic. The party has housed radicals and mavericks and had periodic hot romantic flushes, but it was born at the same time and under the same utilitarian star as the country itself.

So what sort of party is it? It's a *Labor* party, the political or parliamentary wing of the labour *movement*. And it's an *Australian* Labor Party, which means it's a federal creature and as sentimental about the nation as it is about the workers. It's the ALP: a broad church or extended family in which ideals of improvement, fellowship and philanthropy live in perpetual struggle with personal ambition and factions and hatreds of almost Balkan depth and mystery.

The national dimension of ALP ideology is something its critics too often forget. From the beginning, the party joined social improvement with nation-building and national security, and it remains an unshakeable fact of its existence. The balance is essential to political success, and so is the inspiration that each side provides. By the time Bob Hawke's race was run, critical sections of the electorate had come to despise, perhaps even more than economic rationalism and its arcane pitiless language, the sanctimony with which the politically correct commended Labor's social policies, as if all moral virtue and political possibility existed in 'access and equity' or 'rich multicultural diversity'.

As Prime Minister, Paul Keating's 'nation-building' economics, independent foreign policy and republican push helped to loosen at least their rhetorical grip and restore the balance of the party. He did the national thing and the 'helping hand' thing in pretty well equal measure. And for two or three years it succeeded.

There was something of the same divide in Labor's recent hideous leadership contest. Beneath Beazley's 'I can beat

John Howard' mantra was the national security ticket, while Simon Crean recited social policy as if he'd been expressly told to go out there and drive us mad – what Australians are really interested in is health, education and saving the Murray. As usual both of them were telling us what the people wanted. As usual they did not tell us in any persuasive or even vaguely interesting way what they believed.

All who aspire to the leadership these days have at least one belief, and they have it in common. They believe in the polling. They draw different inferences, but they believe in it as passionately as they believe in anything in the world. They believe in staying on the message that the polls determine. And all seem to have decided in the present affluence that, be it ever so myopic, misinformed, prejudiced or disagreeable sometimes, what the people take to be self-interest must in no way be offended.

Imagining half-mistakenly that socialism might bring about similar material conditions, Wilde asked what would happen to the human soul when folk were secure and pain and necessity no longer governed human life.

It was a good question for socialists then and, since free markets delivered about three-fifths of the deal that socialism failed to, it remains a good question for Labor now. On the face of it, Wilde's answer was much more like a neo-liberal's than an old socialist's: he saw the prospect of universal personal security as an opportunity for unprecedented individual expression and fulfilment.

But before our local Tories rush to get him on their think tank, Wilde was a neo-Hellenist, which is a very different thing to a neo-conservative or a neo-liberal. Wilde was for art. For pleasure. He loathed virtually everything that neocons love or depend on, including the state (and let no one tell you that neocons don't love state power), the media, public opinion, sentimentality and the 'sickly cant of duty'. For old Oscar it was not a question of what human beings can have, but of what they can be. It wasn't about security, but boundless possibility.

Forget for now that the present affluence might not be as extensive or as permanent as it looks, or that personal security is not for everyone another word for happiness. Wilde warned about the tyranny of the people, which he said was as brutal as the tyranny of Popes and Princes. The tyranny, of course, is exercised over themselves; or, rather, over their potential as individuals. 'They have marred themselves by imitation of their superiors,' he said. He imagined the state and the press as the agents of this tyranny. He knew from brutal personal experience that, combined with public opinion, they could destroy anyone who broke the rules. He did *not* know about opinion polls and focus groups.

He was an innocent in politics, but certain depressing themes in the history of the 20th century suggest that Wilde's analysis was pretty right. It is a pity that more old socialists didn't listen. And modern Labor could do worse than listen now.

It must be gratifying to echo the people's voice as your focus groups define it. The tactic might encourage you to think that in this way you make yourself a servant of the people's will; a blessed state because it feels both honourable and savvy. But in so far as this 'will' is defined by polls, and polls are much influenced by interpretations of events that are substantially those of the government and the media, and not influenced by any creed of your own because you have substituted polls for original thought, just whose 'will' are you obeying? A loose reading of the Wildean argument would tell us that, far from acting in the people's interest or their own, Labor's poll-driven politics connives in the oppression of both.

If Labor fancies that through obedience to polls it is less the servant and more the *incarnation* of this confected general will, much the same applies: it has only joined the people in 'imitating their superiors', which is to say those who wield power over the people, including the government and its most influential thinkers and supporters. With this strategy, Labor imitates those whose great effort in life is to oppose them in every way they can.

We citizens are obliged to ask much the same question about 'the people' that Wilde asked. He asked, 'Who told them to exercise authority?' We might add, 'Who are they, that they should have authority over the rest of us?' Their authority might not be 'blind, deaf, hideous, grotesque, tragic, amusing, serious and obscene', as Wilde said it was: but 'narrow, short-sighted, uninformed and actually hostile to the public and national interest' are all possible. It might be prejudiced or mad. For all we know these people might be the type who would put Oscar Wilde in gaol, or children behind razor wire at Woomera.

'They called up the street and the street despatched them,' Max Weber said about the German revolutionaries, Karl Liebknecht and Rosa Luxemburg after they were murdered. We might wonder if there are not post-modern equivalents. Of course you can't ignore the polls, but if you make yourself their dummy you will look at best characterless and silly, at worst downright craven. In your earnest demonstrations of respect for the people and their wishes, they see a lack of self-respect. You bring yourself into contempt. You will be despatched.

Here is Wilde again. 'But the past is of no importance. The present is of no importance. It is with the future that we have to deal. For the past is what man should not have been. The present is what man ought not to be.' The future, he says, is 'what artists are', a notion that will not recommend itself to any political party. But Labor must try not to be pedantic. It really must. Wilde means that an affluent future contains an opportunity for happiness. To 'think anew', Lincoln used to say. It is the possibilities we need to dwell on; even the possibility of changing human nature. Wilde says that the only thing we really know about human nature is that it changes.

Labor needs to think this way. Perhaps a 'change' in human nature is stretching things, but it has to play to the better side of it. Kim Beazley was perfectly Wildean last election night when he talked about the better angels of our nature. So why, every other day in the election cycle, bury it like a bone on the dark side? One day you won't be able to find it.

More than a plan or a strategy or a tactic, Labor needs a philosophy. Nothing comprehensive: just a few sentences that reveal what it thinks about the way things are. Calwell did it in 1965 when he declared against the war in Vietnam. He lost the election but that decision helped set Labor up for years. Whitlam did it when he talked about national possibilities in 1972. Hawke did it when he talked about summits and accords in the interests of national reconciliation. 'Speech maketh a man,' Ben Jonson said: 'Speak that I may see you.' Labor needs to speak.

The difference between Labor and its opponents has always consisted in this. The successful conservatives like Menzies – and now Howard – spoke to a philosophy. So did Deakin in his prime. Curtin, Chifley, Whitlam, Hawke and Keating spoke in the same way for Labor, though with each the terms were different. The two who won elections from Opposition, Whitlam and Hawke, both embodied a set of ideas about the future of Australia. They had words for thought and belief. And through those words they revealed a bit of what someone noticed in Abraham Lincoln some years before the Civil War: 'a vein of sentiment', he called it, and he thought it might take Lincoln a long way in public life. Joined to astute reading of public opinion, it did.

For seven years Labor has read public opinion and lost the vein of sentiment. It has not had the words. Few outside the party and not so many in it could tell you what it is they think. They seem to think only what they think the people think. In all this recycled focus-group opinion, people who have had a passion for Labor all their life no longer see in it any of their own sentiments and beliefs. It is not just the more notorious compromises, or the disaster of Knowledge Nation, or the gruesome leadership struggle. What hurts more is that while Labor has been picking its way through the polls, Australia has become a different place.

This is the radical consequence of poll-driven politics. You lack definition. You say: I have a plan. I have a policy. I have what Australians want. You don't say what you hold to, but instead offer your take on what your audience holds to. You don't define your intellectual position, even though it means next time you tell them what you intend to do they'll know *why*. They need that much to believe you.

Oscar Wilde can no more give him the words for that than he can give him the policies; but Wilde sounds a lot more modern than Labor has sounded for years. He talks about individualism *and* unselfishness; a love of tolerance and a loathing of cant and sentimentality; sympathy with suffering and an even greater sympathy with happiness; delight in the social, and hatred of arbitrary authority. He talks about defining yourself by your future.

This last is a very good idea for Australia. It ought to be Labor's idea, and until quite recently it was. But they are *all* good starting points, especially if taken together with the recommendation that any plans should ignore existing conditions – because 'it is exactly the existing conditions that one objects to'.

A weekend retreat in this frame of mind might have a marvellous cleansing effect. It might oblige Federal Labor to see that in pursuit of the existing mean average Australian reality – the battling, aspirational, non-chattering, family Australian – it has become a rarefied almost-unrecognisable extension of it, as a garden gnome is to a suburban garden. A highly professional gnome, no doubt, but just as inarticulate and inspiring only to a few. And this is not the worst of it: the worst of it is that Labor only *looks* like the gnome and is judged to be the gnome, while the real gnomes look like the government.

I went to a lot of ALP functions last year, in every state. At one of them in northern New South Wales, a man who was not a member of any chattering class asked rhetorically: isn't it true that if Kim Beazley had confronted Howard more forcefully over the refugees he would still have lost but he would also still be leader and people would be joining the party not leaving it? The room applauded. I don't know if the man's inferences were right, but every time I repeated his question at other ALP gatherings, it was greeted in the same way. Without exception.

Perhaps they were *all Wildeans*. They didn't look like it. And they didn't look like they were about to abandon the country to its enemies. They seemed like typically Labor people: more typical and just as patriotic as many of the people who compose its public face. No doubt they hadn't been shown the polling. But had they been, I suspect they would have said: What would you have us follow – what we believe or what these other people believe? If those meetings were anything to go by, the irony was positively thunderous: in trying to connect with some abstract representation of the people's will, Labor had stopped connecting with itself. What could be less utilitarian? You want to plug in, but you're not a plug anymore. You're just a wish.

It won't help to argue about the decision to give way to vicious, and viciously manipulated, public opinion in the last election campaign. In letting go of their initial 'principled' stand, Labor only continued the strategy of 'finessing' their way back to power. It would be nonetheless unwise to fool themselves that no choice existed, or that they were the first to suffer such savage opprobrium. Evatt got at least as bad for opposing the bill to ban the Communist Party, and Calwell was treated no better over Vietnam. They paid a political price: but Hawke was paid a dividend for refusing to compromise on Asian immigration; Keating won an election with the republic, reconciliation and an explicitly social democratic program on full show, and Kennett was not punished for telling Pauline Hanson that she was not welcome in Victoria.

Virtue is optional and not its own reward: but it does help with definition. Labor might start defining itself by declaring itself once and forever unequivocally opposed to the present policy on refugees from dictatorships. It might call itself what essentially it must be to win by means other than default, a social democratic party. It could declare that it will relentlessly oppose the drift to vassalage, with or without a deputy's badge. It can do any, all, or none of these things, but it must say what it thinks about the country. This is what a national party does.

If an Irish genius shines no light for them, perhaps a French one will. Alexis de Tocqueville visited the United States in one of those times when 'societies come to rest and the human race seems to draw breath'. It was a good time for small parties, not great parties.

And what was a great party? 'What I term great political parties,' he wrote, 'are those committed to principles rather than their consequences, to general considerations rather than to individual cases, to ideas and not to men. These parties generally have more noble characteristics, more generous enthusiasms, more genuine convictions, a more open and bold approach than the others.'

That is not all Tocqueville says about great parties, but it is all Labor needs to remember. Labor cannot be a small party. If it is not a great party, it is not a party at all.

The Bulletin, 2003

National Trust Heritage Lecture

I have a waking dream, more of a nightmare when I'm doing mundane things like sleeping or listening to a speech or standing in a lift or opening a can of tuna. I'm in a nursing home – a patient, or rather a *customer*. I'm sitting there with a rug on my lap and some fading entertainer is trying to cheer us oldies up by singing 'I Still Call Australia Home'. And we are all expected to sing along. And everyone is singing except me. I'm convulsed with the most profound misery, a weeping refusenik – which only makes them look at me with more sickening sympathy, and sing more loudly. I can't tell them that I hate the bloody song, and I can't believe this is how life in Australia ends. With this empty dirge. I'd rather sing 'God Save The Queen'. Anything but the Qantas advertisement.

It's an elitist view, I suppose: as Tony Abbott or Paul Sheehan or Keith Windschuttle or Richard Alston or Geoffrey Blainey – there are so many of them – would say. They'd say these are the views of someone who hates his country, his fellow Australians and mateship. And they would say that very likely he is anti-American as well – because anyone base enough to hate his own country and the principles of mateship is bound to hate America.

My second nightmare is that somewhere on the balcony of an inner-city apartment, a young man is saying to his partner as the sun sets over the harbour, 'It would enhance our BBQs going forward, Jennifer, if you would more proactively oversight the chops.' And the children – if there are any children – are listening. Or perhaps there are no children, and she replies, 'In terms of value adding, do you think we should have a baby or a miniature Schnauzer?'

This also is elitist, I suppose.

Around the time of the Paris Commune, Flaubert wrote a letter to George Sand in which he said that he had become aware that all his life he'd been indignant. He was indignant in his marrow. Indignation held him up and drove him along, he said.

His indignation just then was understandable. He couldn't stand the philistine middle classes and the idea of a philistine *and stupid* working class replacing them was too horrid to think about. But Flaubert's protest was more than indignation: or rather I'd suggest a definition that takes in more than annoyance or pique. Let's say indignation is a hopeless entanglement of thought and feeling, of mind and emotion – it is when we feel displaced by someone or something: unable to recognise what was once familiar, or the authority of those who are telling us what to do. Old people and children – and those who never grow up – particularly suffer from it. It is like coming home and finding all your furniture has been rearranged and a stranger is lying on the couch. Like being a rat in a maze, and all around it men in white coats are watching. Or, if not a rat, an old man in a nursing home and the men in white coats are trying to make him sing that song.

Indignation is a close relative of despair, longing and confusion. It's one of the emotions brought on by feeling that you don't have a home – you are not *at* home, you are not easy where you are, you are not competent.

'Home' is a very potent idea. All those warriors in 'The Iliad' cut down; in every case the sadness is they will never see home again. Ulysses trying to get home. Penelope waiting at home, protecting her honour, which is, after all, home. 'Man goeth to his long home, and mourners go about the streets.' I know a man with Alzheimer's disease who every evening when the sun sets becomes convinced that this place where he has lived for 50 years is not his home, that he must *go* home. It goes on all night until he falls asleep. His mental confusion, his discombobulation takes the form of homelessness. It's as if he knows that he 'goeth to his long home'.

I confess to feeling a sense of homelessness – of bamboozlement. I feel 'exiled at home'. This is not uncommon in Australia, especially among writers and artists. But it's just as true of those people who supported Pauline Hanson a few years ago. They fought back – as anyone who feels exiled at home has a right to. The Prime Minister and his various spokesmen would doubtless say if you don't like it, clear out. If there were enough of us they might come up with a Pacific Solution. But I don't want to go. As Henry Lawson said a hundred years ago – I know no other land.

So what's different about it?

Around the time of the Second World War, Simone Weil asked herself what sort of society would develop when economic necessity ceased to be the dominant force in ordinary life. Weil thought that some form of socialism was likely to bring this about. In fact a lot of free market and just a little bit of socialism seems to have done the trick, at least for a fair proportion of the population. Weil answered her question by saying that, freed of the necessity to put food on the table, people would retreat to a world of the emotions. She didn't want to live in such a society. She said there could be no good society where there is no life of the mind as well as the emotions.

That seems to me to broadly describe the society now emerging in Australia. We thrive on celebrity and the emotions of celebrities; on public grieving; on reality television; on all the varieties of narcissism that anyone ever thought of. It's very like confirmation of what Tocqueville said when he was in America: that in 'democratic communities, imagination is compressed when men think of themselves; it expands indefinitely when they think of the state'.

This, by the way, is not a socialist argument. It might help to explain what sort of argument it is if I tell you what home used to be. I grew up on a farm of 140 acres; steep hills infested with bracken, rabbits, blackberries, thistles and cows. With the aid of subsidies, 40 cows raised four children. There were about 20 farms and families like this stretched along a six-mile road. A state education system enabled a large proportion of the children to matriculate; in every case they were the first in their families to do so.

We all thought that this was progress: that the natural trajectory of Australian society was towards better and better education, more opportunities and more prosperity for all. If anybody had told us that the state education system would decline relative to the private one, we wouldn't have believed them. If anybody had said that the schools we went to would be worse not better in 30 years' time, we would have taken it as a sign of madness.

We were monarchists, loyal to Britain and the ABC. We depended on the ABC: for stock-market reports, weather reports, news – especially national and international news – for comedy, for music, for the essential sense of nationhood, for knowing that we lived together on this continent with other Australians. Believe it or not, we depended on the ABC for *culture* – that is to say, for ideas, comforts and the sense that our lives had a wider meaning than the cows, the family and, perhaps, the Church.

If anybody had told us that 40 years later the ABC would be under almost perpetual attack and always fighting to justify its role in Australia, we would have said they were mad too.

Now, if you take these things away – I mean if you shrink the public sector; not only shrink it, but consistently deny the validity of the public realm, as if it has no future – then you have to expect a certain amount of shock. Not for a moment would I dare suggest that the economic reforms of the 1980s were anything but necessary and generally for the good. But something in my sense of home makes me resist the calumny heaped on public enterprise, and the dogma that nothing good ever came or will ever come again from the public realm.

On the face of it, it seems to me ludicrous to think that you can apply to this country the same free-market dictates as America applies without thinking seriously about the possibility of incorporation into that union. It's hard to imagine that mateship is enough to string the country on – with or without a Free Trade Agreement. There is a law of uneven development hiding in there somewhere. Not only do we lack America's power, America's GDP and America's military might, there is a sense in which we lack their historical and intellectual development. The Americans have been examining their intellectual origins for decades. The American film industry has looked at the American frontier in a dozen different ways. Whole genres of film have grown up around their cities, their farms, their crime, their notions of family and religion, their ethnic groups, their history and their ambitions. It is not just that the American entertainment industry is so vast and so predatory; it is that their industry is so highly developed and so central to their culture. An Australian industry cannot hope to survive in the face of it. Not at least without some public determination to *see* that it survives. But all the time a little voice says, why resist when rolling over is all 'upside', and meets all the requirements of the doctrine of pragmatism by which we now live.

Our alliance with the United States is almost as old as I am and for that reason I should feel at home with it. But I don't. Foolishly it turns out, I imagined that Australia's natural tendency – as if there is any such thing – was towards a more independent foreign policy, an independent posture in the world. I am not uncomfortable with the alliance, but surely there are other Australians who feel like me that there is something unhealthy and demeaning about the relationship as it now exists. Does it mean that we do business with the Americans regardless of who is in the White House, whatever ideology or interest may be driving them, even if lunacy overtakes them – even if our own interests are different, in even the most subtle ways? That's what a deputy does.

It seems to me a puny return on a hundred years of nationhood – to be a deputy. Like singing that song at the end of a lifetime. It seems to me more honourable to be a state.

So this leaves me feeling not at home and feeds my indignation.

Here's something else: it must be taken as given that this is a country where people can and do invent themselves, and for that astonishing privilege we pay a price in tradition, permanence and respect for the intangible, impractical and profitless world of ideas. The price of our freedom is a little philistinism and a lot of pragmatism. This has always been the way in New World societies, including this one. Of the two of three great ideas that moved Australia, the idea of the 'fair go' is perhaps the strongest and the one with the longest provenance. 'That better country', it was sometimes called in the 19th century; or 'the land of the better chance'. The generalisation does not hold in every instance of course, but where America has tended towards the ideal of individualism, the Australian ideal has been more collective. We thought the distribution of wealth was as important as its creation. Perhaps we got the balance wrong. Perhaps, on the other hand, we have overcorrected: because it seems now that we are creating wealth so widely, our resolve to distribute it fairly is weaker.

I think it is reasonable, even sensible and not at all anti-American to ask what it will mean to shift our ideal along with our economic model. Thirty per cent of Americans earn $8 per hour or less. That figure translates at one level into something like full employment, at another into crime, sickness, homelessness, misery and exploitation. Nearly 20 per cent of American homes now employ people who are effectively their servants, and the number is growing rapidly. Barbara Ehrenreich recently joined the working poor and wrote a book describing her experiences; cleaning toilet bowls after middle-class children had used them, picking up their pubic hair, dusting their bad-taste furnishings and objets d'art. I know people with skills and education who are paid $12 or $13 an hour. We all know people working three or four casual jobs. We know that is the trend. When we get to 30 per cent working for $12 or $13 an hour, will we still be able to talk about the 'fair go', as if this country was still essentially different to America? Will our Prime Minister still talk about 'sticking to our mates' when 20 per cent of us employ other people to clean our toilet bowls and pluck our pubic hairs from the floor of the shower? Or is there some hitherto-unspoken definition of mateship now upon us? Non-core mateship. I would propose that the ideas of mateship and the fair go – if they mean anything – mean that we clean our own toilet bowls and pick up our own hair: even when we stay in hotels.

In these things and several others I feel less at home. It is not all demonstrable reality: it's the direction we are going, the rhetoric (if you can call it that) of our political and business leaders, a general apprehension that a new and uglier society is being born.

And then there is the language.

Nothing makes me feel less at home than the public language. Try writing a song called 'I Still Call Australia Home' in managerial language. Try expressing any sentiment, including the most vapid, in managerial language. Try this as a poem:

> from the strategic management point of view, customer-focused differentiation effected through design can be a source of competitive advantage. From the user-centred design and customer-centred marketing point of view, market based practices can be developed that inform the strategy formation process, especially in the transaction from planned to emergent strategy. This systematic production of design information can support the creation and iteration of all customer interactions manifested in the design of products, services, environments and communications.

Try telling me what I just said. Or try this:

> In defining our values now, to live these values, they must be incorporated into organisation systems and processes as well as the day to day activities of all staff. In defining our values we have formed a range of acceptable and non-acceptable behaviours which contribute to the success of implementation. For example, our key contra behaviour that we are currently focusing on that was identified through our values is employees displaying disrespectful behaviour towards clients, and/or other staff members. The department is committed to providing a positive working environment free from ridicule, intimidation and harassment. Disrespect or behaviour of this nature does not match this commitment, nor does it meet our organisational values, therefore it will not be tolerated.

You see – the only way you can recognise bad behaviour is to see it through your organisational values and match it to your commitment to these values. No proposition can exist that cannot be reconciled with a dot point in your mission statement. Try it on the dog: 'Rover, my organisational values compel me to focus on your lack of commitment to putting yourself in place in the back of the ute'.

The language of management – for which read the language of virtually all corporations and companies large and small, public-service departments, government agencies, libraries, galleries and universities, the military, intelligence organisations, and increasingly politics – is language that cannot describe or convey any human emotion, including the most basic ones like happiness, sympathy, greed, envy, love or lust. You cannot tell a joke in this language, or write a poem, or sing a song. It is language without human provenance or possibility.

In his book, *The Gate*, François Bizot describes three months he spent as a prisoner of the Khmer Rouge. He was the only westerner to survive the experience. Bizot was chained to a post in a Cambodian forest with 50 or 60 other Cambodian prisoners in shelters around him. Every few days one or two of these prisoners were taken away and killed with a shovel. You can see shovels like this in the school in Phnom Penh that the Khmer Rouge used later as a torture chamber. It is now called the Museum of Genocide. Bizot's captor, a man called Duch, moved on from the forest to run the torture chamber. Duch was a mathematics teacher. He was fluent in French. They had long discussions about politics, Buddhism and the revolution. Duch's superiors wanted Bizot executed as a CIA agent, but Duch managed to save the Frenchman's life.

During their discussions, Bizot said, Duch would talk intelligently up to the point where his faith was challenged by reason or sentiment. Then this lips pursed and he exploded in a barrage of revolutionary clichés and brutality. It came in waves of platitudes: opaque, abstract, depleted, impenetrable. At such times Bizot knew he was a breath away from the shovel. He was no longer in conversation with another human being, exchanging thoughts as a means of living with one another: he was a prisoner, a victim, an exile.

This is an old story – we read of the same in Stalin's Show Trials, the French Terror, the Inquisition. Language tethers us to the world and to each other: its mangling always means those tethers are broken.

When Jean Amery, an Austrian Jew, was captured and tortured as a member of the Belgian resistance, he felt most acutely the appropriation of his language. He felt also his arms being torn from their sockets by his German torturers at a place they called the Reception Centre. But when he came to write about his experience as a victim of torture and a prisoner in Auschwitz, he wrote a good deal about the sensation of exile, the loss of home. Amery lost everything, but he counted language among the most crushing of his losses. The Nazis vandalised, corrupted and shrank his native language. They shut him out from his home.

The arguments are more complex than I have portrayed them, but we can see the parallels with George Orwell's warnings 60 years ago and also with the public language that we now endure – as citizens, students, library users, voters, aspirationals and battlers, employees – especially as employees, because the poor employees have to write and think in it. But let's be managerial about it: let's put all those categories together and call them all 'customers'. Friends, Romans, customers . . .

I don't mean that we live on the verge of despotism. I don't mean to equate the Khmer Rouge with McDonald's or even the CIA – although McDonald's and the CIA have very similar mission statements. But that's the thing about mission statements, they are all much the same. Here's a dot point from the CIA:

'What We Stand For: Our Core Beliefs and Values

- Objectivity is the substance of intelligence, a deep commitment to the customer in its forms and timing.

Here's another one:

- Intelligence that adds substantial value to the management of crises, the conduct of war and the development of policy.

You will find those phrases in the public language of every significant organisation in the country, including quite possibly your local school, library and swimming pool. I am sure it is efficient language, developed to satisfy the needs of the Information Age and the management models emerging from it. In fact it is to the Information Age what machinery and the assembly line were to the Industrial Age. That is to say, it is efficient but dehumanising, functional but alienating. And as with the Industrial Age, a good society in the Information Age will try to limit its excesses, preserve what is valuable about the culture it is replacing, compensate us for the destruction. After all, we are asking people to use every day of their lives a language with no life in it. A language without force, one driven by process not by verbs. In its mechanical aspect and its ubiquity, managerial language resembles the language of the communist functionary: all those nauseating flourishes of revolutionary hope for 'continuous improvement going forwards' to a world where everyone's life is 'enhanced', 'flexible', 'innovative', 'vibrant' and 'committed'. As if that is all life needs to be.

Listen to this from an Australian university. Under their 'program quality management system' students will graduate as 'professionals'. This means 'they will participate actively and innovatively in their professional and social communities of practice in the context of the developing knowledge economy. Meanwhile they will also reflect as citizens. They will reflect upon their actions as engaged citizens in the context of local diversity and multi-culturalism, increasing globalisation and the universities [sic] commitment to awareness of global sustainability and indigenous issues. They will learn from experience to make context-sensitive judgements that enable them to continuously develop and transform their practice and themselves.'

Well, it's one thing to do with an Arts degree.

Politicians are attracted to managerial language because it is an endless fund of clichés; of interchangeable phrases that can be rolled out interminably. The pressure of the media makes these instant weasel words – words with the meaning sucked out of them – invaluable. And the media, for reasons I don't quite understand, play along with it. They never ask what these vacuous phrases mean. They never object to them on our behalf. They seek the truth in a language that has no truth in it. When a politician says 'at the end of the day', why don't they say – what bloody day? What sort of frame is a 'timeframe'?

We must not become obsessive about these things. It will only get us into the nursing home sooner. But we're entitled to resist. Even in this Berlusconi-style democracy where anything is okay so long as 50 per cent of the people support it, we have a right to resist. And the best place to resist I think is the language. We have a right to verbs; to active sentences not passive ones.

In the beginning was the Word. And in the Word was the truth – and the heart and the mind. And if you take it away from us we are poorer and the democracy is weaker. If anyone else feels that this country is not the home it was, I think they should go to the words, before we lose the power of sensible speech altogether.

November 2003

driver – key, core, critical, etc.

1. Someone or something that drives; or, as with a golf club, is used for driving.
2. The most important forces or factors for *change* or growth in a business, department, economy, school, hospital, football team, etc. Hence also *change drivers.* Talent, effort, *productivity improvements, enhanced skill sets,* teamwork, *international benchmarking,* loyalty and accounting processes that focus on *outcomes*, are all *key* (or *core*) *drivers* at various times.

Blind faith, greed, jealousy, favouritism, luck, bribery, covetousness, sociopathy, fawning, social aspirations, the primitive urge to win at all costs and performance-based salary packages including allocations of shares are not called *key drivers*. Nor are sabotage, murder, etc.

> '*Commitment* and discretionary effort as *key drivers* of *competitive advantage*.'
>
> Corporate document

> 'The most contested value *driver* in the knowledge economy is the new real estate of intellectual property.'
>
> Terry Cutler, *Making Australia a Knowledge Economy*

> 'Infirm of purpose! Give me the *drivers*!'
> 'May the *key drivers* be with you.'

From *Weasel Words*

What Will History Make of Us?

Should there be any historians left to write it, history might decide that ours was the age when Australians began to live as tropical fish do: off each other, aware only of what they need and what threatens them, changing colour with their emotions, lacking any sense of provenance or Fate or life on either side of the 'moment' in which they live.

They were free of all faith, the historians might say; and they gave up on collective ideals, history and language all at once. They fashioned their lives according to their self-interest and their vanity. It was the point when living became a lifestyle. Indeed, in time, the words became interchangeable and people came to speak of 'laying down their lifestyles for a friend' and the prospect of 'lifestyle after death'. Some went about saying without quite knowing why: 'There is no king in Israel and every man does what is right according to his own lifestyle'.

Should there be any historians 50 years from now, they will notice that around the beginning of their century, Australians stuck as close as ever to the shibboleths of the old one, but the shibboleths were sunken wrecks. They were rusting relics sheltering people who did not understand their meaning.

What could 'mateship' mean in a society stripped of the kind of public policy that favours roughly equal opportunity, rights and dignity? How could anyone profess belief in the 'fair go' while the social gap between rich and poor – and even men and women – grew wider, and people wanting sanctuary here were treated like criminals or dogs? What did these old expressions of the collective will mean now the ethos was furiously individualist?

Future historians will have to reconcile these national clichés with the fact that the more they were recited by the nation's leaders, the more people were working three or four jobs to make a fraction of what others made from one; and ever more citizens were employing fellow citizens to clean their lavatories and make their children's beds.

And what of 'Anzac' when they see the more we honoured it the more egregiously we boasted of being someone else's sheriff, and became so frightened of the unfamiliar we locked up foreign children?

Conventional interpreters of history are bound to conclude that there was a great difference between what was officially said and what was actually happening. Clichés by their nature do not reflect reality: they don't reflect anything; they're dead and have no lustre. For this reason the more anthropologically inclined historians might say that in our time Australia entered an era of spiritual dysfunction; the old gods had lost their meaning and the rituals of worship had become base and ludicrous.

But these are familiar and predictable conclusions. Sifting through the written evidence, including conference brochures, police files and media transcripts, more perceptive and original minds will discern that one traditional attachment had survived intact and swallowed all the others – pragmatism, Australia's oldest, most pervasive and profound belief.

There's nothing wrong with pragmatism. Unlike most philosophies, at the very least it works. But in Australia – and other New World societies – pragmatism has always gone together with a few high ideals and a belief that communities, nations and political parties ought to make an effort to pursue them. Not 'implement' them, as everyone now insists about any 'strategy', 'goal' or 'value'. Just incline to them, hold to them. Erect the stockade and grow the potatoes and keep everyone fed, certainly: but you must also feed their hearts and minds. Their souls need sustenance too. That was where mateship came from.

No ideal will be to every generation's taste, but they do bind the people in some aspiration beyond their own self-interest. Directly or by implication, they express a belief that there *is* such a thing as society and that human beings are capable of being more than customers. They do provide for people, especially the young and the old, some comfort and sense of worth that they can't find in the marketplace, and often not in families.

It will be hard for future historians to find in the public record convincing signs that such ideals existed in this Australia. No 'New Britannia in another world', or 'Australia for the White Man', or 'Workingman's Paradise', or 'Australian Settlement', or nice little post-modern republic in the South Seas. It is suggested instead that we aspire to share-ownership.

Some of us – quaint humanists and religious nuts mainly – will think that unadulterated pragmatism is poison. It leaches the life from democracies and truncates human possibility. Societies of people – unlike societies of fish – cannot survive, or at least cannot be happy, without nourishment for their brains or souls. Marvellous as a nice portfolio of shares would be, or having the kids in private school, the human imagination is more marvellous still and will never reach its full extent in the pursuit of wealth and status.

Surely historians will notice how far we have retreated: how all the talk about 'outcomes' is the managerial way of saying the end justifies the means, and the means include lies and smokescreens; how 'core' and 'non-core', and 'moving on' are weasel words from the same Machiavellian stable. And how the media did not stand witness, but let it pass, almost admiringly it seemed sometimes. Any halfway good historian will see the blatant sleights of hand. They'll have to say that in the age of triumphant pragmatism, when everything was in our favour and anything was possible, Australia slummed it.

Still, hindsight is another marvellous thing and can't be second-guessed. It might turn out that this is truly the post-modern condition: self-enhancement through technology plus reality TV. With hindsight, historians might say that it is one of the better conditions achieved by humankind, and thank us for putting Australia on the pathway to paradise. So what if it needed hypocrisy to grease the wheels. Lies are okay so long as they're part of the strategy, and the same goes for sanctimony. We move on. The only thing that matters is the outcome.

Good Weekend, 20 December 2003

From *Death Sentence*

> Wheresoever manners and fashions are corrupted, language is. It imitates the public riot.
>
> Ben Jonson

Parrots, when they are separated from their flocks, know by instinct that they must quickly join another one or they will make a meal for hawks. It is from this understanding that their mimetic skill derives. On finding any other horde they try to blend by mimicking its members. They do as the Romans do. If it is a Catholic household in which they find themselves, they might recite 'Hail Mary's. Among blasphemers, they'll blaspheme. Where it is customary to curse the dog or tap the barometer, they curse the dog or tap the barometer. Whatever is most frequently repeated sounds to them definitive, and this is the one they imitate. Every day for 40 years, regardless of the context, a bird might screech, 'Don't forget your hat!' or shout 'Oh what a feeling!' all day long, much as advertisers do. Parrots never learn the language, but are smart enough to know, like people involved in marketing, that one or two catchphrases will satisfy most people.

Our language grows, mutates and ossifies in a similar way. We are all inclined to imitate the sounds we hear. Fashion dictates many words and phrases. In foreign countries we pick up accents and inflections. We tune ourselves to the cadences of unfamiliar dining rooms. Politicians go amongst the people primed with local knowledge and saying 'Gidday' or 'How do you do', according to the prevailing custom. Priests murmur Latin phrases that are full of meaning even to their non-Latin-speaking flocks. Street gangs, sports clubs, political parties, families, people who for all kinds of reasons are regularly together, naturally develop a vernacular as a kind of bonding and those who want to join must learn it. Ideologues speak in language best understood by ideologues of like mind: it is called 'preaching to the converted' and it is probably a species of narcissism, like a budgerigar talking to itself in a mirror.

Organisations frequently impose a language of a certain shape on members and employees. Military forces seem to have done it always, and now companies imitate the military example, and all kinds of other outfits imitate the companies. Politics got slogans from military battalions – the word 'slogan' comes from the Gaelic and literally means a battle cry. No sooner were there slogans in politics than there were also 'weasel words': sly words that do not mean what they appear to, or have an unseen purpose. To be involved with politics is to make a pact with the devil, Max Weber said. Should we then expect the language of politics to have something diabolical about it? And if politicians can't resist temptation, why should advertising and marketing? Why should companies? The company is a miracle of the modern world: in fact it is almost true to say that the limited liability company was the beginning of the modern age. The point at which the age becomes *post*modern is marked, perhaps, by companies taking their liability for the language to be limited.

The English language has always been prey to fashion, and on the evidence so far we should not fear for its survival. Fashions come and go, but the language moves on, taking with it whatever remains useful or interesting, discarding what is colourless or vain. The language has proved much stronger than any human attempt to contain it: Samuel Johnson and, on the other side of the Atlantic, Noah Webster, both tried to tie it down and both failed magnificently. Waves of grammarians have followed them. There have always been people to declare that this or that is the only definition of a word, and this is the only way to pronounce it; this is the only way to arrange a sentence and this the only way to punctuate it. These people are essential, but only in the way that lifeboats are to an ocean liner.

The historical view suggests we can relax. English has survived everything that's been thrown at it: political and social revolution, industrial and technological revolutions, colonialism and post-colonialism, mass education, mass media, mass society. More than just surviving these upheavals, it adapts and grows, is strengthened and enriched by them. And never has it grown more than now: by one estimate, at the rate of more than 20,000 words a year, and for every new word several old ones change their meanings or sprout additional ones. It is wondrous on this level.

And yet, as it grows it is depleting. In the information age the public language is coming down to an ugly, sub-literate universal form with a fraction of the richness that living English has. Relative to the potential of language, the new form approximates a parrot's usage. It is cliché-ridden and lacks meaning, energy, imagery and rhythm. It also lacks words. It struggles to express the human. Buzz words abound in it. Platitudes iron it flat. The language is hostile to communion, which is the purpose of language. It cannot touch provenance. It stifles reason, imagination and the promise of truth. Look at a block of 1960s Housing Commission flats and you have the shape and dysfunction of it. Listen and you can hear the echoes of authoritarian cant. Our public language is becoming a non-language. Errors of grammar are irritating; slovenly, colloquial or hybrid speech can be gruesome; but English also gets much of its vigour and resilience from spontaneous invention and the colonial cultural mix. Compared to the general malaise, even the language of the law is harmless and at least amuses those who practise it. These are to the language as a few biting insects are to the tsetse fly: as an itch is to a slow, sleeping death.

There have been signs of decay in the language of politics and academia for years, but the direst symptoms are in business; and the curse has spread through the pursuit of business models in places that were never businesses. Universities that once valued and defended culture have swallowed the creed whole. Libraries, galleries and museums, banks and welfare agencies now parrot it. The public sector spouts it as loudly as the private does. It is the language of all levels of government including the very local. They speak of *focusing on the delivery of outputs* and matching decisions to *strategic initiatives*. Almost invariably these *strategic initiatives* are *key* strategic initiatives. In this language, schools, bank branches and libraries are closed down. In an education curriculum or the mission statement of an international fast-food chain you will hear the same phrases. Military leaders while actually conducting wars sound like marketing gurus, and politicians sound like both of them. If one day in the finance pages you encounter *critical deliverables,* do not be surprised if it turns up the next day when you're listening to the football. The public language has all these variants and all of them are infected, if not dead. It is the grey death of the globalised world.

Those in the vanguard seem determined to create a new language for the new times they are bringing into being: new words to describe the new machinery, new words for the new processes, new words for leadership and management, new words to measure value and priority, new words to govern behaviour; slogans to live our lives by. Inevitably, those who follow the business model follow their lead in language: and while it is partly to imitate, to impress or to melt into the milieu, it is also because this is the language in which they are taught. It is part of the package.

In this revolution we are encouraged to take up the new, like those chimps who took up fire millions of years ago. We learn the laws of the free market as an earlier generation learned the laws of selection: that we must be competitive, that the adaptable survive and the rest are swallowed up. We are so thoroughly persuaded that everything depends on adapting to the new, we are letting go of the language for no better reason than that it is very old.

Political terminology is never adequate to the multitudinous reality it seeks to define. Likewise, political leaders, staring down forests of microphones and lenses while journalists quiz them about that reality, invariably lack the inhuman skill to give answers that are both definitive and truthful. They develop other skills instead. They learn to say, 'We are committed to this, yes, at this point in time, absolutely, Michelle.' Politics is a wrestling match with chaos (or smoke), and it prizes those who seem best able to impose their will upon the impossible. Successful politicians are those who can come up with a picture of things that approximates the view from where the rest of us are standing. Good ones do this by changing our view to theirs. The hacks seek out our view and try to make it their own. In Australia, for more than a decade, a government made the reality economic. Anyone who stepped outside was declared exiled, feral or wet. This was the political reality of the phrase *the main game*. No game is quite so 'main' today. The government keeps redefining the reality: one minute it is *battlers*, then the economy, then the bush, then immigration, personal security, national security, war. The political expression is *setting the agenda*. Every time a government succeeds in *setting the agenda*, or resetting it, they reset the language.

The Labor government, particularly its Treasurer, Paul Keating, introduced dozens of new words and phrases to the public language, and almost all of them at least putatively described an economic reality. To be part of the political culture, to be able to have a say, you had to master this language. Bob Hawke, the Prime Minister in those revolutionary times, was famed as an advocate, but sometimes it seemed that words were less the medium of his expression than just so many bloody obstacles placed in the way of making people see what he bloody saw. When speaking off the cuff he embarked on his sentences like a madman with a club in a dark room: he bumped and crashed around for so long his listeners became less interested in what he was saying than the prospect of his escape. When at last he emerged triumphantly into the light we cheered, not for the gift of enlightenment, but as we cheer a man who walks away from an avalanche or mining accident. And he raised his tremendous eyebrow as if to say, 'Now you see, for I have told you.' For a decade R. J. Hawke murdered speech, and politically it cost him nothing.

2003

Why We Loved the Other PM

> You know you don't have to act with me, Steve. You don't have to say anything and you don't have to do anything. Not a thing. Oh, maybe just whistle. You know how to whistle, don't you, Steve? You just put your lips together and blow.
>
> Lauren Bacall to Humphrey Bogart,
> *To Have and Have Not*

To judge by the volume of press reports, Steve Waugh's retirement from Test cricket is the most important event of the year so far. Consider the other stories he knocked off the top of the news when he played his last innings in Sydney. Some of the 50,000 or so victims of the earthquake at Bam were still being dug out of the rubble; the leaders of India and Pakistan were meeting to reduce the threat of nuclear war between them; refugees were still on a hunger strike in their compound in Nauru; an inquiry found that the White House systematically distorted the truth in making its case for the invasion of Iraq (not that this was news); and it was revealed that Princess Di once jotted something down about Prince Charles plotting to kill her. Typically, the London tabloids put this item ahead of Steve's farewell; but in Australia he buried it along with everything else, including the one about the crocodile man and his baby. Not bad for a batsman who didn't hook or pull.

Steve Waugh is famous well beyond Australia. In India taxi drivers can tell you that he has a wife, two daughters and a son, and what their names are. Being famous in a country with a billion citizens probably makes Steve Waugh the most famous Australian alive. And the most liked. There are billboards on Indian roadsides showing him with some of the orphans he cares for in Calcutta. In India he appears to be regarded as a 'good man', and this summer's farewells suggest Australians feel the same way.

But why? True, no right-hander ever played a better square drive off the back foot than Steve. But his brother's cover drive was just as good, and one of the most beautiful things in the history of cricket. Steve's was like a shotgun blast.

We can't have loved him just for his square drive. That would be like loving Humphrey Bogart for the way he shot people. Come to think of it, there was something wonderful in Bogart's cold stare into the eyes of his adversary and the way he fired from just in front of his coat pocket, as if taking a man's life was just a variation on the handshake.

Waugh had that merciless gaze in common with all heroes of film noir. He had the swagger as well. His swagger was more like a duck's than George Raft's, but he was also the cricketer most likely to tell someone, as George Raft did in *Nocturne*, that if he didn't shut up he'd wrap a piano round his neck. You had to like his style.

As with all film-noir heroes, the good lay half buried in the dark side. To like him, you had to look past the scarred, hard-boiled bits. And he *was* scarred. In his youth he played like a prince. After the Lord's Test in 1988, the once-dashing English opener Denis Compton thanked him for reminding us how the game should be played. Compton spoke for the MCC, no less. But after he was dropped from the side, Waugh shed all the graces, until at times he looked plain ugly at the crease.

He became immovable and indestructible. Fearless. That was the attraction. He was Steve Waugh and you could take it or leave it. So he was the sort of man who wouldn't give you the skin from a grape: that's better than one who gives you the whole thing and thinks he's bought you with it. It's better than being a hypocrite, or a crawler, or a preacher, a pimp, a chump or a politician, etc.

It was because he was Steve Waugh that we forgave him things we didn't forgive in other players; we justified them, or we decided that with Steve Waugh no justification was necessary. He claimed a catch that the cameras showed wasn't clean. He was an inveterate, unapologetic sledger. Even his most ardent fans suspected that once or twice he batted for his average. As captain he didn't discipline delinquent players. It seems he thought he was paid to solve the case, and it was no one's business how he did it. Did his critics want him to go soft? Was that how you won? Well, we could save our oil, as Alan Ladd once said. He didn't get where he'd got listening to clucks like us.

It has often been said that the captain of the Australian cricket team is the other Prime Minister: the one who expresses more of the country's prevailing character and who is better known abroad. Both Prime Ministers were at the Sydney Cricket Ground last week. The one on the ground was playing his last scene, and like the stars of film noir, he was playing it exactly as he always played it, by being himself. The other one was in the stands, method acting as usual at a game he shows few convincing signs of understanding.

In real life, of course, the one who looks less like Humphrey Bogart or Robert Mitchum, and more like the bit player who opens the safe at gunpoint and is left tied up and gagged, is the real Prime Minister and Steve Waugh is now a private citizen. And even as the PM cheered away it might have crossed his mind that he, the old bit player, was seeing off yet another star.

That's the joy in those old films: immortality depends not on the length of your life, or your success at it, but on what it stands for. Perhaps it was for his cricket that Steve Waugh was loved. But if it was also for his character, then truth is alive and there is still something good in sport. It means that artifice and narcissism are not essential, that blandness is only optional, and to feel something for the people of a very different country is not unpatriotic.

The Age, 15 January 2004

Dead Language

Ten years ago Toni Morrison devoted her Nobel Prize speech to 'systematic looting of language' and the almost universal indifference to it. She spoke of 'tongue suicide' and 'dead language'.

Dead language, she said, 'is not only one no longer spoken or written, it is unyielding language content to admire its own paralysis ... Ruthless in its policing duties, it has no desire or purpose other than maintaining the free range of its own narcotic narcissism, its own exclusivity and dominance. However moribund, it is not without effect for it actively thwarts the intellect, stalls conscience, suppresses human potential. Unreceptive to interrogation, it cannot form or tolerate ideas, shape other thoughts, tell another story, fill baffling silences.' This language, she said, was common among 'infantile heads of state and power merchants'. It leaves them with 'no access to what is left of their human instincts for they speak only to those who obey'.

In describing the language of tyrants, ideologues, megalomaniacs and bullies, Morrison offered a near-perfect definition of the contagion that now reaches into every nook of our lives.

Education, for instance, is thoroughly infected. In Queensland the people responsible for the senior secondary English syllabus describe 'High Achievement' in these terms: 'At High Achievement, the student has consistently shown knowledge and understanding of how texts are constructed across a range of texts in a range of social and cultural contexts.' Nineteen bullet points follow this sentence under three separate headings: 'Knowledge and control of texts in their contexts', 'Knowledge and control of textual features' and 'Knowledge and application of the constructedness of texts'.

Read that first sentence aloud and you are likely to find yourself wondering how anyone charged with educating children could write it. And this is no idle sentence: it has been considered by a whole committee of educators. We must assume they decided this particular arrangement of words was the best way to express whatever was in their minds.

It won't do to blame any educational or literary theory on which the syllabus is based. It's not the thought that resists us and excites irritation and contempt. The first protest comes from the ear, and only afterwards from struggling cognitive faculties. It's the language. We can't get at the thought: the language puts it into a sort of holding pattern and there is a fair chance it will never land.

Queensland should not be singled out. The Victorian English curriculum includes a Plain English Speaking Award which is described in the syllabus thus: 'The award provides opportunities for all students to demonstrate outcomes in speaking and listening in a variety of ways, including observing speakers' strategies, preparation of speeches and delivery of speeches in public settings.'

We can assume that in both Queensland and Victoria the curriculum is 'outcomes-based'. In various degrees they all are. Everything is. That is why the word 'outcome' appears with such mind-numbing frequency in modern public language. Every day in government departments throughout the Commonwealth countless sentences are built around 'outcome'. The same happens in the big corporations. In fact government departments learned 'outcomes' from business, and small companies and little local government agencies, and quite possibly bridge clubs and church auxiliaries, are all committing themselves to 'outcomes' – 'going forwards'. Poor fools, I'm told among the really cutting edge these days 'outcomes' have been superseded by 'outputs'.

Outcomes are not the only thing, of course. 'Working with the passion, commitment, enthusiasm, committed to teamwork to fulfill our company needs', says the mission statement of a sticky note manufacturer. 'We use our time to enhance our skills with the passion and desire of self-fulfillment.' The CIA's mission statement says something remarkably similar.

'Respect for the individual's personal journey and traditional beliefs is given high value amongst all participating chaplains. Therefore, policies, strategic initiatives and operational plans will be put in place to ensure that a quality service, relevant to this vision and mission statement, are [sic] maintained.' So concludes the mission statement of the Multifaith Chaplaincy Service at James Cook University.

These words, 'value', 'strategic', 'quality', 'commitment' and 'outcome', are almost to modern management what 'glorious', 'proletarian', 'revolution' and 'marching forward' were to copywriting in the old communist states.

Infected organisations and the consultants who serve as plague rats will sometimes concede that the new language might be infelicitous, *as language*, but never that it is less than functional and efficient as . . . well . . . *a key driver of communication.*

Compounding cultural vandalism with intellectual slumming, those who are still capable of being embarrassed by the sludge – in universities for instance – have been heard to say that the language employed in their mission statements and other public documents has no connection to what the organisation actually thinks or does or hopes for.

But we might wonder how language that circumscribes or clouds thought can be more efficient than language that expresses, clarifies or enlarges it. Efficient by what measure? The measure of an assembly line, perhaps. Efficient in the way that containerisation is an efficient means of transport? Efficient as a way of containing human beings? This is what this streamlined (or mutilated) language strives to be: the machinery of the information age.

Even if we allowed this depressing possibility, there is little to suggest the mechanical version is more efficient than one that respects a few rules and allows a freer flow of words and thoughts. If depleted language depletes an organisation's ability to think, might it not be *less* efficient? What if the managers were wrong, and it turned out that a bullet point is no more likely to be true than an original sentence? An American guru of the information age, Edward R. Tufte, has come to just this conclusion. Bullet points are 'faux analytical', he says, and he illustrates his case by reducing Lincoln's Gettysburg Address to a PowerPoint presentation. Naturally it doesn't work. Not as language as such. Not as a speech. Professor Tufte maintains that the language of management is depleting our cognitive powers.

There is one other thing practitioners of the new public language will not admit. They will never say the language is coercive or oppressive. I would be more inclined to believe them if, since the publication of *Death Sentence,* I had not received so many letters from people who have been compelled to write in the prescribed way. They feel tyrannised and abused by it.

Almost as abused as those Victorian primary-school children who last year were compelled to write their very own personal mission statements, with their own core values, key goals and preferred outcomes. As soon as they've got their lives sorted in the managerial context they'll be ready for those texts.

Sydney Morning Herald, 2 March 2004

The Turf

A friend of my father had a racehorse. It was a big chestnut gelding called Goldbao and in the winter of 1956 he won three races on end. The third of them was a two-mile event at Flemington. He won it by ten lengths. It was inevitable that my father's friend, whose name was Reg, dreamed about winning that year's Melbourne Cup, but Goldbao broke down. It was a year before he started again, and when he did it was at Yarra Glen. His trainer, Owen Lynch, said it was not worth backing him because he wasn't fit enough to win. But the horse, as they always say, never knows such things and Goldbao won at tremendous odds. Reg listened to the race in our kitchen and when Goldbao won, a packet of cork-tipped Turf hit the wall beside the wood stove with great force and spilled bent cigarettes all over the place. Perhaps it broke the spell, because the horse did not race again. Reg bought another horse and called it Dlaniger, which is Reginald spelt backwards, and Dlaniger went in much the same direction.

Overall, Reg didn't have a lot of luck with horses, but in those six weeks when Goldbao was winning it was as if he had literally been touched by Fortune. He bought a big Ford

Customline and bags of Violet Crumbles. Photos of Goldbao's victories hung on the walls in their sitting room. The one of him ten lengths clear in the Flemington straight and nothing else in the picture, R. Hutchinson perched quietly behind his pricked ears, made an impression on me that has lasted all my life.

Humans have been enchanted by horses since the Stone Age. They are engraved on the walls of the caves at Chauvet with leopards and bison. In a 30,000-year-old chamber at Lascaux, Stone Age people imposed four horse heads upon each other to give the impression of a photo finish. It is unlikely that anyone was riding them. The first convincing signs of equestrian humanity were found by archaeologists in the Ukraine in the Bronze Age grave of a horse now known as the Dereivka Stallion. This 14.2 hands, 6000-year-old horse had been buried with two dogs and several clay figurines, such as one might expect to find with the remains of a notable warrior or prince. The Dereivka Stallion was not only the first horse we know to have been ridden with a bridle, the figurines and dogs in the grave with him suggest he was also the first to be revered.

A racehorse is a kind of talisman for people who normally don't believe in them: like those riders on the Ukrainian steppes, owners hope that their horse might pass on some of its power and grace and the wild spirit inside. Failing that, a fat wallet and a good night out will do. With horses you can at least imagine crossing over. Goldbao's winter of success brought briefly into our lives and imagination Pimm's, cocktail cigarettes and a shadowy racing man with a noirish, Camusian Robert Ryan look about him, who kept a form guide in one pocket of his gabardine overcoat and in the other a jar of mussels in brine – the kind you used to see lonely and gathering dust on the shelf in fish and chip shops – and every so often he would take a mussel from the jar and slip it down his throat whole. A child could not help but be impressed. These early childhood experiences are critical in our development, and in my case help explain why since I was seven years old form guides have been symbols of liberty unrestrained.

All my life I have browsed them, and all my life I have listened to the races, even in Japan where I could not understand a word. Once the habit forms you listen without listening. I heard Fr Edmund Campion say in a Sydney pub one Saturday that hearing Johnny Tapp calling the races was like the national anthem. It is true: there is always that stirring arc between start and finish, and always the climax, hour upon hour, day after day. It grounds us, means life goes on. Race calls are for some of us what evensong is for Anglicans: a refuge, rather like the TAB is or the stables at Caulfield on race day. There is something about these horse-connected places that restores human equilibrium.

Jockeys are unsuitable role models for boys that grow to normal size or fail to develop the smile of an assassin, and I could not go on forever wishing to be R. Heather or N. Sellwood. I transferred my allegiance entirely to the horses like Todman, Tulloch and Sailor's Guide. But jockeys can get a grip on your imagination. The two unforgettable faces of my childhood were Peter Lorre and W. Williamson. And then there is the way they ride. The Ukrainian stallion no doubt felt like a winged arrow to his rider, but at up to 70 kilometres per hour a good thoroughbred is faster. Put 20 of them into a race together and you have a partly controlled stampede. It is one of the marvels of human competence to see a jockey, weighing all of 50 kilograms, spring onto one of these beasts and with ease command it. And then when the race begins, rate the horse's speed, conserve its energy and, keeping its rhythm even as it plots a course past slower and rapidly slowing horses, time its run to the finish. Watch them as, with their hands, their knees and thighs and feet, with the whip – with all these things at once – they search for whatever it is in the horse's genes that might get it to the line first. Men less than four-feet-ten are unlikely heroes, but jockeys frequently make a case. Watch Steven King on Fields of Omagh in last year's Cox Plate, or Frankie Dettori leading from beginning to end down the wavy mile-long straight at Newmarket, and you will see skills that rank with any in sport. See a horse snap its leg and fall and watch the others come down over it and you can't question the courage of these small people – and even when you can, you can hardly blame them.

Naturally a jockey's task is made possible by the horse's training, and that in turn is easier because once out of the herd horses like to bond. They will make an inseparable friend of the stable pony, or a cat or a dog or a rooster. Of course they will also mate up with the trainer, and the trainer, with a stick in one hand and lump of sugar in the other, makes the most of it. The smartest horse may be less smart than a border collie or a good parrot, but it is smart enough to learn who its friends are. It can also tell who is competent around horses and who is not, and will frequently make the incompetent pay. The extraordinary thing is the great differences between the smart and the less smart, the passive and the cranky, the beautiful and the plain. That some beautiful-looking horses can't gallop and some plain ones have been wonders of the turf is axiomatic. It is just as true in reverse: among the legions of slow horses are countless plain ones, and among the few champions are such beauties as the black Octagonal and the golden Vain.

It is in the ability to gallop that the most astounding difference lies. With a few friends I have had an interest in several horses, and all of them by the standards of a Cox Plate field were hopelessly slow. But over 2000 metres the fastest of our horses would have beaten the slowest by half a circuit: though it has to be said that the slowest we had, a gelding with one floppy ear that lifted its feet as if it were stepping over snakes, would have been beaten by an elderly man on foot. R. Heather would beat him were he still with us. We whistled him one day from a hundred yards away and, though he came at a gallop, I had rolled a cigarette and lit it before he reached the fence.

On the other hand, the best of our horses, a grey mare who won six races in the country and twice was city placed, would have been lapped by two other grey mares, Emancipation (who was as plain as a horse can be) and Surround (who looked like Natalie Wood). Then there are horses which can run like the wind for 1000 metres and stop as if shot when they reach 1050. And there are stayers that don't get up momentum until they've gone a mile or more. The real duds are very fast horses that only go for 900 metres, and stayers that never get going at all. But all these are revealed characteristics and owners and trainers and punters can make allowances. So can handicappers and the people who devise races for horses of all classes except the supremely hopeless.

What are much harder to measure and understand are those innate characteristics of horses that no amount of human intervention can change. Herein is the mystique of the thoroughbred. Training regimes can increase a horse's stamina or speed, and teach it to conserve its energy, but only rare horses can do both and not even the best trainer can turn the others into what their genes insist they are not. Nor can training overcome the genes that make some good horses hopeless if the ground is wet or muddy, while some slow ones seem to go much faster in it. And no trainer could do for the attitude of a 17-hand horse we had: at the first of its two runs it threw the jockey in the mounting yard, savaged the clerk of the course's horse, and pig rooted most of the way round Cranbourne. With horses as with people, some are just born evil.

The genes that determine attitude are the most important ones. Why do some horses with great ability never produce it in a race? Why do some always run well but not well enough to win, while others win every race until the handicapper beats them? Some horses give in easily or seem to beg other horses to pass them, while others – such as Manikato and Northerly – fight furiously all the way and refuse to let anything get past. Some are Chamberlains and some are Churchills.

Then there are those like Better Loosen Up who repeatedly finished races like a train to win by the smallest possible margin.

The answers might lie in those herds on the Ukrainian steppes, where some horses were dominant and many more knew their place. By this reasoning the squibs and the ones that could win but won't are imprinted with the thought that they're not supposed to, and for the same reason they never learned to put up with pain. In other words it is not always the fastest horse that wins, or the one with greatest stamina – it is the horse that is, genetically speaking, meant to and therefore has the will to do it. This is, I admit, a very poor guide to punting – but show me one that works.

The really telling fact about thoroughbreds is that, unlike humans, they are not getting appreciably faster. It is as if the dominant racehorses of each year are the equivalent of the horses that dominated in the wild, before thoroughbreds were invented. The mare that wins the race is the mare that would have led the stampede. It is probable that all the great and charismatic horses, the horses that people have revered, are great and charismatic because they are *by nature* dominant. This is the horse that all breeders try to breed, all owners hope to buy, all trainers want to discover in their charges.

The pity is they can't tell you. Good judges can see signs, but nothing's certain till they reach the racetrack, and that won't prove much until they're in a race, and most times it will take a dozen or more races before it's clear to everyone concerned that the horse just doesn't have it. Between that moment and his first morning in the trainer's stable large sums of money go down the drain. On balance the horse with the floppy ear is the best kind of horse you can have, because it was clear from the start that he could not get out of his own way. It's the ones with a glimmer of ability that bring you undone. The merest sign it might be able to gallop and the pain begins.

If it is 'forward' enough to race by the age of two, it is almost certain to go shin sore and have to be turned out again until it is three. Then it starts again. Horses' eyes provide almost 360-degree vision and are situated at the top of their long heads so they can see approaching wolves and sabre-tooth tigers and eat at the same time. This is essential in the wild but less useful in a race. It means they tend to see things everywhere; they get spooked by horses coming up behind them, or imagine a mammoth in the car park. If your horse shows these symptoms, the trainer will use blinkers on it. Horses can't see things immediately beneath their heads or just in front of them, so if yours starts looking for objects that might need leaping, the trainer might use a nose roll on it. The blinkers might work, but they might also have the effect of putting the horse into a kind of coma, of taking the wild energy out of it; and whatever the nose roll does to the horse's line of vision it's not proof against its imagination.

Once you have sorted out the equipment best suited to your own mad animal – and I have not mentioned lugging bits, tongue ties, half blinkers and other devices including bicarbonate of soda – experience will tell the trainer if the horse's potential lies in sprinting, staying or middle distance. More experience will tell you if the horse is the kind that likes to lead, sit just off the pace or come from behind. And yet more experience is likely to reveal to you whether your horse is the kind that does not like to go between other horses; or does not like other horses on the outside of him or on the inside of him; or is frightened of other horses; or is more interested in biting them than beating them. If within 12 months you have definitive answers to all these questions and have found the means of dealing with them you will have done well, especially as it means that your horse has not bowed a tendon, got a chronic mysterious cough, gone sour, died of colic or – as one of ours did – broken its neck on the wire stay of a power pole in a storm.

Your trainer has the horse as fit as man can make it, he's picked just the right race for it, worked out the right gear, it's drawn the kind of barrier that suits its style of racing, the going is of the right consistency. Still the chocolates are not yours. The horse might bang its head on the barrier and be scratched there and then. (This happened to one of ours.) The jockey gets it trapped in a pocket and only gets out when the race is over. (This happened to another one of ours.) It gets a check just when it's gathering momentum. (This happened just about every time our horses raced.) The jockey has taken a sling to lose the race. (We suspect this happened once.) Or the most likely thing of all – there is a better horse in the race. Slower than yours perhaps, but with something in its genes – or in its bloodstream – that yours lacks.

The possibilities are without number and should persuade any sensible person not to gamble on horses, much less own one. For all the science and knowledge that has gone into it, there is still enough of the stampede about most horse races to leave almost nothing that is not open to chance.

And therein is the attraction. There is no equivalent in golf to the Dereivka Stallion. Nothing about Ernie Els connects to the wild in the way it did in Manikato or Might and Power. Very little in life does. I have never seen a golfer who looked half as interesting as W. Williamson, or as beautiful as Vain. And among those who follow golf – or football, or poetry readings for that matter – you never see the variety of class, character and existence that you see on racecourses. Picture a man leaving a golf course. Now picture a man leaving Sandown on a wet winter evening trying to convince himself that he didn't need the money. A battling trainer driving 200 miles home with his horse that got held up for a run and was beaten by a nose. And the owners with the horse that won. Everyone who goes home from a racetrack goes home with a story.

Long after my interest in other sports has faded, I remain riveted by horse racing. Not everyone can understand this, but the same people would likely forgive Degas for the same fixation. For all his famous ballerinas, Degas painted at least as many jockeys and horses. For every painting in the Paris Opera there is one of the racecourse at Longchamp; and it was for much the same reason that he painted it – for life's spectacle. His pictures connect horse racing to the landscape and thus to sport's pastoral roots, and for this reason he might not have liked Randwick or Flemington quite as much. But everything else about the scene is essentially the same: the jockeys' insouciant grace, the owners representing all the species of vanity, hope and anxiety, the colour, the clip clop, the smell, the punters and bookies and touts and experts, the ones in the know and those who know nothing – and those marvellous beasts.

Good Weekend, 22 October 2004

Once a Jolly Lifestyle

Early in the new year I entered a hairdressing salon in the main street of the Victorian Wimmera town of Horsham (not 'Sirs and Hers' but the one next to it, if ever you're looking). At 9.30 in the morning the place was empty, and in no time the hairdresser was fluffing the hair around my ears in the familiar way of her profession, and I was about to say, in the familiar way of the country, 'Hot isn't it, but I suppose we should expect it at this time of the year.' But before I could begin she said, 'So, how's your day been so far?'

There was a time – a very long time – when country people rarely asked more of another human being than how he or she was going. In this same time there was often a whiff of damp hay, dogs or sweat about country schoolrooms, churches and picture theatres. Country people – this was before they were called rural and regional Australians – were the living embodiments of their work and environment, somehow even of their faith. They were as seals are to rocks and owls to the night, the elemental Australians.

Media celebrity has had some say in revising the ideal from, say, a sheep shearer to a crocodile wrestler. But a much more general and probably unstoppable change is underway too. The country, you see, is going forwards, which is to say it has joined up with the rest of the economy, the rest of the economy has joined up with the global economy, and when that happens 'So, how's your day been so far?' becomes pretty well mandatory. It is the standard greeting of all customer-focused businesses, worldwide, and the world now includes the Wimmera. For hairdressers it is doubtless as much part of their training as scissor technique. As I left this hair-care centre of excellence I thanked her. 'Not a problem,' she replied, 'have a nice day.'

Cruise control and empty roads create a state of mindlessness that is perfect for getting round Australia. Think of a Fred Williams or Arthur Streeton if you will – or in the Wimmera, Sidney Nolan – but the pleasure is in not thinking. Thinking is a form of resistance. Let the emptiness swallow you alive. Time and the miles will simply fly by.

Yet enough remains in the Australian countryside to occasionally disturb the driver's trance. A glimpse of a house in ruins can do it, a tank toppled off its stand, an overgrown domestic fence or fowl-yard can provoke the subversive thought that something once happened here. What we see now was once something else. Children slept beneath that collapsed roof, were conceived beneath it, climbed in the shattered cypress.

You know it is the quaking of your own childhood that the house in ruins provokes, and the empty schools and halls remind you of the thin, brief shadow your own life throws. A glimpse of rusted iron and flaking weatherboard can hollow you out for half an hour. Or it can set you thinking of the ping pong that was played inside that hall, the dances, weddings, meetings, baby shows, the young men gathering to enlist for wars. You can suddenly find your mind in full-blown worship of these ancestors: the prodigious work they did which their children never thanked them for; the faith no longer comprehended; the lives lived with no certainty of reward or sense of entitlement.

Those old halls with the broken pine trees round them speak for vanished communities and their secular spirit in the same way that the abandoned churches stand for an age when people, though they rarely got excited about it, practised religion in the hope of salvation and, if not that, for the good it did their souls, its restraining force and the pure energy it mined. Along with work, cooperation and religion were the eternal verities and the conditions of success. Those public buildings might now be forlorn monuments to these beliefs, but for the people who built them they were also the reward, the proof of their devotions.

It was natural for pioneer communities to erect the essential markers of civilisation's progress, and the pioneering went on long after those inveterate builders, the Victorians, had departed. The Great War demanded monuments and every second hamlet got one. They will last as long as the civilisation, unmistakable evidence of a strange, Homeric event and the myth it engendered. We should genuflect twice every time we pass one; the first time for the dead and the second for the builders who imagined something permanent, secular and noble.

The Great War also demanded post-war settlement schemes which created new communities, and wherever they survived up went public buildings. The halls, libraries and mechanics institutes, post offices, churches, banks, butter factories, grandstands, rail stations, wheat silos and war memorials – just about everything that is substantial in form and meaning – were built before World War II. And apart from swimming pools just about everything built after it is gimcrack and suburban.

Put the difference down to the spirit of an imperial, pioneering age when stone, bricks, skill and labour were much cheaper. Wherever the need occurs and funds allow, no doubt public buildings still get built. But it is rare to see a modern one of imposing substance or of deeper meaning than a shopping mall, perhaps with a McDonald's in the middle puffing the fumes of frying oil into the air. The absence of substance or any sign of an aesthetic also exemplifies an age – our own, the one ruled by market ideology and private taste. Market ideology deplores public investment. It rearranges the cosmos on post-modern lines. Those old banks, courthouses, post offices and churches now do for hairdressers, beauty salons, pancake parlours, estate agents (known in some places as 'lifestyle merchants') and people exercising various lifestyle options. No one can miss the irony, and nor should we miss the fact beneath it – that the first language of the post-modern is accounting.

There are no less than 18 hairdressers in Horsham (population 13,000), and in January local ABC radio reported that the shire intended to teach them drought counselling. They have 'a one-on-one relationship for half an hour to an hour and it's important that they know how to listen and respond', a shire spokeswoman said. It seems when your customers are going through a drought – or, one assumes, a flood, bushfire or locust plague – it is not enough to ask them how their day has been so far. It might seem curious that the man on the land must now have the spiritual as well as the physical comforts all farmers since Job have had to do without. But much more radical is the idea that people need to be trained before they can take a sympathetic interest in their neighbours. Soon there will be diplomas in it, diplomas of mateship, perhaps. The cost of course will have to go on the price of the haircut.

Hairdressers occupy the old Bank of New South Wales building in the once grand Murray River town of Echuca. They have adopted the familiar marketing strategy of keeping a blackboard on the street outside and every day writing on it a homily or maxim of their own invention, much as Cicero might have done had he been in retailing. The one I saw in January was perhaps a taste of the counsel farmers can expect next time they go in for a tint. It said: 'Never put limits on yourself. Just be free at all costs.' It must be that the booze got to Henry Lawson before he could think of that.

This is the bush, the mighty bush; crucible of the nation's spirit, imagination and binding beliefs. The legends were born in these places. Mateship was born here, and Anzac was born of mateship they say. So were Carbine, Bradman, the Drover's Wife, John Curtin and Black Jack McEwen all children of the bush and all chips off the country's block because, as the legend says and our media and leaders would very often have us believe, it was from the bush that Australia's character and traditions came.

Some readers might remember a few of them: a collective rather than individualistic ethos; an aversion to boasters; an outlook more fatalistic than optimistic; laconic, sceptical in most things, practical, more inclined to admire physical than intellectual prowess and achievement. In all but the last of these traits our New World society was believed to be different to the American one. Readers might note as well that Australia's traditional 'values' in no way resemble the values of what contemporary commentators and successful political parties call 'values-based' politics, which is said to be the most suitable variety in the current social climate.

As far as it is possible to tell with such an abstract term, 'values-based' politics is concerned with other abstractions such as religion, the proper role and entitlements of fathers, the entitlements of the unborn child, the entitlements of the born ones, lifelong entitlements and what are called lifestyle choices. In vain will our political leaders and their ideologues search the Bulletin school, the collected works of Paterson and Lawson, Weary Dunlop's memoirs, the school readers, Mary Grant Bruce or the words of 'Waltzing Matilda' for any sign of such 'values'. Too bad, we might say if they got on with their 'values-based' politics and left the ancestor worship to those who know they have them. But they won't of course.

Despite all the evidence to the contrary, they'll pretend that mateship is alive and readily seen in the nation's juice bars, that it is more than a male thing, that it has something to do with what the media and politicians would have us believe is a unique determination to save our homes from bushfires, and that it has nothing whatever to do with trade unionism, the welfare state or any species of big government. They will make themselves and their words heirs to mateship, or any other traditional 'value' they can convert to the narcissistic prism essential to marketing and personal enlightenment. Who can say for certain that the swagman's defiant leap into the billabong should not be understood as a lifestyle decision? A values-based decision? It is tempting to believe that they are wasting their time; that you cannot invent or reinvent tradition. But you can of course. You just need to say the same things often enough, starting with the ones who don't know better and shutting up the ones who do.

That life in the country is sweeter and richer in choice than it used to be is not a reason for the rest of us to feel gloomy. Why should the gentle breezes of air-headed aspirationalism caress only the suburban dweller? May they all be cabled to the World Wide Web until, in the name of individualism, freedom and choice, the dream of sameness is made real. Not a problem. May they plant the nation's cereal crop while watching Foxtel in the air-conditioned cabins of their mobile power plants. But deliver us from the refrain about traditions. Spare us the sacrilege.

In Wentworth, at the junction of the Darling and the Murray, a little grey Ferguson tractor has been hoist high on a pole to memorialise the heroic little machines that in the 1950s saved the town from floods. When I first looked up at it, a kookaburra was sitting on the steering wheel. It's impossible not to like Wentworth with its old gaol, its tractor worship and its junkyard museum. By these small gestures a town says it is a town, a conscious culture, a place with a memory. And Wentworth seems to say it as it should be said in the bush, without taking itself too seriously.

You go down to the Wentworth Club for tea and eat your steak and chips and out the window, pink in the sunset, the Darling flows on its immortal course. A cormorant crouches on a dead branch and hangs its wings out to dry. Downstairs young couples are playing the machines and older ones are dancing evening three-steps nose to nose. It is Austral bliss. But on the big TV in the dining lounge *A Current Affair* is covering the tsunami. Ray Martin and his team are up there in devastated Aceh and Phuket and the message keeps coming at us: our Aussie generosity is awesome and unmatched; it's amazing how we Aussies pitch in when there's a crisis; it's the Aussie way, the Aussie spirit, and Aussie tradition akin to mateship and our long history of fighting affliction.

It can only be to make us feel good, as if we need to feel dividends from kindness. As if, unlike the people who lived in those crumbling houses by the roadsides, and the people who built those public halls, we can't do things or face things without this constant stroking, without reward. We need the warmth of mutual self-congratulation, to see ourselves in everything, to be wrapped in the story of our life's progress every day. We need to be customers, valued customers. So we always have an answer to that question – 'How's your day been so far?'

The Monthly, May 2005

War on Terror

The 'war on terror' is officially over. Last week, after consultations with Madison Avenue, the US administration declared that the 'war' had been rebranded as the 'global struggle against violent extremism' (Global SAVE). It is common with wars that not all of the belligerents know at the same time when they are over and this might be why on the day that John Howard arrived in Iraq in a helmet and camouflaged body armour, Donald Rumsfeld arrived in a suit. In these matters it does take a little while to adjust the mindset and realign one's symbols and rhetoric.

The need for rebranding became desperately clear on 7 July when four terrorists failed in their attempt to blow up themselves and hundreds of others on the London public transport system. George W. Bush, Tony Blair and John Howard expressed their sadness at the loss of life, their loathing for the killers and unshakeable determination to win the 'war on terror'. We will win, they said, and let no one suggest that we might not in every regard be going the right way about it.

It seems that like the successful suicide bombers a fortnight earlier the failed bombers were British Muslims. In Egypt in the same week suicide bombers killed 89 local Egyptians and foreign tourists and injured hundreds of others. To this point the identity of these bombers remains unknown, but three groups have so far claimed responsibility for the atrocity on the internet. Of course in Iraq that week, as in every other week, suicide bombers killed and maimed scores of people.

What they didn't get round to was telling us who or what precisely the enemy is. In Iraq they are generally called 'insurgents' but the word 'terrorist' is used almost as often. People who commit acts of terror elsewhere are always 'terrorists', though President Bush seems to prefer 'people who hate our freedoms and way of life'. We know that they are not all 'insurgents' in Iraq: the people who captured Australian construction engineer Douglas Wood were simple criminals although one would have thought from the reporting that they were driven by the same religious and political demons that possessed the four suicide bombers from West Yorkshire. In Iraq, among the ones to whom the term 'insurgent' might sensibly apply, there are local Sunnis, foreign revolutionaries and the disaffected leftovers from the Hussein regime that Donald Rumsfeld used to call 'dead enders'. And doubtless there are others engaged in violent resistance for different motives and beliefs, including resentment of the occupation.

The point is we don't really know who it is we're fighting in the 'war on terror'. Not in London. Not in Iraq. Dick Cheney or Donald Rumsfeld or George Bush might know. It's possible that Blair and Howard know. But if they do, they have not told us in a way that is believable. In Iraq we are saving the government there; we are keeping faith with the brave Iraqi people who voted in the elections: they seem like good reasons, but they are also old and notorious reasons for occupying armies to stay on and on until there is nothing left to defend and face is all there is to save.

At a press conference with Tony Blair in London the Prime Minister told us it was folly to imagine a connection between the occupation of Iraq and the London bombings. And then he went off to Iraq. The sight of the Prime Minister getting out of a Black Hawk in a helmet and body armour was in keeping with the idea of a war on terror. It was also in keeping with the idea of another Vietnam, but this is the wrong idea, and the same goes for the idea that the war in Iraq had anything to do with the bombings in London or with the risk of something like it in Sydney.

As it did for so long in Vietnam, in this 'war' any old thing will do. The lies that made it possible, the tens of thousands of civilians killed, the damage to the United States' reputation, the fact that the occupation daily incites the rage of young Muslims everywhere and that while it continues at such obscene cost Osama bin Laden has gone free – all this ought to make journalists hyperactively sceptical and probing. But no: at the Blair and Howard press conference in London, Paul Bongiorno tried bravely but the rest of the pack were overwhelmed by five minutes of artful and passionate vapidity from the Prime Minister. In war you don't ask questions.

It's the word 'war'. From the moment the 'war on terror' was declared everything went fuzzy. Australians persuaded themselves that refugees from terror might be agents of terror. American soldiers went to fight in Iraq believing they were avenging 9/11. The whole world was conned into believing Hussein had weapons of mass destruction. The consequences of these now well-known delusions are still with us and compounding. No one responsible for creating them has been punished or paid the smallest price and it seems unlikely that they ever will.

So long as it is a 'war' on terror we are easily persuaded to do and think all sorts of other things that in normal times we'd shun. It's a war so we'll put it down as collateral damage. We will give up civil liberties as Philip Ruddock says we should, for instance. We will find reason where there is none to speak of, and cling to beliefs despite the evidence against them. We will render our enemies monolithic and insensate like a thing, rather than pathological like human beings; we'll flaunt our own anger but never recognise theirs. We'll condemn suicide bombers as subhuman filth who kill civilians, but not Stealth bombers which also kill them. We'll conceive of them as cowards or at best poor deluded fools and never think that wars have always required young men to give their lives in battle and young men have always done it. It is war and nothing can compromise our righteousness.

We'll call it a *just* war, which of course is what the terrorists believe it is, and so we'll join them in the folly of forgetting that there is no such thing. There are just causes and necessary wars, but no war is just. Read Homer. Ask the dead. Ask the family of the young Brazilian held down by British plain-clothes police and shot eight times in the head. And then ask if Simone Weil did not have a point when she said that war – or 'force' which is its stock in trade – 'petrifies the souls of those who undergo it and those who ply it'.

The 'war on terror' is a convenient brand, but it is also hard to think of a better way to elevate the enemy's self-regard and, in the long run, through lies, hubris, monstrous acts, eroded rights and self-deceit, lower our own. The British fought the IRA's bombers without doing them the honour of calling it a war. Better to say we're just defending ourselves and the things we believe in.

You might ask why our political leaders are so keen to be fundamentalists when fundamentalism is what we are said to be fighting. Muslims might see it as consistent with the 'crusade' that President Bush said we were on. They might imagine it gives substance to their belief that they are indeed at war with Christians and Jews. And believing they're at war is almost certainly the essential precondition of recruiting young troops, including suicide bombers, to the struggle – and keeping their minds shut and imagining they can smell the perfume of heaven.

It's a pity they caught our politicians unprepared and still firing the old belligerent salvos, but at last the American administration seems to have realised that declaring a 'war on terror' was pure counter-productive folly. It is now a 'struggle against violent extremism'. And hallelujah to that: but expect them to take a little longer to get the fundamentalist rhetoric and the egregious hypocrisy out of the system, especially when their most faithful ally is just getting the gist of it.

Peter Costello says it's all about strength. He told Hillsong that nations needed to be strong and a nation gets strength from 'the heart and commitment and the faith of its people'. But – faith in what? Some of us remember young men in the sixties who went with faith in democracy and the domino theory to Vietnam; and others with faith in the class war and Mao Tse-tung. Like the soldiers in Iraq and the bombers from West Yorkshire they had enough faith to kill and be killed.

New Matilda, 4 August 2005

Judaeo-Christian Mateship

From the experience of Australian men at war and otherwise in extremis, the creed of mateship took on a sacred quality that is not to be mocked or belittled. That is why prime ministers should not make idiotic claims for it. If you want to kill mateship, make it a cliché. If you want to subvert it, render it an article of the national faith where it can invite ridicule. If bringing it into contempt is your aim, utter it as a mantra as you go about doing the opposite of the few precious things it stands for.

The creed itself is not immutable, but elements of it are. To begin with, it's masculine. If we must have national values and mateship must be counted among them, it is a national value for men only.

But not all men. Most men in relatively normal circumstances will settle for friendship, with which humanity made do for many years before mateship. But the cult of mateship has its origins and its most eloquent expression in circumstances that were not normal: most famously, among soldiers at war and bushmen in the bush.

These were men without women: not 'good women' at least, and where there were not even bad women (which is to say prostitutes and 'gins') there was, as one 19th-century settler put it, 'alas . . . the sin for which God destroyed the doomed cities'.

The idea that there is something homosexual about mateship is a familiar sacrilege that we need not entertain. But we do need to recognise that the meaning of the word 'mateship' is plainest when it describes the attachments and the needs of men struggling in a common cause.

In simple terms, while mateship might justly be applied to relations between shearers or miners during a strike or lock-out, it is a corruption in a day spa. The second definitive element of mateship is collectivism. It is an ethos of mutual aid and support, and no more compatible with a creed of self-interest or what today is called aspirationalism than liberalism is with fascism.

This is why, despite the efforts of politicians, talkback hosts and other purveyors of popular fantasy, mateship is now all but obsolete. It is not suited to the times. The segregation of men and women and the divisions of class do not exist as they once did, and it is not in the nature of modern warfare to create the episodes that might give it a second wind. Trade unions that have some claim to be expressions of the creed are declining, and may well be snuffed out by a government that professes faith in mateship.

It also happens that we are less provincial. Exposure to the world likely makes us less inclined to believe that loyalty to friends is an exclusive Australian principle. Americans talk of sticking by their buddies, the English by their chums. Europeans have been familiar with the concept for some time now. It is not unknown among the people who live in Africa. Why, even our own Aborigines seem to have grasped the idea.

Mateship was born about the same time as Australia's racial laws, which, it is worth remembering, pre-dated Germany's by 40 or 50 years and outlived them by another 25. It is not of itself xenophobic, but seems happy in that kind of company. This might be why the PM fancies its chances in the present environment. But what he encourages is less mateship than mateshipism. This requires little more than calling everyone 'mate' and ascribing everything that's good and true to that 'peculiarly Australian value of mateship'. Anything more in a post-modern world is probably psychosis.

The Prime Minister's own Education Minister must have been aware of this when he decided that the second of his nine values for schoolchildren should be: 'Seek to accomplish something worthy or admirable, try hard, pursue excellence.' Brendan Nelson must know that to pursue this perfectly reasonable (some might say breathtakingly fatuous) ambition often requires that we ditch less inspired or dull-witted mates. Nor does mateship allow us freely to cast off mates who have no respect for the minister's other eight values, which include honesty, integrity and tolerance. It is no accident that the creed is often professed among both the criminal and political classes.

That's the other unchanging thing with mateship. Essential and ennobling as it has been in some dire moments of our history, in ordinary times it is a bulwark of mediocrity and slumming. Can this be why we hear so much about it from our Prime Minister?

Well, he can't go on forever. When Peter Costello is Prime Minister we can expect less mateship and more your Judaeo-Christian/Chicago School of Economics national values. Mind you, anyone who can put that package together can probably squeeze in mateship as well. Look out for a kind of trickle-down mateship.

And then there's the possibility that, consistent with his devotion to mateship, John Howard will outsmart his Treasurer, who is not a mate of his, and engineer the elevation of his Minister for Foreign Affairs, who is a great mate. Now there's a prospect: perhaps only when Alexander Downer is Prime Minister and telling us to practise mateship will we give it up forever.

The Age, 2 September 2005

The Treasurer and the Awesome God

Like Harold Holt, Peter Costello has waited a long time for an ageing Prime Minister to move aside and it is no surprise to hear him recently taking comfort from Holt's example. People say that even if Menzies had stayed on for another decade Holt would not have challenged him. The same seems to be true of Costello and Howard. But the comparison ends there.

In the early 1950s, when the White Australia Policy was still an article of national faith, Harold Holt wanted to end it. He backed the 1967 referendum that passed responsibility for Aboriginal affairs to the Commonwealth. In the McCarthy era he enjoyed cordial relations with union leaders and dined with left-wing radicals. No wonder the story got around that he had been spirited away from Cheviot Beach by Maoist submariners.

Where Holt maintained a sufficiently open mind and generous spirit to imagine a different kind of Australia, Costello still gives no convincing sign that he has the same capacity or inclination. Perhaps a true liberal waits behind the epic mask of loyalty. Perhaps we should put aside the nine years serving the most radical right-wing government in Australia's history without once raising his hand to deflect it from its reactionary course.

He marched across the bridge for reconciliation, didn't he? He declared himself a republican. And he once said that he wanted a 'tolerant Australia'. Small 'l' liberals desperate to be rid of Howard and despairing of Labor's prospects might construe these gestures into some reliable indication that enlightenment approaches. And pigs might conquer the heavens. And Harold Holt really is buried near Shanghai.

The idea that a Costello government will have a softer liberal glow than a Howard government comes from the same fog-bound school that gave us the one in 1996 about a Howard government being much the same as a Keating government.

Peter Costello wants us to believe that he will 'regenerate' the government after Howard as Holt did after Menzies. And by way of illustration he tells Hillsong Church he shares their faith. Hillsong's 18,000 worshippers, 35 million TV viewers and $100 million turnover are figures to impress any Treasurer, and might suggest to a Baptist that this church does something right in the eyes of the Lord.

The faithless cannot safely say if he goes there in search of votes or grace. Political and religious euphoria are such he may not know himself. A man accustomed to the speech patterns of business, bureaucrats and Amanda Vanstone might conceivably be moved by Hillsong's: 'Let's have an attitude of being appreciative of where we are because we know where we have come from, and let's never fall into the trap of being satisfied with where we are at and stop growing.'

Hillsong's head honcho holds to the ancient belief that it's okay for Christians to get rich. While it has always required a considerable imaginative feat to find evidence of this in the gospels, the Treasurer would be a pretty poor sort of politician if he spent his days looking for something that might not be there instead of paying attention to what happens in the real world.

Remember we are talking about a Treasurer whose government has borne more false witness than any since Federation and attached itself to a Washington cabal that lies through its imperial teeth. If you can see your Saviour's hand in these places you can see it anywhere.

The miracle is also manifest in a man responsible for the operation of a free-market economy yet, believing in Jesus and the Ten Commandments, recommends meekness and love and not coveting anything our neighbours have.

Good luck to them if they want to clap their hands and sing 'Our God Is an Awesome God'. Hillsong is whatever members want to make of it. But Hillsong is at base a variety of religious fundamentalism that maintains the Bible is literally true and 'our eternal destination of either Heaven or hell is determined by our response to the Lord Jesus Christ'.

Even if this were not the age of global jihad it would be strange to see our leaders suddenly joining in the chorus of Psalm 20 and signing up to a creed that seems to condemn non-Christians to hell. That we do have jihad and they're doing it is plain bizarre.

Peter Costello told Hillsong a nation gets its strength from 'the faith of its people'. He also told them that our Judaeo-Christian civilisation was built on the Ten Commandments. Don't think George Bush: the most striking comparison is with Margaret Thatcher. Thatcher was a crusading Christian, devoted equally to the Ten Commandments and the trickle-down theory and repelled by welfare and collectivism. Raised in the same sort of evangelical household as Peter Costello, she too believed that faith was everything, the Judaeo-Christian tradition was pretty nearly without flaw, and unionists and Tory wets could go to hell together. It is Margaret Thatcher not Harold Holt we should expect when Howard goes. He might change of course, but men who reach 50 still holding to the doctrines of their childhood rarely do.

People who do not find religious fundamentalism especially miserable, nonsensical and offensive should be nonetheless concerned about religion's encroachments on Australian political debate. The evidence suggests that far from regenerating a country it perverts policy, stymies energy and stunts growth.

It is hard to escape the feeling that in this Costello and his colleagues are once more taking their cue from the US – and once more getting it the wrong way round. True, the religious right is on the march and the President is backing them; but the American *tradition* holds with Jefferson that a 'wall of separation' must stand between politics and religion. Thirty or so years later Tocqueville noted that this 'wall' was why the US prospered and Europe decayed, and this observation is well remembered.

You may think the 'wall' is an invention of the faithless, but as a US Appeals Court judge (and Baptist) has pointed out, Jefferson borrowed it from a 17th-century clergyman and founder of Providence, Rhode Island. And the clergyman got it from John 18:36.

Sydney Morning Herald, 10 March 2006

Faith, Freedom and Katrina

> Also it is very important that time is allowed for Mr Brown to eat dinner. Given Baton Rouge is back to normal, restaurants are getting busy. He needs much more that [sic] 20 or 30 minutes. We now have traffic to encounter to get to and from a location of his choice, followed by wait service from the restaurant staff, eating, etc. Thank you.
>
> Text message from Mike Brown's Press Secretary to Marty Bahamonde in the New Orleans Superdome, 31 August 2005

> Oh my God!!!! . . . Just tell her that I just ate an MRE and crapped in the hallway of the Superdome along with 30,000 other close friends so I understand her concern about busy restaurants.
>
> Marty Bahamonde replying, 31 August 2005

Cutting through New Orleans on the freeway that runs above the tattered rooflines the Superdome looms out of the dusk, a monument less to Hurricane Katrina than to the bewildering paralysis that preceded and followed it. The press had arrived two days before the marines, the marines before the head of the Federal Emergency Management Agency (FEMA) and five days passed before the President arrived from his ranch in the neighbouring state of Texas. Because a large part – the poorest part – of the city had not been evacuated large numbers of people had died. More died because help was so late arriving. The President when he finally showed up made a point of telling Mike Brown, the old buddy he had appointed to head up FEMA, that he was doing 'one heck of a job'. Then standing in Jackson Square with civic authorities and press all around he declared that the rebuilding of New Orleans would be 'one of the largest reconstruction efforts the world has ever seen'.

Two months later, there is only one lane open on the bridge out of New Orleans across Lake Pontchartrain. The traffic slows to a crawl. We sit and watch an orange moon climb into the night sky and drop a dozen shimmering reflections in the water. As it rises, so does a smell: of something like sewage but something less organic and fouler. By the time we've crossed the lake to Slidell the moon's turned pearly – 'soft and copious' as Walt Whitman called it.

Another 40 minutes down the road we turn off Highway 10 into Pass Christian, population until two months ago, 7000. The New Orleans gentry kept substantial houses in Pass Christian for 150 years. One of those houses is now jammed under the awnings of a Shell service station. Large houses rest on top of smaller ones. There are houses without roofs and roofs from which the house has gone and left it spread-eagled on the stumps. It is a work of magical realism: here one night not long ago houses roamed around scuttling buildings like Confederate raiders.

Katrina's wind ripped large trees from their trunks three feet from the ground and left jagged stumps as proof of its brutality.

It made houses disappear. Yet clusters of smaller trees are standing and for every half dozen houses in pieces, as if by an arbitrary exercise of will – or the grace of God – a flimsier structure has survived the wind. But nothing survived the sea surge. Pass Christian is 10 feet above sea level. On the night of Katrina it was several feet below. When the sea came ashore it moved concrete slabs, washed asphalt roads away, flattened buildings made of brick and flooded every building.

Refrigerators line the streets, all of them taped up because the smell which was intolerable inside the houses polluted the air outside as well. Rubbish mucked out of the houses and stuffed in plastic bags lies on the roadside like heaps of innards. Signs are painted on the wall, a circle with quadrants indicating the day of inspection, the organisation that inspected it, the number of human corpses if any, the number of cats, dogs or other pets found dead.

Somewhere along the road a light glows under awnings stretched across makeshift kitchens and trestles loaded with groceries. In the tents and vans around the awning volunteers and refugees are sleeping. The vans wear the badge of churches from Florida to Minnesota. One says 'Pastor and People, one in the spirit seeking a more excellent way'. Another says 'Thank God I'm Episcopalian.' The light is on for security, but it is also the light of American Christianity.

Biloxi is 20 minutes up the road from Pass Christian. It's easy to miss on the highway strip of fast-food franchises, Walmarts, Walgreens, real estate outfits, drive-in banks, mortgage houses, credit agencies and churches, all in much the same architectural style and all set on profligate amounts of land. The strip runs for miles along the Gulf Coast and it makes you wonder why on the night of Katrina the Holy Comforter didn't take the opportunity to make a more comprehensive town-planning statement. Some of the big signs are still bent at 160 degrees, but corporate America is indestructible and the really big ones like Walmart, Wendy's and McDonald's replaced their tattered roofs and straightened up their signs within a fortnight.

Evangelical America is no less indomitable. Katrina had hardly blown out to sea before a wave of volunteers of all denominations from all parts of the country descended on the coast. At 11 pm in the Lutheran Church only a half dozen of 65 volunteers are awake. The rest are sleeping on camp stretchers and inflatable mattresses on every bit of floor that is not taken up with makeshift doctors' surgeries and donated groceries: breakfast cereal, toilet paper, AAA batteries, canned fruit, mops. When I ask who donated these supplies I'm expecting her to say Walmart or Dixie but the lady says, 'God. God our Guide.' Next morning God made the pancakes as well. He works through our hands, the lady said as she mixed them. Beside her the polystyrene cooler is marked 'The Lord is Life'.

In April 1960 some blacks protesting at segregation were driven from Biloxi's beaches by a gang of white folks. Those days are over, and if the descendants of those protesters still live in Biloxi, chances are they work in one of the 13 massive sky-scraping casinos. Biloxi's big thing is gambling. But Mississippi's lawmakers don't hold with gambling and they made the operators build the casinos on concrete barges in the water, spitting distance from the beach. They employ thousands of people, about half of Biloxi's residents – or they did until Katrina came ashore. Most of them won't open for a year, but when they do at least they won't have to be in the sea any more. The storm surge drove them as far on to the land as they had previously been off it. Recognising necessity, or perhaps sensing a Biblical dimension to this jaw-dropping phenomenon and seeing no other sense to make of it, within a fortnight the city fathers made the casinos' new onshore location legal.

Naturally the sea that drove the casinos onto land also surged into the residences of those who worked in them. It first knocked down the more opulent houses along the beachfront. The brick walls and everything inside them have gone, leaving only the swimming pools and the crazy paving. Massive oaks lie hundreds of yards from where they grew. They say there used to be a couple of grand antebellum houses, but there is no sign of them. Down by the casinos, an area still cordoned off by the army, a green fishing boat is hard up against one of the walls from the old part of town. Look down towards the water and you can see the path its skipper took when the surge picked him and hurtled him toward the shore: through a two-lane driveway under the casino, past the five-storey-high guitar of the Hard Rock Cafe and a quarter of a mile inland till it hit what might have been the post office. In the rubble between the boat and Hard Rock Cafe a waitress from the nearby Waffle House found a Fender guitar signed by Johnny Cash. Hard Rock headquarters in Florida promised to pay the shipping costs if she sent it back.

In the hours that Katrina raged along the coast sea birds turned up hundreds of miles away in the car parks of Tennessee supermarkets. They stayed for the day and then went home. But the people have no homes to go to. A lot of them never will. Drive around the streets of Biloxi and you can see why.

Once it got past the bricks the water surged unrestrained into black and Vietnamese communities in the weatherboard bungalows behind them. Every house was inundated. Of those that survived, most have been mucked out. Houses still standing have a pile of plasterboard, floor linings and furniture heaped beside them. The air is full of mould and then, as you feel the temperature rise in the mid-morning, the other incomparably worse smell rises with it. For every three houses there are two useless, abandoned cars grey-brown with salt and dirt. There are tens of thousands of useless cars on the Gulf Coast. The houses have the signs on the front walls. An odd one indicates a corpse was found, but that story is not over – in the last week eight more bodies have been discovered including two children. No one knows how many more they'll find, or how many were sucked out to sea when the surge retreated.

No one really knows where everyone's gone. More than a million have left the coast, many more than left the 'Dust Bowl' in the 1930s. They are living in hotels and motels, temporary shelters, trailers, state parks, with relatives and friends. Birmingham, Alabama has organised accommodation for 3000. The schools took in the children. The local chamber of commerce found 3000 jobs. In total Alabama registered 22,600 evacuees but authorities think the real number is at least 60,000. It is the same with the 26,000 registered in Baton Rouge and the 150,000 in Houston.

Each of 419,000 registered families has been given $2,358.00 by the government. The money is to keep them in food, clothing and rent, if they can find an apartment or a motel room. But life's hard in America without a car, a credit card, a computer or cash. Cities that used their own resources to accommodate Katrina's victims can't sustain the effort forever. They expect evictions to start this month. They say some of the trailer parks are becoming ghettoes. Utilities are breaking down. Only a fraction of the trailers needed for evacuees have been provided.

And winter is coming. No one questions the generosity or the resourcefulness of communities across the US. And of course no one questions the churches. But just about everybody questions the Federal government.

Loaded with bottled water, nurses and supplies the Red Cross van crawls around the streets like Mr Whippy, looking for people. Whole blocks are deserted. Then a spectrally thin woman appears on a porch. The volunteer driving the van is a handsome grey-haired Vietnam vet from New York whose father was in the landing at Guadalcanal. He has a brittle military courtesy. He stops and says through the window, 'American Red Cross. Is there anything you need, ma'am, anything we can help you with?' 'Batteries,' she says. 'We've got batteries, ma'am,' he says. And his assistants get out of the van and fill a box with flea powder, apples, bananas, crackers, chocolate, a mop, vacuum packs of Alaskan salmon, toilet paper, diarrhea formula and batteries. Another woman appears and a young man. 'Y'all need anything?' asks the New Yorker adopting the local style.

Over the next couple of hours the Red Cross van finds about 20 people living strangely dignified lives in the mess. It's a great coming together. A volunteer nurse who drove down from Connecticut replaces the dressing on a young man's wounded foot, while another one from South Dakota watches on. A woman caring for a diabetic multiple amputee describes her devotion to the Lord and the understanding of His ways that her mother taught her, while a young man from Phoenix who is serving ten months in what remains of one of Bill Clinton's national youth programs ferries groceries into her trailer. A soft-spoken immaculately groomed woman who looks about 35 takes what she is offered reluctantly. She says

'Yes' when she is asked if she has children, but 'No' when she is offered an armful of soft toys: one of her children is 30 and the other 25. Her sister-in-law is much more enthusiastic and bounds into the Red Cross van to kiss the people in it. There are smiles and hugs and blessings all round until the groceries run out and the van goes back to the church on the highway. It was a good day, says the team leader, 'we emptied the van'; and it seems churlish not to share his sense of satisfaction, or allow any doubt about whose souls – ours or theirs – had been ministered to that afternoon.

In New Orleans alone there is 22 million tons of debris to clear. The devastation along this part of the coast must have produced at least that much again. It is a monumental task. And yet it does seem strange that after two months these people are still living in mounds of rubbish. Could someone not bring in a bulldozer and clear *their* streets at least. You sense paralysis. And you wonder why they are being given snack food and not generators and coolers and meat, barbecues. Why they get diarrhea medicine and not portable lavatories. Why when doctors are expecting an outbreak of scurvy people are being given Honey Smacks. In an atmosphere almost palpable with faith, hope and charity you don't want to be critical, but you can't help wondering.

The saying goes in Louisiana and Mississippi that if you're a Lutheran you must be from somewhere else. But Katrina has done a bit for the Lutheran profile: or, as the pastor's wife insists, God has done it through Katrina. Not only did He bring together so many people in a spirit of Christian love, He created missionary opportunities for the Lutherans. So while groceries and medicine have been dispensed and teams from their little church alone have mucked out 30 houses, there has also been the opportunity for what she calls 'mission fill'. When God sent Katrina he sent miracles, she says. She wants to stay and talk but has to leave for the first meeting of Interfaith, a body representative of all the denominations working in the disaster areas which has been established to decide who gets what from Federal government funding.

On public radio a leader of a Louisiana Church with 250,000 members also speaks of the opportunities created by Katrina. Far from weakening faith it will strengthen it, he claims. What if fear knocks on your door and faith does not answer? Martin Luther King answered his own question: Faith *must* answer, only faith *can* answer, he said. The Louisiana minister agrees. He thinks Katrina might be the beginning of an ecumenical awakening and an opportunity for his church and the more traditional evangelicals to take back some ground from the religious right. In the face of such need he believes all the churches might find common cause and in finding it will recognise that they must resist hypocritical governments that, claiming to be Christian, give $50 million with one hand, and claiming to be fiscally responsible with the other, take $50.6 billion from health care, housing and other programs that assist the poor.

People from countries where religion long ago retreated to the background might be surprised to find evangelical churches in the front lines of disaster relief. But religion is in the front lines of everything in this country. The first people to be consulted about Supreme Court nominations are religious leaders, and the first question to be asked of nominees concerns the separation of church and state. It's a country where God is in both the storm and the pancake batter. He is present at rodeos where successful contestants give thanks to the Good Lord for protecting them and 'helpin' me hold on' to bucking bulls. 'All credit to Him,' they say. He's in football stadiums where national teams, in breach of their Lord's injunction to pray privately and without display, go down on their knees and pray together. He's in the White House as we know, and in congressional, gubernatorial and every other kind of election many of the candidates also go down on their knees.

There is certainly anger at the failure of government to carry out its responsibilities or even accept them. It is a disaster as great as Katrina itself, one national newspaper said last week. Another commentator said that in the government response one could see 'all the symptoms of a failed state'. Marty Bahamonde, the FEMA man who was in the Superdome, called it 'systematic failure at all levels of government'. It didn't help that the President who stayed on the ranch for Katrina was in Florida eight weeks later, with his sleeves rolled up within hours of Wilma going through. Nor have the critics been mollified by the release in recent days of emails sent by Mike Brown and his press secretary, Sharon Worthy. The emails give the impression that Mr Brown, his wife and secretary were less concerned with the emergency than the shirt he chose for television and that he rolled his sleeves up to show he meant business. As people drowned or waited to be rescued from attics, in the Superdome Bahamonde sent texts on his BlackBerry telling Brown they were running out of food and water, that many would not survive the night, that the situation was 'post critical'. Brown replied, 'Thanks for the update. Anything specific I need to do or tweak?'

Even before these made the news if you asked four Americans what they thought about Katrina, chances are at least one or two would pour forth the rage and shame they felt when they recalled the time it took George W. Bush to even seem to notice what was happening in New Orleans. But these days ask four Americans to recall *anything* about George W. Bush and you will get much the same response.

And yet the anger is tempered by the common belief – much older than the modern free-market fashion – that sensible citizens should not expect very much of governments. It helps to remember that in general where there is more faith in God there is less faith in government, and less reliance on it: or as Tocqueville put the equation 170 years ago, '. . . if faith be wanting in him, he must be subject, and if he be free, he must believe.' Tocqueville said it and so did Walt Whitman, democracy is inseparable from religion. 'At the core of democracy is the religious element,' Whitman said, and he meant 'all the religions old and new'. That is the sense one had among all the religions old and new on the Gulf Coast, and in the meeting of social justice and religious ecstasy in the Biloxi church. In experiencing Christian fellowship and purpose they were experiencing America as a place that filled needs beyond the self. And in experiencing this, it seems reasonable to think, those people felt they were experiencing democracy as God intended it in their country.

The churches are carrying so much of the responsibility in part because they never ceded it to government and they are big and strong and fervent enough to fill whatever vacuum the government leaves them. It is as if Katrina recreated the original ground for Christianity: God rained on rich and poor alike, on the just and the unjust. Divided on false lines they can now unite in the common cause of human need. When everyone's lost everything the words of the old spiritual apply to everyone:

I got shoes, you got shoes
When I get to heaven I'm gonna put on my shoes . . .
And walk all over . . . heaven.

If for the churches Katrina is a kind of cleansing, a chance to see in the murk and devastation a light of opportunity, for many in the secular end of town it's a great moment of truth. There are people who say Katrina will have a more profound and lasting effect than 9/11; that it laid bare all the fault lines of American society: race, inequality, energy, the environment. That might explain the seeming paralysis in the place where decisions about such things are made – the Federal government. Everything since the dim-witted insouciance of the President in the first few days suggests that Katrina created problems beyond the government's reach and comprehension. They might wish to leave as much as possible to the churches, state and county authorities and the good will of communities but they cannot escape all responsibility. For one thing they built the levees that collapsed. Two months later no one has decided what is to be done: about the levees, about the rubbish, about the evacuees, about what sort of rebuilding there should be, and in much of New Orleans if there should be any rebuilding at all.

There is no leader. On television last week, John Barry, the author of a book about the 1927 Mississippi floods, remarked that the then President, Herbert Hoover, evacuated 300,000 residents in the time it took President Bush to get Brown into New Orleans after the hurricane. People who know about disasters and people who know New Orleans and the environment of the Gulf Coast cannot understand why a 'Czar' has not been appointed – a Giuliani or a Bloomberg for instance. Why the Academy of Science has not been called in to work with such a 'Czar' and the Army Corps of Engineers. Why no one in government seems to be addressing the questions that are addressed in the opinion pages and letters columns of newspapers every day. The church speaks of grasping opportunities that Katrina created, but the government, when it speaks at all, speaks increasingly of retreating from the big promise that the President made in Jackson Square. Will they take the opportunity to rebuild the regional ecosystem from the ground up or just rebuild the levees, but sink them deeper this time? Will they make a Venice of New Orleans as some writers have suggested, or as another wrote to the Birmingham paper, 'a slum of the future . . . hastily and shabbily reconstructed on sinking earth . . . prepared for suffering souls to live out their lives, periodically casting their votes for morsels that promises entice.' Conservative republicans now say that the parts below sea level should not be rebuilt at all. Suddenly they're worried about the deficit.

Newt Gingrich was on television the other night telling young people at a business school that wherever government went on the Gulf Coast there would be failure. He asked his audience to imagine New Orleans if Fedex were in charge. Or McDonald's. Or Travelocity, an internet travel company. It's easy to see that it's been a long time since Newt made his own bookings – and easy to point out companies generally go where there is profit rather than need. Gingrich however was making a different point: US government departments and agencies don't work, he said, because they are built on obsolete models that go back to civil service regulations devised in the 1880s and revised but not fundamentally changed in the 1930s. Government in his view is now constitutionally incapable of providing the services people need.

Gingrich's student audience, it goes almost without saying, were all ears and among them not one could think of a single thing to say in favour of government at all. You wondered what they might think if they had heard a ghostly voice saying the citizenry 'must effectively control the mighty commercial forces which they themselves have called into being'. If out of the blue they heard it call for 'a far more active government interference with social and economic conditions in this country'. What outrageous liberal would they think it was? Paul Krugman? Susan Sarandon? In fact the words come from the old tiger of American individualism and imperial can-do, Theodore Roosevelt. Obsolete model or not, it's hard to imagine the rubbish would still be lying in the streets if Teddy Roosevelt was in charge of the government. Or FDR or LBJ, for that matter.

What no one seems to be able to decide is if the government is incompetent because it's a government, or because it has been put in the hands of incompetent people – for which, very often, read cronies. The debate does not always divide along the familiar ideological or party lines: conservatives and republicans have been among those arguing that government failure with Katrina goes much further than cronyism or the inexplicable sluggishness of the White House: that it is a symptom of general decline in the status and abilities of government over the past 25 years. They wonder aloud about such a government's ability to cope with a bird flu pandemic.

That feels much closer to the truth, perhaps because it is where the failures of the White House and the bureaucracy converge – in the apparent absence of will, of purpose, dispatch. After Katrina it is impossible to imagine a modern US government of either stripe having the capacity for a New Deal or even a Great Society. It is easier to imagine that these were aberrations which for the last three decades governments intent on satisfying the wants of the white middle class have been determined to pull down. Katrina was not a failure of government per se, but a failure of a government compromised, run down and badly led. It was the failure of government in an era when government is out of fashion. Perhaps the whole story is contained in one article that appeared in a Gulf newspaper recently: in it a local contractor complained that every day he looked around and saw what he could be doing with his fleet of bulldozers, but he can't get a tender. How come Halliburton can get them, he asks, and I can't?

Downtown New Orleans and the French Quarter are functioning again. The hotels have pumped out their basements and got the worst of the stink out of the elevators. Not that it is easy to get a room: they're full of insurance assessors and FEMA people. It's only when the train pulls out and gets beyond the Superdome that you see the meaning of Katrina – and the statistics: nearly half a million people lived in New Orleans before Katrina; going on for three months later there are only 70,000. Mile upon mile of gutted houses, useless cars, empty streets. Here and elsewhere on the coast it seems incredible that the country which took Baghdad in a fortnight and nearly 40 years ago landed two men on that soft and copious moon can't move the rubbish. That nothing seems to be happening.

There is a black man on the northbound train with his five-year-old daughter. The mother left when she was six months old. His house in Slidell was washed away and all he owns is in the US Navy duffle bag on the rack above him. He's going to Maryland where a couple of old friends think he might be able to get a job. In front there's an extended poor white family of eight. Seven feet of water went through their house. They're going to start again in New York or maybe New Jersey. An old black couple tells them that New Jersey is better for bringing up kids. None of them are ever going back.

Good Weekend, 24 March 2006

empower, empowered, empowering, empowerment

Key goal of all organisations. Employees are *empowered* when they *take ownership*, usually by becoming *competent*. Customers are *empowered* by *choice*, *shareholders* by profit, dividends, etc. Thus is the *triple bottom line empowered*. (See *ducks in a row*.)

We are all *empowered* by employment, education, a win at the races, a new set of spectacles or teeth, etc. Some are *empowered* by God; others are *disempowered* by Him. Faith *empowers*: the loss of it can *empower* equally. Ditto Reason. Hitler and Stalin were both *empowered* by 'transforming unwanted beliefs into beliefs that *empowered* them'. An *est* word.

'*Transform* unwanted beliefs to beliefs that *empower* you.'

Neuro Linguistic Programming

'To reach and influence the world by building a large Bible-based church, changing *mindsets* and *empowering* people to lead and *impact* in every sphere of life.'

Hillsong Church Mission Statement

'*Empower* thy sheep.'

From *Weasel Words*

The East Timor Problem

Take a poll and ask the people if they like brute violence. If they care nothing for justice or seeing the weak ground down by the strong. Are they for torture, rape and murder? Who favours terror? If as we might expect only a few cranks answer 'yes', it follows that the great majority of Australians must have deplored Indonesia's 25-year occupation of East Timor and the way their governments turned a blind eye to the crimes. And, were they to read Mark Aarons' article in the last *Monthly*, they must now feel ashamed. It's not as if they didn't know. True, the story faded for long periods, and there were times when the matter of East Timor seemed to be concerned less with the East Timorese than the murders of Australian journalists during the invasion. But no one who read the Aarons story can say with honesty that he was surprised by the horrors it contains.

How much we knew depended on how much we wanted to find out, but we knew. And knowing, we were happy to trade with Indonesia, go there as tourists, and without demur vote for governments that wanted to make friends with the Suharto regime. Nothing we knew about East Timor persuaded us that the relationship with Indonesia should be curtailed. This is not to say that Australians don't deplore tyranny, but rather that they deplore it at their own convenience and they don't deplore it any more than the people of other countries and other times who notoriously turned their backs on it.

In the early nineties I could find out about East Timor just by visiting the struggling supermarket across the road. It was run by an East Timorese man who had fought in the resistance to the invasion and remained a part of it in Melbourne. He could not go back to East Timor because he would be killed. He was a cheerful man. He had a quick smile, even when he was telling me that the East Timorese were being systematically terrorised and dispossessed; that they were being killed, tortured, starved, disappearing; that people who went into hospital in East Timor did not come out. Many of the things the report of the East Timor Commission has chronicled, this man said to me among the supermarket shelves. It *was* genocide, he said.

Though he admired Paul Keating, the Prime Minister for whom he knew I worked, he could not understand how a man as smart as Keating could be so wrong about Suharto. But then Suharto was a smart man too. Maybe too smart for Keating, he thought.

The truth is Suharto did not have to outsmart anyone. By the early 1990s when this East Timorese man was running his supermarket, everyone in a position to influence policy in Canberra was persuaded that pursuing close and friendly relations with Suharto was the only sensible way to pursue Australia's interests. Taken together, their arguments for all but unrestrained 'engagement' took the form of an impermeable, self-reinforcing world view.

The central premise of the pro-Suharto ideology was that we could not make such an important relationship as the one with Indonesia hostage to events in one of its minor provinces. Around this article of faith – or dogma – layers of seemingly self-evident truth accumulated, and through them no countervailing thought could seep. A believer in the policy was like any other believer, including old communist believers. All evidence that could be denied was denied: that which could not be – corpses for instance – was duly deplored, but as aberrant rather than typical of a thoroughly vicious regime. And then there was the old one about history's often brutal course with which no wise person argues: the corpses washed away by historical inevitability are numberless.

Indonesia was important as the most populous Muslim nation in the world; as a developing country offering numerous 'complementarities of interests'; as a precondition of successful Australian engagement with Asia. Immeasurable economic and geopolitical benefits would come of advancing this relationship, and none would come of retreat. In speeches we would recite the ways we'd profit like lines of doggerel and leave listeners to reflect upon the costs of inaction. But East Timor was as good as any other measure of the dictum: the more we talked to Suharto, the more trust and mutual dependence we established in Jakarta, the more the future of the two countries became entwined, the more chance to have some influence on the matter of East Timor.

For people who said that 'engagement' really meant 'appeasement' there were several standard ripostes. What would they prefer? A military invasion? Trade sanctions against our nearest neighbour, a third world country? Or did they just want more and more John Pilger-like moral denunciations, to which Suharto would respond with his usual impassive stare, or leave the room, or read you his non-aligned nations speech on comparative national development, pointing out that there were no journalists and photographers making the case for human rights when the western countries were colonising the world, including Indonesia, and exploiting and brutalising large numbers of its inhabitants. Indonesia did not lecture Australians on their treatment of Aborigines. Indonesia did not question the integrity of Australia's borders. And so on: butt out! It was not beyond the right-wing general, the man most responsible for the deaths of hundreds of thousands of alleged communists and sympathisers at the advent of the New Order, to outflank the Left on the left.

Besides, the pro-engagement people said, unless the East Timor lobby had evidence that Suharto had designs on Darwin or other parts of South-East Asia, the charge of 'appeasement' was hyperbole, a conveniently misleading anachronism. Whatever else might be said about the realpolitik of recognising the occupation, East Timor was not granted to Indonesia as Poland and Czechoslovakia had been to Hitler, to stem his appetite for more. While all exercises in the realities of power that do not end in full-blown war or perfect peace may be to a greater or lesser extent morally deficient, they do not all constitute appeasement. On the contrary, in an imperfect world decent people frequently do best by minimising the number of the victims.

What was more, the policy advocates argued, in an imperfect world Suharto's Indonesia was a lot better than its critics were willing to concede – or able to see from their moral high ground. It was hardly an open society but nor was it entirely closed. True, from time to time, the military cracked a few heads in restive provinces. True, they periodically turned on the press, foreign and local. And by western standards the regime was corrupt (though the beneficiaries might say that nothing they were ripping from the national wealth compared with what Europe had taken). But this country of 18,000 islands was home to 240 million people, whose standards of health and education were improving and who were for the most part free to practise their various religions and live according to their various traditions. Indonesia was a stable, advancing and moderate Muslim nation.

In this another part of the argument lay. Paul Keating had always believed and as Prime Minister publicly said that Suharto's control of Indonesia had been of incalculable benefit to Australia. To understand this one only has to think of what it would have meant had Indonesia remained unstable after Sukarno fell in 1966. And it was not just the economic opportunities and the military savings generated by the pro-investment, anti-communist Suharto: it was that so long as those 240 million Asians on Australia's front doorstep were under the General's heel we slept soundly. We recoiled from the massacres of communists, but once they were gone we had less to worry about and we soon forgot the manner of their going.

A stable Indonesia, moreover, made it easier for us to shed our ancient fears of Asia. Suharto was not why we dropped the White Australia policy and began to take in Asian migrants, but he made acceptance easier. It is surely more than a coincidence that the generation of Australians who took such pride in open immigration policies, multiculturalism and the value of tolerance and diversity corresponded to the rule of Suharto. And when Suharto fell and Indonesia began to register in Australian minds as it had back in the Sukarno days, as problematic and unreliable, our xenophobia returned; we put the borders up, replaced the value of tolerance and diversity with chest-beating about Australian (and 'Judaeo-Christian') *values* and, before you could say 'Pauline Hanson', proposed 'citizenship tests' for migrants.

That courage should desert us so quickly and the era of openness and diversity should be so brief is hard enough for liberals to swallow. Harder still is the idea that liberalism in Australia profited from despotism in Indonesia; that what we took for our own courage and optimism, what we took for change in the national temperament, was really just the profit on Suharto's ruthlessness. And isn't this the rub? Countries only get that sort of courage when every now and then they abandon sophistry and confront tyranny without compromise. It was the lesson Lincoln taught Americans. And it might yet be the lesson of East Timor.

The Monthly, June 2006

Situation Ethics

When Abu Musab al-Zarqawi was killed on 7 June, United States military officials at first said he was dead when they found him, which is no less than one would expect after two 500-pound bombs landed on the house he was in. Two days later, however, the same officials told journalists that the Iraqi police were the first to reach the site and found the terrorist alive: he 'mumbled something . . . indistinguishable', and he 'attempted to roll off the stretcher . . . and get away'. 'Everybody re-secured him back onto the stretcher, but he died almost immediately thereafter . . .' The military spokesman told how they washed the blood from al-Zarqawi's corpse before taking photographs; because, '[d]espite the fact that this person actually had no regard for human life, we were not going to treat him in the same manner'.

As the US military offered this revised account, an Iraqi witness told a different story. A man identified as Mohammed or Ahmed Mohammed told Associated Press reporters: 'We put him in the ambulance, but when the Americans arrived they took him out of the ambulance, they beat him on his stomach and wrapped his head with his dishdasha, then they stomped on his stomach and his chest until he died and blood came out of his nose.'

In view of al-Zarqawi's atrocities and the part he played in what is at present called the 'insurgency', we might ask if it matters how he died. The man was a vicious thug. Spare a thought perhaps for the two women and the child who also died in the air strike, but al-Zarqawi killed a lot more than that and doubtless would have killed many more. It is just as fair to ask why we should believe an Iraqi witness – especially one who, it seems, lived near al-Zarqawi's hideout – before we believe the American military.

The problem with the first of these two apparently reasonable points of view is that so many civilians have now been killed and wounded – at least 50,000 have died since the invasion began – the word 'atrocity' as aptly describes American conduct as al-Zarqawi's; if not for us, then surely for those on whom the phosphorous bombs are being dropped. As for the second, such has been official American deceit about the war in Iraq, by now we might as well believe the most partisan bystander as their military – or their administration or much of their press.

Or their President, who declares and believes himself a war president in a 'war paradigm' – which is to say in a situation where normal democratic standards, including standards of truth, may be suspended in order to deal with the (unending) emergency. And the press fall into line 'in this very serious time' (*New York Times*) and describe his lies as '. . . the President just being the President' (CNN).

The alleged massacre by US Marines of 24 civilians at Haditha on 19 November 2005 is one more case in point. The dead included a 76-year-old in a wheelchair and four children under five. Within 24 hours of the shootings the Marine Corps said a marine and 15 civilians had been killed by a roadside bomb. Soon after they said the civilians had been inadvertently killed in a battle with insurgents. The cover-up lasted until March this year when *Time* magazine broke the story with compelling evidence from eyewitnesses, and they followed up with a cover story on 12 June. The military did not act alone in the cover-up: al-Jazeera ran the story of Haditha on the day that it occurred and shared its information with the western media. But the western media ran the Marines' story and went on running it for four months.

At least 14 US soldiers are now serving sentences for killing or abusing prisoners in Iraq. A dozen or more incidents involving murder, rape and 'voluntary manslaughter' of civilians are being investigated. Four were announced last month, including one into the premeditated rape and murder of a woman and her family. After Haditha broke, retired Air Force Colonel Mike Turner, a former planner at the Joint Chiefs of Staff, offered this interpretation: 'What we're seeing more of now, and these incidents will increase monthly, is the end result of fuzzy, imprecise national direction, combined with situational ethics at the highest levels of this government.'

Situation ethics seems not to have reached Australia yet. Not officially. We're a practical people and never did like doctrine. If you've not heard of it, it's a theory first proposed in the mid-1960s by Joseph Fletcher, an Episcopal minister. The argument in essence is that the ethics of any course of action depend much less upon an external code than the state of things at the time – just ask yourself whether you should bear false witness when the truth will cost your life or a loved one's, and you have the gist of it.

Proponents of situation ethics insist that it is nothing like moral relativism. Moral relativism is a notorious nonsense of liberals who recognise no moral truth at all. Nor are the situational ethicists to be compared to folk who justify foul acts by reference to revolutionary as opposed to reactionary truth, or any other species of fanatic or Machiavel, including Richard Nixon, who ever found in doctrine a convenient justification for committing crimes. There is nothing wrong with situation ethics *per se*: the problem began, as Colonel Turner seems to have decided, when rather like Marxism it fell into the wrong hands.

It was inevitable that Haditha should arouse memories of the massacre of Vietnamese civilians at My Lai in 1968. Twenty times more were killed at My Lai; it was a village not just three houses, and rape, torture and mutilation accompanied the killing. Regular soldiers did the business, not the venerated Marines. But then as now, the affair was covered up by the army – the 'investigation' was led by (then) Major Colin Powell – and the administration and the press joined in the whitewash. Then as now, patriotic Americans (and many like-minded Australians) tended to see the men responsible as the real victims: victims of a war in which very often the enemy could not be distinguished from the civilian population; men under extreme stress; men for whom normal standards of judgement and behaviour had with good reason broken down.

At Haditha it was 'purely shooting people', the Democratic congressman and Vietnam veteran, John Murtha, said after being briefed 'at the highest level' by the Marines. 'Marines overreacted because of the pressure on them, and they killed innocent civilians in cold blood,' he said; and thus in a single sentence both condemned and, as if ordinary ethical considerations did not apply in their situation, excused them.

This is no redneck's view, and it wasn't when My Lai was in the news. Then as now, the men responsible were either a few bad apples, or good men made momentarily bad by bad situations, and if they were guilty so were the men who sent them. Sympathy for the soldiers went far and wide and to the top. William Calley, the only man convicted of murder at My Lai, served just three years – not in gaol but under house arrest. During his trial all over the country banners hung in the streets demanding clemency. Calley claimed he was just doing what he was told to do: 'Nobody in the military system ever described them as anything other than Communism. They didn't give it a race, they didn't give it a sex, they didn't give it an age. They never let me believe it was just a philosophy in a man's mind.' The public thought this a reasonable defence. Richard Nixon said the telegrams were 500 to one in Calley's favour, and so he pardoned him. You'd swear they had all been reading situation ethics.

More people would have been killed at My Lai had not a helicopter pilot, Warrant Officer Hugh Thompson, risked his life and career to forcibly bring it to a halt. For this most soldierly action Thompson was persecuted by the army, vilified in the media and before Congress, and shunned and threatened in his home state of Georgia where Governor Jimmy Carter urged citizens to drive with their headlights on to show their support for Calley.

Thompson was shot down five times in Vietnam, the last time breaking his back. When he died at the age of 62 in January this year, the media replayed a shattering interview he had given a year and a half before. He wept as he told the interviewer about what he saw at My Lai and his subsequent treatment by his army and his country. But the most telling thing he said was this, about Calley and his men: '. . . I wish I was a big enough man to say

I forgive them, but I swear to God I can't.' For Thompson the situation did not change the ethics – soldiers do not murder, he said. Simple as that – and the same as the old Generals Grant and Sherman said. Situation ethicists might say that love led him and his crew to stop the massacre, but it seems much more likely that it was an external code, a belief in something unshakably true.

The idea of 'situation ethics' had not long been born when Calley's ethics were judged to be situational and Hugh Thompson unethical in his reading of the situation. But something (the situation or the ethics?) must have changed because in 1998 the men who had stopped the slaughter at My Lai were given medals for valour. The army changed its rules and made it unlawful for a soldier not to intervene if he came upon unlawful acts. Thompson spent the last years of his life giving talks to young soldiers on 'doing the right thing'.

Before he died he said he felt ethics were now 'all but tattooed on their foreheads'.

And then there was Abu Ghraib. Thompson, by now a hero of sorts, said by their obvious unconcern the soldiers in the photographs revealed that they were acting with the sanction of their superiors. The situation was not of the soldiers' making. And we know that to be true: the situation was the making of people higher up, as high as the US Attorney General Alberto Gonzales, who said, 'In my judgement the new paradigm renders obsolete Geneva's strict limitations on questioning of enemy prisoners,' and abandoned any attachment to an external code. As high as Donald Rumsfeld. As high as the President.

Now, in contrast to My Lai, the US army is sending offending soldiers to gaol. It is insisting on the application of a code. In recent weeks there has been talk of the death penalty.

Maybe it's not the same thing, but situation ethics doesn't seem to work very differently – or much better than moral relativism. This might be because it's the President and the military and the cabal around them, and the press embedded with the cabal, with the 'war paradigm' and the lies it sanctions, who decide what the situation is and what it's not. After that, stuff happens.

The Monthly, August 2006

Aussie Icons

Imagine for a moment that George Orwell was right when he said that words have precise and specific meanings and we should do our best to stick to them when we speak or write. Orwell argued that 'slovenly' language made it harder to think clearly, and as clear thinking is a precondition of enlightened and functional democracy language is not a frivolous concern. Let's say we took Orwell seriously for a moment – *only* for a moment because the time we spend on taking language seriously is time we cannot spend on taking 'real issues' such as 'Aussie values' seriously. It 'mitigates against' them, as they say sometimes on the ABC. But spare a non-frivolous moment for the language and think about the way we use 'icon'.

Two or three days after Steve Irwin died, while standing in an airport queue I heard a man behind me say to his companion that Germaine Greer had 'tried to gut an Aussie icon'. His companion was astounded to hear that anyone should be so insensitive. 'I mean,' said the man, 'I wasn't a big wrap for the bloke, but he was an icon and you have to respect that. You don't go gutting an Aussie icon.'

Language proceeds by imitation and it's a safe guess the traveller thought of Irwin as an icon because that is the cliché everyone in the media had chosen. They did not call him a naturalist or a blowhard, and he had got beyond 'celebrity'. Some stressed he was a 'family man'. But above all he was an 'Aussie icon'.

Back in 1946 when Orwell wrote *Politics and the English Language*, icons did not wrestle with crocodiles and pythons. Icons were still as they had been for the previous two millennia; sacred images, usually of saints, venerated by Christians, especially in the Eastern Church. They were mute and inanimate *representations*, though granted they spoke plainly to the faithful.

The sorts of people who are now called icons in Orwell's day were called national heroes or stalwarts or giants or lions, or citizens much loved and looked up to. Explorers, soldiers, political leaders, entertainers, scientists, sportsmen: the world was not short of what are now called 'icons' just because that was not then the word for them. Take Field Marshal Montgomery, for instance, or Edmund Hillary, Albert Einstein, Winston Churchill, Eleanor Roosevelt, Douglas Bader, Don Bradman, Gary Cooper, John Landy, Jane Russell, the Queen and Rising Fast. For some people, Orwell was one. Stalin was another, for some people. It was more than admiration. They were people who represented to us something elevated, if not perfect; people in whom we saw ourselves as we would like to be. They embodied our personal or national ideals.

We went some way to making icons of them if we had a photo or poster above our beds, or a little bust on the mantelpiece; but the person and the representation were kept distinct. A pepper shaker was not Winston Churchill, nor had it any of his powers, just because it was in his likeness. This was for the same reason that Winston Churchill was not a pepper shaker, and had none of a pepper shaker's powers. There must have been some general intimation that there was peril – and possibly madness – in failing to distinguish between the reality and the representation. Some people might hold that a little gilt-framed, hand-painted image of St Anthony and a photo of Stalin are both icons, but even if we accept that questionable proposition we are not therefore obliged to believe that St Anthony was in his own person an icon of Christianity and Stalin an icon of Communism. Andy Warhol knew that he was making icons of Marilyn Monroe and Campbell's soup, not making Marilyn and the soup icons.

There is of course another reason for taking Orwell's advice and reserving 'icon' for its original and accepted meaning: this was that the photos of Stalin and Hitler and the badges of Mao were created in imitation of icons to encourage quasi-religious veneration. They were mass-produced facsimiles designed to invest the Fuhrer, the Great Leader or the Great Helmsman with perfect wisdom and seeming divine powers. This was Orwell's very point: slovenly language and slovenly thought live in permanent and dangerous embrace.

The *American Heritage Dictionary* of 20 years ago defined 'icon' as a representation or symbol. The latest one includes two new meanings: the picture representing a file or program on a computer screen and 'One who is the object of great attention and devotion; an idol.' Most, though not all, other dictionaries have done something similar. The English language is of course forever changing; often for the better and just as often for the worse. In both cases, as followers of Orwell know better than most, it is all but futile to resist.

Yet we might as well mark the changes. Before those popular heroes became icons we had, in addition to a language with more variety and life in it, a more general freedom to dissent. One did not have to like Don Bradman or Winston Churchill in the way it seems one has to like these modern 'icons'. They were legends in their ways and it was common for bits of myth to attach to them. But our attitude was not religious. In the end they were what they were, and if they were transcendent it was only as a cricketer transcends the demands of that game, or a general an enemy with the high ground, or a nurse septicemia, or a horse the limitations of most horses. There was no heresy or threat of damnation in ignoring them.

Still, it is hard to put a finger firmly on the difference. Three quarters of a century ago almost a quarter of Melbourne's population turned out for the funeral of Sir John Monash. No one called him an Aussie icon. Or even a war icon; or an engineering icon; or a Jewish icon. Is it possible they mourned him as an icon while thinking him a mere national hero, or a good man who had served his country very well?

It is more likely that our democracy had not evolved to the point where, for want of a local Monarch, Messiah or Patron Saint, by means of these icons the people had taken to granting themselves the same sovereignty. What are 'Aussie icons' if not likenesses of the people at large? And from what do they derive their authority – not to say, majesty – if not from 'Aussie values'? The very alert will notice the switcheroo: where the old icons reminded the faithful of their relative weaknesses, in the new Aussie icon Aussies see confirmation of their strengths. The Aussie icon is, as one would expect, an enhanced icon.

Let no one – no one who does not wish to be nailed by the ears to a gum tree – suggest that this phenomenon runs in any way parallel to one observed in the United States by H. L. Mencken: 'As democracy is perfected,' he said in 1920, 'the office of the President represents, more and more closely, the inner soul of the people. On some great and glorious day the plain folks of the land will reach their hearts' desire at last and the White House will be adorned by a downright moron.' We can ignore Mencken, like any other bitter old curmudgeon. He was a notorious elitist, blind to democratic progress and could not tell an Aussie icon from a catfish.

But we are trying to honour Orwell here, and all the others including Mencken and William F. Buckley Jr, who say that while language is by nature inexact, we should strive for exactitude. With 'icon' the heart of the difficulty is the matter of representation. Even computer science keeps the original sense of 'icon' as an image or symbol of something else. But the Crocodile Man, though an idol, remains himself and not a symbol in the sense that an icon is. It was the same with St Anthony. That is, we do not make the saint an icon; we make icons of the saint.

And here is the opportunity for the Leader of the Opposition, Kim Beazley. The following proposal could in a single stroke do a service to plain English, make a lasting contribution to Australia's national security and dig him out of a hole. Let us make a real icon of Steve Irwin, a framed engraving or photograph with a crocodile, much as St Patrick is with a snake and St Agnes with a lamb. Make another of John Howard and a random third, and let our customs officers show them to all visitors and intending immigrants. Demand either that they name all three, or by some non-verbal means such as kissing or weeping or pressing to their brows, prove their respect for the Aussie values these icons symbolise. A simple test and those who pass it will enter with our blessing. Those with whom it draws a blank shall be turned away.

The Monthly, October 2006

A Never-Never Land for Sense

Three and a half hours westward from Gove, the half-dozen houses of an Aboriginal outstation lie baking in the scrub. At certain times of the year about 80 people live here. In addition to the houses, there is an airstrip, two school buildings, a workshop and a phone booth: and a story attaches to each of them.

A couple of weeks ago, police arrived and searched the place for drugs. They had no reason to think they'd find any and they didn't. When the place was established nearly 40 years ago the community banned all drugs, including alcohol and kava, and the rule has applied ever since. There is no gambling. And if the police were looking for signs of domestic violence or molested children, they weren't going to find them either. It's not paradise, but these things don't happen here.

They are Yolngu people. To judge by the rock paintings and mythology with which they identify, it is likely they have been on these lands for 4500 years. As with other outstations, this one was set up to maintain the culture and language and the land from which they are inseparable. The white Australians of those times thought this was reasonable. The feeling was that enough damage had been done to these people, and that less might be done in future if they were given their ancestral lands and, as far as possible, allowed to live according to their customs and beliefs.

It is hard country and it has made them resilient people. The chief custodian was raised in keeping with the laws and rites of his ancestors. He grew up nomadic and can give the Yolngu name to every species of plant and animal that lives there; every rock and every painting, every waterhole and every kind of fish. He is a tiny, impish man; alternately anxious and laughing. He also looks indestructible, and if he proves not to be in the next few years, it will be the tobacco and not the country that does for him. Tobacco is the only non-medicinal drug allowed at the outstation.

The great objectives of the outstation movement were to protect the cultural traditions and pass them on to future generations, and to keep the young people away from the chaos of the larger settlements where drugs, violence and despair devour them. Go to one of these settlements and then go to the outstation and you can easily conclude that the objective has been met. The young people of the larger centres know nothing of their traditions, and look unhealthy. The children of the outstation know something and look healthy and happy. The teenagers and adults carry no surplus fat. Their skin shines.

They would be even healthier if the contractors who put in the septic tanks and drains had done their work more conscientiously: a real septic tank instead of the 44-gallon drum they used, and agricultural pipes to drain water away from the taps, would have eliminated the pools of stagnant water where parasites gather. They would be healthier still if the health department had held the contractors to account: or if they had not taken the view that the people's rotten teeth should not be treated because then everyone else would want their teeth done, and excused their own neglect on the grounds that Aboriginal people can tolerate more pain than whites.

The people at the outstation go hungry sometimes. This is partly because the habitats of the animals they once hunted are being destroyed by exotic species. Cane toads have killed off the goannas and pythons that were once an important part of the people's diet. Water buffalo and pigs gouge the land, rip out vegetation and erode and foul the creeks.

They also go hungry because their supports fail them at nearly every step. The half-dozen houses are as if expressly designed to be unlivable in the sweltering climate and perfectly unsuited to the inhabitants' way of life. No breeze can blow through them. Most of the solar panels only worked for a few weeks after they were installed and no one ever came back to fix them.

The tractor provided to maintain the airstrip is a rare Korean model without spare parts. For more than a year the people asked for someone to come and fix it. Three months ago a volunteer overhauled it, but it lacked two parts. It still does. The community generator was running the batteries flat. The community was blamed. But the volunteer found that the person sent to repair it had assembled the alternator the wrong way. The daily life of the people is conducted in the shadow of this incompetence, waste and neglect. The stories are funny in the manner of Russian satire; but the reality, like the Russian one, is corrosive and dispiriting.

Dr Neville White is a biological anthropologist. He is also a Vietnam veteran. He drove up from La Trobe University 35 years ago and has been there for months at a time every year since. He persuaded Rotary and other philanthropic bodies to put up the money for a school and a workshop, and he took up a team of Vietnam veterans to build it with the young men. When the workshop was finished, at a cost of several thousand dollars, a bureaucrat flew out from Darwin to supervise the installation of an illuminated 'Exit' sign.

The vets teach the young men various mechanical skills; how to repair houses, how to paint them. The young men are keen to learn. Until recently a teacher came each week from the regional college – a teacher with trade skills who could work with the teenagers and young men. Two young women from the outstation were trained to be assistant teachers. Enrolments at the school more than doubled. A second, larger school building was erected.

And then, after a few months, the trade teacher was taken away. The young men who had been learning how to repair LandCruisers and plumb houses found themselves in class with six-year-olds being taught how to make pizzas. Enrolments halved. Most have gone into the centres where the drugs and chaos are. Some of them went because they were frightened by stories that the police and soldiers were coming after them. The Yolngu often use signs to communicate with each other: to signify police they cross their wrists, as if handcuffed.

The difference between the efficiency of the volunteers and the ineptitude of the bureaucracy is startling – as startling as the difference between the volunteers' generosity and the paltriness of the bureaucracy and the contractors. Next time Australians congratulate themselves on their work in Aceh or East Timor, or deplore the American response to Hurricane Katrina, they might reflect on the Northern Territory.

No white community would stand for it. But then, in general, white communities are not so heavily dependent on the government. Some are, of course; and some, like the Aborigines of the outstations, choose to live in remote and unproductive places.

But the white people who do this are commonly esteemed as authentic, if not 'iconic', Australians, and the passing of their way of life is reckoned a national tragedy. There was a time when it seemed possible the country would think this way about the Aborigines living on their homelands, but it now seems certain that this time has passed.

Even if the services intended for the outstations actually reached them, life on the outstation would still fall well short of perfect. When the sun is setting and the kids are playing football or hanging from the mango trees, and the men are hunting and the women tending fires, and the bee-eaters are whizzing about and the old custodian is wandering up the airstrip on his nightly search for tracks and taking the odd potshot at mudlarks with his shanghai, it comes close to *seeming* perfect. But of course it's not: it wasn't before the Europeans, it wasn't after them, and it's not now.

Yet it is so much better than the bigger centres. And it would be so much better still if the promises were kept; the humiliations and disappointments were kept to a tolerable minimum and the people were not obliged to be always asking – like children – for their recognised entitlements. It is not just the impression of relative health and happiness: there is hard data to say they are healthier. And while government surveys never seem to ask the question, the people on the outstations will tell you that they feel healthier, happier and safer there.

The practical skills the outstation residents want, and the vets and the government teacher were beginning to provide, are precisely what the government says *it* wants. Being able to fix their own and others' vehicles would not only provide income and employment, but also free them from the grip of town repairers who charge them what they like and do not hesitate to confiscate their cars if they cannot pay their bills. Local Yolngu work teams can maintain the buildings, machinery and roads at a fraction of the cost of contractors. Providing guided tours of their country for scholars and students would make for useful jobs and income and maintain the connection with the land. Everything the people of the outstation want, the government says *it* wants for Aboriginal people. Everything the people have conscientiously shunned for 35 years, the government says must be shunned now.

So why would the government abolish the permit system that protects the land against degradation and the people against booze and drugs? No one seems to know if the system still applies or not, but tourists and hunters are assuming that it doesn't and heading into the lands for the first time in 40 years. Why would they cancel CDEP on these outstations? Why would they tell the people that they must be economically self-sufficient, yet deny them the means they have chosen to do it? Why tell them – as the Yolngu say they have been told – that they must set up a shop and sell drinks and artifacts to motorists passing on the Katherine road? Or dance for them at night? Why, when the centres are plagued with booze, dope and violence, force the outstation people back into them? These are not my questions: they are what the local administrators and educators are asking.

Whatever the particular merits of the present Federal government intervention, there is no question that the big centres needed drastic action. They have needed it for many years. But why starve the people out of the homelands? The old custodian speaks just enough English to make his view of these things clear. It's not for drugs or for children, he says. It's for mining. He has always said 'No'. But they never stop asking. And they'll win in the end.

That is one plausible explanation. There is another one which he cannot know: that they have put themselves beyond the reach of booze and drugs, but they could not escape the culture wars and the Carlylean tenet of their chief protagonist – that history is always right and just and the vanquished have no cause worth defending.

Sydney Morning Herald, 20 October 2007

Society of Birds

E. E. Cummings prayed that his heart would always be open to little birds. My family, the maternal side especially, has always shared some of his sentiment. It goes back to the clearing of the forest. As the trees went, the little birds came and dwelt in the hydrangeas under the window. Fantails, wagtails, blue wrens, scrubwrens, honeyeaters, eastern rosellas, finches, silver-eyes, robins, thornbills, mudlarks and thrushes: generations of us have watched them from the kitchen and talked to them as if to friends or children. If it is one of the last pagan associations in what remains of the rural Protestant, or has a more philosophical origin, I do not know.

I do know that Cummings' line does not ring quite true. Birds are less a matter of the heart than of the senses. We are not talking about commitment, but rather the pleasure a bird's shape and sound affords us, and the wonder of its aeronautics. These things might be surrogates for something deeper (try holding a grey thrush in your hand and see if it doesn't stir something) but the first conscious sensations that birds create are aesthetic ones. A hovering kite, an egret by the water's edge, a thrush singing by the window – in every bird's construction there is first an irresistible line.

Consider that thrush. It is a very ordinary flyer, yet in appearance it is at least as pure a bird as the swallow: a swallow, in truth, is such an aerial acrobat as to seem part bat.

'Whatever the bird is, is perfect in the bird,' Judith Wright wrote. And no bird is quite as perfect as a thrush. In the same verse Wright also talks of parrots and kestrels, but I think it's a fair bet that a thrush – 'round as a mother or a full drop of water' – inspired the line about perfection.

'Whatever the bird does is right for the bird to do,' Wright says, and contrasts that happy state with her own, which is 'torn and beleaguered'. It's a beautiful line, but like the one of Cummings, as untrue as it is true.

This spring, whenever I opened the back door, a magpie took off from its nest in a gum tree half a kilometre away and came skimming over the grass, arcing over the fences, zooming beneath the branches down the drive and veering straight at my brow, before braking impossibly late and landing on the porch rail beside me. It all took about five seconds. I've no doubt the magpie was showing me how exhilarating flying is for the creatures that can do it. And then it carolled.

Another magpie with a nest on a higher branch always followed the first, but it did not fly with the same élan or straight at me, and it always pulled up a metre further away. It was a shyer bird and its carol was more guttural. The first took the meat from my hand, the second only when I put it down. Both flew straight back to their nests, fed their pleading young with my mince and came sailing back to the porch again.

The young have now left the nests. In the morning they follow their parents to my back porch and whine for food while the adults warble away in their mezzo-sopranos until I come out. No unprejudiced human being could fail to be improved by the presence of magpies. They are fearless, resourceful, amusing and melodious; and, above all – as all birds have to be – stoic. But they also contain complexities of character: not in the multitudes of some humans, perhaps, but not that many less than the average. And, just to go on the sample at my door, between one magpie and another there are differences as pronounced as they are between, say, the Three Tenors or two modern political leaders when there is an election on.

Last week on a local road I saw a kookaburra dive from a fence post on one side to the verge of the other; in pursuit of what I don't know, because in the instant that it dived, a man on a motorbike roared round the corner and the bird's head struck the front wheel. The collision killed the kookaburra: it bounced back across the road and lay there on its back, quite still. What Australian does not love kookaburras? To be truthful, in that moment I would have been no more dismayed if it had been the motorcyclist on his back and the kookaburra flying on down the road.

What this bird did was *wrong* for the bird to do. Yet it was only a minor departure from the normal drama of bird life. Watch birds for a while, and you begin to see that what is natural for the bird is perpetual menace, frequent terror and sudden death – much of it inflicted by other birds – and to all this they must find solutions.

Around midnight a couple of nights ago, a honeyeater of some kind crashed into the wire-screen door and clung there shuddering. There was an owl in the trees outside. If owls are wise, it must be only in the daytime. When darkness falls they are ruthless, havoc-creating monsters. The owl and the pussycat went to sea, and when night fell the owl tore the cat to pieces.

Every day in the society of birds down by the lake, harriers, kites, falcons and eagles glide among their fellows, brazenly looking for one to kill. Patches of feathers and down on the ground – all-white, pink and grey, red and blue, green and yellow – are all they leave of any bird they catch, and the proof of their efficiency. They are the SS of the lake. Like owls, they use not just the weapon of surprise, but that of terror. They hunt in pairs or trios: hovering over the marshes on the edge, or sweeping and swerving low over the gums and willows in the hope that their sudden appearance, or the equally potent effect of their shadow, will frighten something out.

They glide and soar and dive in accordance with their natures and our ideal of them. But they also concoct, invent and improvise. On windy days they let the air carry them wildly from tree to tree, as if to use unruliness as a disguise and to heighten the terrible effect of their shadows.

At dusk, when flocks of galahs, corellas and cockatoos go screeching home, the hawks station themselves in trees, or glide and swirl about looking for their chance. But at the same time of the day, I have watched a falcon stand for 20 minutes in the reeds by the edge of the lake. I thought it was counting on ducks or cygnets coming ashore, but when a flock of parrots flew overhead the falcon climbed into the air – and into the parrots – like a surface-to-air missile. On another occasion, it hid for a long time in the grass on one side of a low ridge, then suddenly soared into the air and swooped down the other side and onto some creature it must have sensed was there.

In response to the raptors' ingenuity, the parrots have worked out their own defences, which amount to a kind of Resistance. They post evening lookouts in the trees and on the ground. They divide their flocks. They fly jagged, crazy paths.

They communicate endlessly. No galah or cockatoo ever seems to move without screeching a message of some kind to every other galah or cockatoo within a kilometre, and none ever hears a screech without replying.

And they are served by other species: by the magpies and mudlarks that spend a good part of every day obeying their ferocious territorial instincts and driving raptors from their airspace, and by crows whose motives might be more subjective.

If there is one bird unloved even by those who love birds, it is a crow. (In fact they're ravens, but in the language they are crows.) Crows are hated because they are black and symbolise death and drought; because their cawing is maudlin and depressing; and because they are eaters of carrion. What is worse, they eat dying animals before they are dead. Unable to pierce the hide of feeble young lambs, they peck out their eyes and tear their mouths and tongues. For this cruelty – which is considerable, but nothing to our own – they are abominated.

Here is something a crow did. One morning three brown falcons were hooning around and wildly diving at every living thing, including a colossal pelican many times their size. It seemed likely they were just enjoying the general commotion their antics were creating, but they must have had a serious purpose because eventually one rose from the banks of a small island with a little egret in its claws. The other two flew off with it to share the meal.

A dozen galahs went back to the dead tree in the middle of the lake where they nest and camp at night. Two others sat lookout on the branch of another tree, 300 metres away; and a metre from the two galahs sat a crow – talking to them. Not cawing – but talking, in a low and irate voice.

It was still talking when one of the falcons returned, flying at great speed towards the tree where the dozen galahs had settled.

The crow took off in hot pursuit, surging to a level a few metres higher than the other bird and then, as the falcon's approach panicked the galahs into the air, the crow dived and knocked it sideways. The falcon recovered its poise, but the crow struck again and again and drove it off the lake. The crow flew back to the two galahs.

Absurd as it may seem, I could only see the crow's behaviour as fulfilment of an undertaking he had given the galahs. It was conscious philanthropy. Later, it also seemed to me to be the antithesis of our ancient belief, alive still in such fables as the Fox and the Scorpion, that animals cannot act outside their (savage) natures. Not for nothing is that view – and that fable – very popular with devotees of the free market.

A couple of weeks after the episode on the lake, I noticed a teal labouring on foot between two dams, when out of nowhere a falcon swept in to kill it. A millisecond before the falcon reached the helpless duck a crow reached the falcon and knocked it to the ground. Another crow followed up. Feathers flew. The duck fled back the way it had come. The hawk went home defeated. The crows hopped off into some cypresses. It was impossible to see what they had gained from the action, unless it had satisfied some charitable instinct or a subjective loathing for the other bird.

> Then I could fuse my passions into one clear stone
> And be simple to myself as the bird is to the bird.

Some birds, maybe, but not quite as the crow is to the crow. Or the magpie is to the magpie. Or the butcherbird with the beguiling song is to the butcherbird with the habits of a fiend. As I stood under a tree one day, a silvereye dropped at my feet. I took it in my hand and, as its chest heaved up and down,

I looked up into the tree from which it had fallen. In the lowest branch a butcherbird was sitting, staring down at me and the bird that he had dropped. A butcherbird would fit in a beer glass, but that stare stood my hair on end. And as it stared, the silvereye's heart stopped beating.

Since then I've looked at many photos of butcherbirds, and none of them has a stare like that. The stare was that bird's and that moment's alone.

And then there is the kookaburra, the larrikin icon of Australia before Steve Irwin replaced it. *Laugh, kookaburra, laugh,* we used to sing. We have in the family a sequence of three photographs of a kookaburra perched in typical fashion on a fence. In the first you can see it has something large in its beak. In the second there is less of the thing. By the third, all that protrudes are a couple of webbed feet on scrawny legs. It's a duckling, a couple of weeks old. If they'd shown that before the Movietone News, this country might have a different view of itself.

The Monthly, December 2007 – January 2008

From *American Journeys*

It was a couple of weeks before Christmas. I had taken the train up the California coast from Los Angeles, where I had gone to attend a wedding. Now I was making for Emeryville and Amtrak's California Zephyr, which runs from there across the Rockies and the heartland to – of course – Chicago. In the fields outside, hordes of labourers were bent to the ground picking strawberries: inside, Herb with bright eyes, olive skin and a white moustache told me about his most recent Pacific cruise. Herb was deep into his 70s but very fit. He looked like Clark Gable might have, had he reached that age. Herb took a lot of cruises; the last, from which he had just returned, was the eighth he'd taken on the one line. When he wasn't cruising he was riding his six-cylinder Honda motorbike with a trailer that converts to a tent in three minutes. He rides it all over the United States.

The 91-year-old man opposite had written a text book on the law 50 years ago, and it was still paying for ocean cruises. Herb had joined the army just as World War II ended and, though he stayed in it until Korea, he never saw any action. But the lawyer saw more than he cared to recall. He had been in Patton's Third

Army and later became a war crimes investigator. In Austria he had had to witness the forced (and frequently fatal) repatriation of POWs to the Soviet Union. Then he'd gone to Korea. He was inclined to laugh at horror, but he also said he thought every act of war was criminal.

His wife was 83. She had once been a marriage counsellor and wrote a thriller called *Motel Murder* in which she killed all the people she didn't like. That 'such a pretty man' as Herb had never married she found surprising. Herb did not blink: it was just a matter of choice, he said. Now, in a broad valley south of San Luis Obispo, hundreds of backs were bent to pick cauliflowers, and thousands of trailers and shacks huddled together on the edges of the fields with American and Mexican flags in a ratio of about 20 to one.

The Supreme Court judge Earl Warren once called Emeryville the 'rottenest city on the Pacific Coast', but it's not rotten any more. It's booming with high-tech. From Oakland it's just a few miles up a local rail line towards Berkeley. Amtrak brought the train into Emeryville right on time, but then a Union Pacific freight train rolled past and we sat there while the conductor recited his drolleries: 'Do not occupy a seat with your luggage. If you wish to buy a ticket for your coat you can do that at the Amtrak office.' We were still sitting in the station half an hour later. Our ambition was to get to Sacramento, where the train becomes the California Zephyr. One of the great train journeys begins in the town where the Central Pacific railroad began in 1863.

We sped through marshland where russet grass grew between the channels and half-hid men standing perfectly still with their shotguns tipped back across their shoulders and pointing to the sky, their dogs just as still beside them. The hunters all wore iridescent orange jackets to reduce the risk of shooting each other. In no time we had crossed California's Great Central Valley, which grows two billion tons of rice each year, and unimaginable quantities of almonds and walnuts, prunes, pistachios, peaches, apples, oranges, turkeys, chickens, eggs, kiwi fruit, lettuces, milk and grapes.

At Sacramento a 200-pound, 18-year-old youth flopped down opposite, drew the curtain on his window and loaded a DVD into his player. He played six before we reached the other side of the mountains, and not once did he open the curtain. An historian from the Sacramento Rail Museum came on the public address system to tell us the story of the High Sierra, which we were about to cross. He had a soft, deep voice and it's possible that his cadences owed something to Shelby Foote: 'In 1867 an immigrant train led by Josiah Stevens reached the shores of Donner Lake after a journey fraught with misfortune and ill-advised turnings. Here they were snowed in and a party of the fittest among them set out for Sacramento to get help.'

Somewhere between Colfax and the highest point in the Sierra Nevada we made an unscheduled stop. In the 1870s, our guide said, mining companies blasted the soil off these hillsides with high-pressure hoses and collected the gold salted through it from the gullies below. It was called hydraulic mining: Clint Eastwood used it as the epitome of evil in *Pale Rider*. It was outlawed in 1884, but not before the railroad company was obliged to employ police to stop the mining companies hosing away the ridge on which the railroad ran. We listened to this while looking out at a scene of utter lifelessness. Not a bird, not even a kite or a crow. Conifers. The gates of hell will stand in the silence of a coniferous forest. And the damned will wait for a Union Pacific train to pass.

As we crawled over Emigrant Gap, my youthful companion loaded yet another DVD. People gathered in the observation car to admire American River Canyon and Bear Valley. It was hard to know which to admire more – the grandeur of nature or the efforts of human beings to cut it down to size. On every precipitous and inhospitable hillside there was evidence of mining, irrigation, hydro-electric power or, for that matter, skiing. And there was the railroad itself. We passed some of the wooden sheds that were built to protect 40 miles of track from the 30 feet of snow that falls in an average year. And at last the train went through the Big Hole – a two-mile tunnel at 7040 feet – and came out on the other side of the Sierra Nevada. We looked down on the Donner Lake, where more than half of the stranded immigrants died in the snow and, we were told, the living ate the dead: indeed, children ate their fathers, wives saw their husbands roasted. It is a story from Poe's imagination. Or the author of Genesis.

For long stretches Highway 80 snaked along beside the railroad, and at Emigrant Gap it seemed to go under it and bobbed up on the other side. The cars zipped, the trucks thundered, the train edged its way, creaking as it went. The highway is more advanced, no question, but the railroad is heroic; and because its engineers had to shape it to the physical environment, people on the train not only see more of the mountains, they feel them. The sublime thing about a train is that you're always dimly conscious of the engineering.

We passed through Truckee and I seemed to hear the guide say it burned down six times in its first ten years. Truckee was a Paiute chief and his father was Winnemucca, which is a couple of stops after Truckee on the Nevada side of the California border; like Emeryville and Truckee and all the other towns on the line, it was a wild town in its day. So wild, in fact, that the Wild Bunch robbed a bank there. We travelled on in pitch-dark, I presumed across the Nevada Desert. There was an occasional light from a house, or a car spearing through the blackness, and every now and then a Christmas tree with a star on top or a couple of flying reindeer.

I had dinner with people who did not like their president or Mr Cheney. Amtrak travellers are everywhere opposed to them. 'We are all neocons now,' an NPR journalist said soon after the fall of Baghdad. Not on Amtrak, they're not. Not now, and as far as I could tell, not then. Journalists might try to explain the abandonment of their critical faculties after 9/11 as a normal patriotic response. The patriots in the dining car wouldn't buy it.

One of my companions said that, like me, he'd been thinking of Humphrey Bogart in *High Sierra* on and off all day. And the thought led him to recall the *Treasure of Sierra Madre* (an altogether different Sierra) and the bandit who says to Bogart: 'Badges? We got no stinking badges!' which was one of the few times a Hollywood lead was worsted in conversation with a Mexican. The people at the table told me Elko was a cowboy town and famous for its rodeo. I'd heard it elsewhere – NASCAR and the rodeo are what every American town wants. Elko also has an annual Cowboy Poetry Gathering.

The lady opposite was travelling to Tampa, Florida. She said to me: 'You could be a cowboy.'

'Surely I'm too old,' I said.

'No you're not,' she said. It was going to take her four days and four nights to reach Tampa.

The train was two hours late into Elko, but there was a taxi waiting at the shed which passes for a station. On the way through the dark to the Stockmen's Hotel and Casino, the driver told me that Elko relies less on cows and cowboys than on gold and gambling. Nevertheless, it was a cowboy I saw when I opened the blinds in the morning: that is to say, he was wearing a white cowboy hat and cowboy boots and a big check woollen coat like the boys wear in Brokeback Mountain. He must have weighed 300 pounds and he was picking his way through the ice and snow in the big car park that divides one side of Elko's main street from the other.

The sun shone weakly as I followed the cowboy's trail through the snow to Leotard Corner, and then past some more casinos until I found a laundry about where you'd expect to find the town hall. It had huge washers and dryers, and I left my clothes with one of the half-dozen nice women who worked there. I imagined they were used to cowboys' and goldminers' clothes and I hoped they wouldn't think mine too girly. Then I went round to a little place called Cowboy Joe's, where they make the best coffee in the United States. They knew exactly what I wanted: two-thirds espresso and a third steamed milk. In fact, they had a name for it – a Tony. I had two Tonys at Cowboy Joe's and took myself down to the Cowboy Museum and bought a Cowboy Poetry Gathering T-shirt. I looked at the old photos of cowboys with their chaps and ropes and lariats and hackamores, their rifles, rifle-holders, holsters, boots and spurs and neckerchiefs and fancy saddles, and wondered how long it took them to get dressed and on their way in the morning.

It seemed to me then that this cowboy thing was all about balancing the wild and the tamed. Among the images and objects at Elko's Cowboy Museum were wild horses, wild bulls, wild jackalopes, wild deer, elk and salmon, on the one hand; and, on the other, tamed, dead or stuffed versions of these animals. Tamed nature and cowboys in their taming gear. It's a delicate balance. Too much wild and you can't make progress or money, the two most concrete expressions of freedom and independence. Too little wild and you've nothing on which to exercise those freedoms and the independence-loving taming instincts which are the hallmarks of frontier experience. The cowboy is caught in this contradiction, which might be why some cowboys, like the one I saw walking across the car park that morning in Elko, bear the same kind of relationship to a living thing as a grizzly bear does to its glass case.

A cowboy is a bit of a hoax; and not only because he is grafted on to the Mexican original, the vaquero. The brands he burned into the cattle he so expertly roped were not his brands. He was a wage-labourer by any other name, but he could kid himself that he was as free as any man because he was engaged in the essential business of taming wild critters. Sometimes, behind the expression of American freedom, you get a glimpse of an illusion – and not only with cowboys. A man can be robotic, ignorant or vicious. He can be timid and pathetic. None of that matters as long as he keeps saying he is free, or that he stands for freedom or represents freedom. A *New York Times* reporter put it to Larry McMurtry that while cowboys were symbols of freedom and self-reliance, one could hardly say they were 'interested in spreading democracy'. 'No,' said McMurtry, the great novelist of the species, 'they were interested in spreading fascism.'

I liked Elko. The women, in particular, were very pleasant. I went into an optometrist's shop and asked the lady there if she could straighten my glasses. She was a handsome, intelligent, middle-aged woman, and when she put the spectacles back on my nose I asked her whether Elko was a good place to live.

She said she couldn't honestly say that she was happy there, and after nine years she was leaving.

Around 5.30 pm I rang Julie. It was dark and the moon was bouncing light off the snow in the car park. Julie said the California Zephyr to Chicago – due at 9.40 pm – was now due at 12.10 am. As it was several degrees below zero and the station was just a shed three miles out of town without so much as a kerosene radiator, there was nothing for it but to kill time in town.

I went over to the Commercial Hotel and Casino and ordered the prime ribs and salad for $7.70 and a glass of red wine. The vegetables came in a bowl of hot water sitting on the plate, with some garlic in a plastic cup and the meat juice in another plastic cup and a potato in a piece of silver foil. I ate every morsel. The wine they brought was white; when I told them I'd asked for red they brought me some and said I could have the white as well, because there was nothing they could do with it now. I drank the red and washed it down with the white, and I was playing a machine when the thing began to jangle and gurgle and spit out coins and an alarm went off. Next moment a young woman appeared at my shoulder and told me I had won 80 dollars. Half an hour later I'd lost it, and another half-hour later I was 80 dollars down.

I walked back across the car park to the Stockmen's Hotel and Casino and lost another 50 dollars, so I sat at the bar in the gloom and drank vodka and read the *Elko Daily Free Press*, whose headline read: INCREASED PROFITS AT ELKO CASINOS. Then I read the back of a Go Mega Bar wrapper: it contained 28 different ingredients, including 16 different fruits and berries. It had vitamin A and vitamin E and omega 3, folate, iron and calcium. A poker machine was inlaid in the bar. I lost some more money on it.

I rang Julie again and this time she said the train would be in at 10.30 pm, which gave me about 20 minutes to get there. The shuttle driver was in the lavatory. He must have taken a book with him because it was 15 minutes before he came out. We raced out to the shed by the tracks, but the train wasn't in. The driver went back to town. A few snowflakes were falling. There's no place as dark as a railway track in the middle of the night, the killer says in *Double Indemnity*. I waited an hour, thinking about the immigrants at Donner Lake; then I rang Julie again. Just as she said, 'Hi, I'm Julie,' I heard the whistle blow and I saw a light in the distance.

The next stop was Salt Lake City, but I had taken a sleeper and missed it. I missed Utah completely. At some point in the night, when I peered through the curtain, we seemed to be skimming across ice, as if on a frozen lake – or a salt lake, I wondered.

In the morning, as I looked out at the landscape west of Grand Junction, Colorado, cowboydom became seductive.

Afterword

> I passed Slimgullion, Morgan Mine, Camp Seco, and the rotting Lode.
> Dark walls of sugar pine –, And where I left the road
> I left myself behind;
>
> Philip Levine, *Sierra Kid*

Around Thanksgiving I took a train south from Oklahoma City. I was aiming at El Paso but a death in the family obliged me to get off in Austin and go back to Australia for a fortnight. Oklahoma was in drought and the land and the lawns were dull brown. The creek beds were dry, silted and eroded.

We passed a few little towns with the familiar towers and church spires and the rest looked like it had been simply scattered on the ground. Horse farms seemed to be the main activity, and oil pumps. As always, the blue sky was shredded with vapour trails, and even the half-moon looked like something a plane had left behind.

Stopped in the middle of a refinery as the train filled with oil fumes, the young man beside me slept with his feet in cowboy boots jammed against the wall in front. Dirty jeans, cowboy shirt and his woollen hat pulled hard down on his head. Every now and then he woke and talked to me about his life. His life was something he was working on. Rich and poor, religious and secular, Americans work avidly at their lives. A 'work in progress', the young man called it.

He had been raised, he said, 'in a kinda cone' and never saw how other people lived. But he was learning. He spent a lot of time with homeless people in Fort Worth and Dallas and travelled with them on freight trains to Colorado and other places. 'They're cool,' he said. 'They don't starve. The charities look after them. You can't die of hunger in Texas, but you can die of the cold or someone might kill you for your shoes.' Then he went back to sleep: he faded in and out of consciousness, like someone who might be about to die.

We got going again, and when we were not far from Fort Worth the conductor, in a voice like Slim Pickens, called our attention to a huge structure on the left of the train: 'That there's the new Texas speedway. Next town comin' up's Hazlitt, Texas. Hazlitt, Texas, is next.'

Sure enough it came up, and we stopped on the site of a new housing estate. They were big plain houses with big charcoal-grey roofs and very big yards, fences with white rails as if the owners fancied keeping a few thoroughbreds as pets. Sprinklers were on and the grass was green but there were no trees, shrubs or flowers. Not a sign of a bird or a birdbath. For the 100th time I wondered why Americans don't grow gardens. Adam was put into a garden 'to dress it and to keep it'. Heaven is often likened to a garden. 'In the place where He was crucified there was a garden.'

We sat there for half an hour and the young man beside me woke up again and told me he was a Christian. Most Sundays he went to one or other of the various non-denominational Christian churches outside the big cities. He was studying other religions, including Mormonism, and he wanted to 'understand' the Catholics as well, he said. He told me that many of the homeless men with whom he spent nights in parks and railway yards and under bridges were middle-aged and middle-class and, until they went bust or their marriages failed, successful in business. It could happen very easily and very suddenly, he said. Others, he maintained, simply chose to leave their conventional lives. They just gave up and walked into the other world.

A mile and a half outside Fort Worth we stopped again. After half an hour or so the lady from the snack bar told us that the driver of the freight train on the track in front had gone home. He had to, she said, because he'd completed his 12-hour shift. There was a cemetery out the window. 'Right now, what we're doin' is watchin' a cemetery,' a man told his friend on the phone.

Slim Pickens came on the PA and said: 'I'm sorry, folks, but there ain't nothin' we can do about this freight train up ahead. We're at its mercy.' He recommended everyone phone

left us with a simulacrum for every occasion. There were a dozen possibilities. He'd lost his job? His wife had left with the children? His bank had foreclosed? Perhaps the hurricanes or capital's 'perennial gale of creative destruction' had blown him onto the street?

Just as it is easy in America to suddenly find yourself in an alien, hostile part of town, you see signs of how quickly the ground can give way beneath your feet. This man looked as if he had just walked into hell. Whatever else he'd lost – his wife and children, his money, his mind – what had most obviously gone was his dignity. He was as if stripped bare to the world.

In nature a thorn in your paw or a broken limb can mean death because you can no longer catch your prey or escape your predators. It means you're not competitive. That, it seemed to me, was why the man was panicking: he sensed his days were numbered. Life is uncertain and disaster is never far away – and sudden when it strikes. Who knows if it is because Americans believe this is the natural – or God-given – way of the world that their legislators seem so reluctant to ameliorate it: or if their prolonged inaction is why, to them, this world seems natural? 'Who provideth for the raven his food when his young ones cry unto God?' So often in the United States the answer is much as it was when God posed it to Job: God provides, if it pleases Him to do so.

It might be that the more 'natural' a society is, the more the need for religion; and the more religious, the more potent the symbols and rituals of the tribe. I may be churned in the economic mill, fall through the cracks, never get a chance, be of no useful account, but I cannot be cast out. Whatever befalls me will be according to the Lord's plan. I have that assurance, if nothing else. And I have the flag. The flag is mine as much as anyone else's. And freedom is mine. I am as free as every other American, and like every other American, I answer only to God.

Freedom is such an old chestnut of American rhetoric that it does not impress outsiders as perhaps it should. The more the President speaks of it, the less meaning it registers. When he says, 'Our enemies hate us for our freedoms,' we cringe, even though we know that, down the years, Americans have died in tens of thousands for the cause. In any case, we think, it's less for the freedoms that they hate you, and more for the influence you exercise. 'Our enemies hate us for our power, our hegemony' would be a truer statement, and little would be lost by stating it in these terms.

And yet, when one travels in America, the chestnut sheds at least some of its shell. You come to see that, to Americans, freedom means something that we incurable collectivists do not quite understand; and that they know freedom in ways that we do not. Freedom is the country's sacred state. Freedom is what must be protected. All over, they will tell you what is wrong with America, but freedom is the one thing they think right. And whatever the insults to my social democratic senses, that is what I find irresistible about the place – the almost guilty, adolescent feeling that in this place a person can do what he wants. He can grow absurdly rich; he can hunt a mountain lion; he can harbour the most fantastic ideas; he can shoot someone. He can commune with God or nature, buy anything he wants, pay anyone for any service and at any fee. He can be a social outcast or even a prisoner and yet, being American, believe that he is free.

If I am American, I am as free as a person can be. If I am free, I can do – or dream of doing – all the things that it is in my nature to do or to dream; no other place on earth need interest me. So long as I am guaranteed this freedom, I will forgive the things my country does that are not in my nature or my dreams. I will be 'spared all the care of thinking about them'. That is, of course, unless my country or some other place threatens freedom.

Sometimes in America, when you are watching television, or a scene on the street, or someone 'creating herself' in a café or train, you wonder if in their minds many Americans imagine they live just the wrong side of a kind of theatrical scrim, a thin floating membrane whose opening is almost impossible to find. *Almost* impossible: but it exists, and if you keep your hope alive and apply yourself hard enough, who can say if one day you won't walk through it and find yourself in the magical kingdom of celebrity – and soon after you will tell a television host how, like revealed religion, it was all meant to be.

It is just as the faithful think: you do not know when the moment will come and you'll wake on the other side. You do not know what you will see. The face of Jesus, or Dave Letterman? You do not know, and because you do not know you figure there must be a plan.

It may seem crass, juvenile and provincial. It has seemed that way to visitors since Tocqueville. But in the midst of this unworldliness, one also sees startling, unselfconscious acts of grace and generosity that might be possible only when something childlike and raw remains in the spirit of the place. Depending on the angle and the light, much that seems unworldly or unformed in America will, a moment later, manifest something older and better in our natures.

On a train between Winslow, Arizona, and Los Angeles, I sat beside a sublime black woman and her two nephews. They had been sitting up all night and were very tired. She asked the ten-year-old to thank God before he ate. When he mumbled, she said in a gentle voice: 'Please say it so that we can hear the words.' And the boy did.

2008

Language Like This Should Be Put to the Torch

'They leapt from mountain peak to mountain peak or far out into the lower country, lighting forests six or seven miles in advance of the main fires. Blown by wind of great force they roared as they travelled. Balls of crackling fire sped at a great pace and in advance of the fires consuming with a roaring explosive noise all that they touched. Houses of brick were seen and heard to leap into a roar of flame before the fires had reached them.'

The fires described here are not the Black Saturday fires, but the Black Friday fires of 1939. The writer is Justice Leonard Stretton, who conducted the inquiry into Black Friday.

When Jack Rush, QC, quoted these passages to the current commission, he intended to suggest to the chief of the Country Fire Authority that last summer's fires were not without precedent, and to ask why its warnings on 6 February 'did not prepare people for the sort of fire that could be anticipated on February 7'. 'All I can say, Mr Rush,' said the CFA chief, 'is that we did our very, very best.'

The matter, of course, has nothing to do with the efforts of CFA firefighters. It concerns CFA management and more particularly what managers call 'communication'. It's unlikely

Rush and his colleagues are wondering if they had anything but good intentions.

With or without precedent, the task on 7 February was complex and immense. They were like Horatius holding the bridge. But with this difference: Horatius had no management strategy. Unschooled in value-adding as he was, when he saw the Etruscans massed on the other side, he resolved to hold the bridge. To go by the commission transcripts, the limits of their language being the limits of their world, CFA managers did not approach the task of warning us with the same spontaneous dispatch.

One CFA manager variously described the business of telling the public as 'messaging'; 'communicating the likely impact'; 'to communicate the degree of the circumstance', providing 'precise complex fire behaviour information', 'to communicate more effectively in a timely manner not just that it is a bad day, but other factors as well'. He spoke of his task as 'value-adding' and as 'populating the template' or 'populating the document' and of the 'document' as an 'iterative type document'. He talked a good deal about 'learnings', 'big learnings' and even 'huge learnings'. 'Of course the learnings from these fires,' one said, 'the scientists will come out and give us an outcome of what sort of messaging and where we can go to better inform communities about what they should do.'

Commissioner Ron McLeod asked the CFA chief if it might not have been more useful to have told people what firefighters in the Yarra region had been told: 'That they were liable to face a fire that could not be stopped, that had a flame height of 35 metres.' He wondered if more 'explicit terms' might have 'added a bit more substance and a bit more meaning' with 'implications . . . for people who might in other circumstances have chosen to stay as their preferred option'.

In reply the chief could not escape the limits of his professional idiom: 'My view of the world is that for those people who are in that environment the weather conditions were very plain to understand. We had very clearly communicated the fuel conditions. I think the bit – if you think about it in terms of the fire triangle – was we had not communicated the likely outcome, if that is the judgement.'

Stripped of jargon we presume he meant to say the only thing they messed up was the bit about the fire. They neglected to tell people in concrete language – the only kind we understand – that any fire on 7 February was likely to be one they could not fight, and might not survive.

If instead of 'fire activity with potential to impact' we had dangerous, unpredictable, deadly fires, fires like the one Stretton described, the CFA's 'messagings' might have persuaded more people to get out of the way. If instead of 'wind events' and 'weather events' and combinations of 'events', the experts and the authorities (including politicians) had said the wind will blow a tremendous gale of searing air through forests so dry they will explode into fires that no one can stop, and that the wind will very likely suddenly blow just as hard from another direction and send these firestorms into the midst of people who just minutes before had thought they were safe – or something like this – perhaps more people would have recognised the danger.

It was not that they did not do their very, very best. More likely, when it came to telling people what they had to know, the management side of their training made their best inadequate. Telling people requires language whose meaning is plain and unmistakable. Managerial language is never this, and being without roots or provenance there is no past from which to learn.

Here is a possible 'learning' for managers. Take Stretton's description of Black Friday and add the word 'event' after any mention of wind or fire – and see if it adds value. Add 'impact', 'outcome', 'activity' and 'asset-protection'. Is the 'messaging' clearer or less clear, would you say? What 'learnings in terms of outcomes' do you take from this? The same test may be usefully taken by managers in other fields.

Sydney Morning Herald, 19 September 2009

From *Bendable Learnings*

Mission statements and vision statements

What is a mission statement?

A company without a mission statement is like an evangelist without the cross or a shaman without her spirit animal. The same goes for any other business, including government departments, schools and kindergartens, hospitals, funeral parlours and nursing homes, cafes, sports clubs and bikie gangs: any band of people gathered for any roughly common purpose. When we lose our way in the world and forget what we're here for, our mission statement reminds us. It tells who we are and what we believe. If one day we don't recognise ourselves in it, then we know that either we *have an issue with alignment*, or the thing is no longer any good and we should exchange it for a better one – just as we would with a mirror.

A mission statement defines your mission, and the reason you exist.

> Writing a Mission Statement for a Business, Charity, Sporting Group or Community Group can be one of the most challenging tasks a group of people have to do . . .

> A mission statement is simply **a definition of your mission** . . . You should believe your mission statement and follow it to the letter.
>
> 1 on 1 Personal Computer Training

> Your mission statement should be a clear overview of your company values and ideals. A well thought out mission statement can convey your business purpose and reason for existence to your customers, suppliers, employees and shareholders . . .
>
> www.businesslifesolutions.com.au

It does pretty well everything, especially if the verbs are pro-active ones.

> An effective mission statement is concise, to the point, realistic, operational, inspirational, informative, and even emotional. It is forward-thinking, positive, and describes success.
>
> USA Swimming

> Your Mission Statement Should:
>
> - Express your organization's purpose in a way that inspires support and ongoing commitment.
> - Motivate those who are connected to the organization.
> - Be articulated in a way that is convincing and easy to grasp.
> - Use proactive verbs to describe what you do.
> - Be free of jargon.
> - Be short enough so that anyone connected to the organization can readily repeat it.
>
> USA Swimming

Never go anywhere without it.

> The mission statement should be referred to continuously. It should be present everywhere: on the letterhead, all communications, all brochures, and all official documents.
>
> Australian Institute of Sport

And remember:

> If you don't believe in your mission statement or you don't believe you can achieve your mission, then don't undertake it as your mission.
>
> 1 on 1 Personal Computer Training

For example, would BAE Systems say 'Our services are grounded in a commitment to delighting customers' if they didn't believe it, or didn't believe they could *achieve* such delightfulness? You don't get to be the world's biggest manufacturer of guided missiles by fooling yourself, do you? But delight is not mandatory. General Motors prefers *total customer enthusiasm*:

> We are working to create an environment that naturally enables GM employees, suppliers, dealers and communities to fully contribute in the pursuit of total customer enthusiasm.
>
> General Motors

Then there's *customer satisfaction*:

> To be the best Fast Food Hamburger Restaurant in terms of customer satisfaction in both product and service and individual restaurant profitability.
>
> Hungry Jack's

And this:

> To provide outstanding customer service and products, in which creates United's point of difference to continue with innovative developments of our fuel and retail offer.
>
> A local petrol station

Markets

People who do not know the market, or play or ride it, might assume it is incapable of ordinary human feeling. Not so. Having to do with money, it shares something of money's character, which the young Karl Marx called 'the alienated ability of mankind'. Were we to accept this, we might see the market as this 'alienated ability' made animate, and those who wrestle with it are in some sense wrestling with themselves. Before you dismiss this characterisation as altogether too silly, watch Jim Cramer on CNBC: that might not be his alienated self he's wrestling with, but it's someone very close to him.

Those who know the market have often ascribed to it a quasi-religious dimension. For a very long portion of the history of capitalism it shared a close relationship with Providence. In a famous phrase beloved of free marketeers, Adam Smith said that when men were allowed to pursue their own self-interest, society was governed by a generally benevolent 'invisible hand'. Smith's 'hand' was God's, 'whose wisdom works itself through competition for wealth'; but the true modern market disciple reckons it a blasphemy to think the hand could belong to anyone or anything but the market.

Listen to them for a while and you would swear the 'invisible hand' was the least of the market's mysterious properties.

The thing has a sort of animal intelligence, corresponding perhaps to that of a Doberman or grey parrot. The market sees things, it senses things, it sulks, it anticipates, it gets depressed, it has friends, it is inscrutable: it understands things that we mortals do not.

> This market is sick of the leadership; not of the stocks like General Electric (GE:NYSE) and Microsoft (MSFT:Nasdaq), but of the President and the Vice President, and nothing that comes out this week or the next or the week after in earnings will change that.
>
> Jim Cramer, CNBC

> I wanted to believe that he could articulate correctly why we went to war in some foreign land where a thousand guys have died and billions have been spent. But he hasn't. He had terrible intelligence and bad homework, stuff I fire people for regularly and always have . . . The market senses this, and that casts a pall over every day's trading.
>
> Jim Cramer, CNBC

> What we see now in the market is a gradual realisation that Bush will be forced out in November and a new man will be President . . .
>
> Jim Cramer, CNBC

> I know that President George W. Bush has been a good friend of the market when it comes to taxing those of us with lots of money. We've done great these last few years. But it is time to recognise that things aren't working. Time to recognise that the stock market is out of favour

because we don't trust it, and that the trust is more a function of the leadership in Washington than it is of anything the companies have to say.

Jim Cramer, CNBC

Markets cause slowdown

The political process started in late 2007. Since that time, the markets have been down 55 per cent. Markets are forward-looking, not backward-looking. They saw what was coming in the election. They were anticipating what this guy would do, and they caused a slowdown.

Art Laffer, CNBC, March 2009

Markets fail to understand

Distressed Securities: Buys equity, debt, or trade claims at deep discounts of companies in or facing bankruptcy or reorganization. Profits from the market's lack of understanding of the true value of the deeply discounted securities and because the majority of institutional investors cannot own below investment grade securities. (This selling pressure creates the deep discount.) Results generally not dependent on the direction of the markets. Expected Volatility: Low – Moderate.

www.magnum.com

Market up, market down

The [Bernie Madoff] strategy is generally described as putting on a 'collar' in an attempt to limit gains compared to the benchmark index in an up market and, likewise, limit losses to something less than the benchmark in a down market, essentially creating a floor and a ceiling.

MAR/Hedge (RIP) No. 89, May 2001

Markets sideways

On top of experiencing relatively weak investment returns in sideways markets, hedge fund investors have many important issues to consider as we enter 2003, including conflicts of interest, regulation, style drift, opacity and capacity constraints.

9th Annual Hedge Fund Managers' Conference, Phoenix, Arizona 2003

Markets not crazy

You can say on one hand the market is crazy but it's not 1999. People have had their medicine from overexuberance.

James Packer

Flipside of downside

In our base case simulation there is an upside case that, er, corresponds on the flipside of the downside case in kind of an adverse direction.

A World Bank economist, 2008

Nature's downtick

[It's] human nature, wanting to get that last downtick.

Bill Griffeth, CNBC, March 2009

Consumers' uptick offset by downtick

Eurozone consumer sentiment eroded slightly in June, according to the Commission. An uptick in consumers' plans for major purchases at present was offset by a downtick for purchases over the next 12 months.

Automated Trader, 5 July 2010

Subtract downticks from upticks

Money flow attempts to measure the capital moving in and out of a security by adding the value of higher, or uptick, trades and subtracting the value of downticks. As prices fall, money flows are usually negative, turning positive as prices rise. A divergence between money flow and price may signal a change in the trend.

Bloomberg Businessweek, 21 June 2010

Market matures into granularity

The key concept is that of risk assessment, and this is becoming more granular by nature as the market matures. The question is, does the industry have the datasets required to drill down into to get the level of granularity required for this and, more importantly, are the data accessible to the industry.

Wallis Advisory Committee

Liberals and pedants might ask if people do not 'cooperate together' in religion, field games, war, mothers' clubs and disasters; if they did not 'cooperate together' to split the atom; and isn't everybody now cooperating together to rescue the market before it dies by its own invisible hand? Silly people.

Alan Greenspan

Not everyone in this life has a put named after him. But Alan Greenspan has the Greenspan Put. What seems strange to people who don't have a put named after them – who would not recognise a put if they stepped on one – is why, when the market possesses a thing as wonderful as an 'invisible hand', it needs a put like the Greenspan Put. What sort of invisible hand can't keep a reliable grip on asset prices? One would think that it could generate its own liquidity, and even manage its own risk.

But these are the wrong questions! The market fails us because *we* have been bad. With our ignorance and doubt and base presumption, it is clear we have offended the invisible hand. We must make an atonement. And if that takes a put, so be it. Trouble is, every time we send up a successful offering it gets factored into asset prices and the credit spreads are narrowed.

> Any onset of increased investor caution elevates risk premiums and, as a consequence, lowers asset values and promotes the liquidation of the debt that supported higher asset prices.
>
> August 2005

No government regulation necessary

Risk in financial markets, including derivatives markets, are being regulated by private parties . . . There is nothing involved in federal regulation per se which makes it superior to market regulation. The risk of a crisis stoked by loose derivative trading was extremely remote.

1994

Risks hedged

I believe that the general growth in large institutions have occurred in the context of an underlying structure of markets in which many of the larger risks are dramatically – I should say, fully – hedged.

2000

No worries

Perhaps the most significant innovation has been the development of financial instruments that enable risk to be reallocated to the parties most willing and able to bear that risk. Many of the new financial products that have been created, with financial derivatives being the most notable, contribute economic value by unbundling risks and shifting them in a highly calibrated manner.

April 2000

Under control

Building on bank practice, we are in the process of improving both lending and supervisory policies that we trust will foster better risk management; but these policies could also reduce the pro-cyclical pattern of easing and tightening of bank lending and accordingly increase bank shareholder values and economic stability. It is not an easy road, but it seems that we are well along it.

June 2001

Innovation has taken care of it

In recent years, we have incorporated innovative ideas and accommodated significant change in banking and supervision. Institutions have more ways than ever to compete in providing financial services. Financial innovation has improved the measurement and management of risk and holds substantial promise for much greater gains ahead.

June 2001

Don't worry – new paradigms

The development of our paradigms for containing risk has emphasized, and will, of necessity, continue to emphasize dispersion of risk to those willing, and presumably able, to bear it. If risk is properly dispersed, shocks to the overall economic system will be better absorbed and less likely to create cascading failures that could threaten financial stability.

September 2002

Only a fool would regulate

But regulation is not only unnecessary in these markets, it is potentially damaging, because regulation presupposes disclosure and forced disclosure of proprietary information can undercut innovations in financial markets just as it would in real estate markets.

September 2002

It's taken care of, I tell you

A major contributor to the dispersion of risk in recent decades has been the wide-ranging development of markets in securitized bank loans, credit card receivables, and commercial and residential mortgages. These markets have tailored the risks associated with holding such assets to fit the preferences of a broader spectrum of investors.

September 2002

Relax

Especially important in the United States has been the flexibility and size of the secondary mortgage market. Since early 2000, this market has facilitated the large debt-financed extraction of home equity that, in turn, has been so critical in supporting consumer outlays in the United States throughout the recent period of cyclical stress.

This market's flexibility has been particularly enhanced by extensive use of interest rate swaps and options to hedge maturity mismatches and prepayment risk.

September 2002

Absolutely no worries

In conjunction with this improvement, both as cause and effect, banks have more tools at their disposal with which to transfer credit risk and, in so doing, to disperse credit risk more broadly through the financial system. Some of these tools, such as loan syndications, loan sales, and pooled asset securitizations, are relatively straightforward and transparent. More recently, instruments that are more complex and less transparent – such as credit default swaps, collateralized debt obligations, and credit-linked notes – have been developed and their use has grown very rapidly in recent years. The result? Improved credit-risk management together with more and better risk-management tools appear to have significantly reduced loan concentrations in telecommunications and, indeed, other areas and the associated stress on banks and other financial institutions.

November 2002

The market has it well in hand

What we have found over the years in the marketplace is that derivatives have been an extraordinarily useful vehicle to transfer risk from those who shouldn't be taking it to those who are willing to and are capable of doing so. It would be a mistake to increase regulation.

2003

The strategy is working

Instead of trying to contain a putative bubble by drastic actions with largely unpredictable consequences, we chose . . . to focus on policies to mitigate the fallout when it occurs and, hopefully, ease the transition to the next expansion . . . There appears to be enough evidence, at least tentatively, to conclude that our strategy of addressing the bubble's consequences rather than the bubble itself has been successful.

2004

How many times do I have to tell you?

. . . private regulation generally has proved far better at constraining excessive risk-taking than has government regulation . . .

May 2005

There could be a problem or two . . .

The rapid proliferation of derivatives products inevitably means that some will not have been adequately tested by market stress. Even with sound credit-risk management, a sudden widening of credit spreads could result in unanticipated losses to investors in some of the newer, more complex structured credit products, and those investors could include some leveraged hedge funds.

May 2005

But I'm pretty sure the market . . .

Risk management involves judgment as well as science, and the science is based on the past behavior of markets, which is not an infallible guide to the future. Yet the history of the development of these products encourages confidence that many of the newer products will be successfully embraced by the markets. To be sure, for that favorable record to be extended, both market participants and policymakers must be aware of the risk-management challenges associated with the use of derivatives to transfer risk, both within the banking system and outside the banking system. And they must take steps to ensure that those challenges are addressed.

May 2005

In any case the benefits outweigh . . .

With these advances in technology, lenders have taken advantage of credit-scoring models and other techniques for efficiently extending credit to a broader spectrum of consumers. The widespread adoption of these models has reduced the costs of evaluating the creditworthiness of borrowers, and in competitive markets cost reductions tend to be passed through to borrowers. Where once more-marginal applicants would simply have been denied credit, lenders are now able to quite efficiently judge the risk posed by individual applicants and to price that risk appropriately. These improvements have led to rapid growth in subprime mortgage lending.

April 2005

Hang on . . .

'I have found a flaw. I don't know how significant or permanent it is.

'I made a mistake in presuming that the self-interests of organizations, specifically banks and others, were such as that they were best capable of protecting their own shareholders and their equity in the firms ... But I have been very distressed by that fact ...'

'In other words, you found that your view of the world, your ideology, was not right, it was not working,' Mr Waxman said.

'Absolutely, precisely,' Mr Greenspan replied. 'You know, that's precisely the reason I was shocked, because I have been going for 40 years or more with very considerable evidence that it was working exceptionally well.

'The problem here is something that looked to be a very solid edifice ... did break down. And I think that, as I said, shocked me. I still do not fully understand why it happened.'

October 2008

Education

'Without a gentle contempt for education, no man's education is complete,' G. K. Chesterton said: but this is taking contempt too far. Says the NSW Board of Studies: 'Outcomes: The outcomes describe what students learn about and what they learn to, as a result of the teaching and learning in the course.'

Of course, they will tell us they are merely describing the curriculum; that they don't teach – or even *deliver key learnings* – in this language. But they do. In the course of the 20th century, humanities education survived punishing encounters with both scientific objectivity and post-modern subjectivity, but it might not survive managerialism. Management language and management practices have drifted as far down as lower primary schools, where they show up in mission statements written by eight-year-olds in Grade Two, and in school reports that parents and students understand no better than the teachers alleged to have composed them. Schools – and even universities – might have seen it as their duty to offer some resistance to the general debasement of the language. Instead they acquiesced. They became *outcomes-based*.

'Oh that the Lord would show me how to think and how to choose!' It is difficult to find in the outcomes-based curriculum a better description of education's purpose or anything so well expressed. The question that no one seems able to answer is this: even if we had to change the way we organise educational institutions and adapt or discard older philosophies, did we have to give up teaching children to write and think in the language of that student writing in his diary 150 years ago?

> Your child is exhibiting ALL key indicators.
>
> School report

You are the parent of the child. Make a list of key indicators she has been exhibiting to you – then a list of the exhibits she's been indicating.

> Essential Learnings identify what should be taught and what is important for students to have opportunities to know, understand and be able to do.
>
> Queensland Education Department

> Essential Learnings clearly focus attention on what is central to the curriculum and help educators determine what learners should know, understand, value and be able to do.
>
> Tasmanian Education Department

Can you think of a reason for the difference between Queenslanders and Tasmanians? Or are their essential learnings essentially the same?

Are your essential learnings different in this example?

> The EsseNTial Learnings are organised into the Inner Learner, Creative Learner, Collaborative Learner and Constructive Learner domains. Each domain has a set of culminating outcomes and developmental indicators to help map a learner's progress through the Key Growth Points and Bands.
>
> Northern Territory Education Department

Do the capital N and T make any difference to the culminating outcomes in your particular domain?

> Essential Learnings form an integral part of children's and students' learning from birth to year 12 and beyond. They are resources which are drawn upon throughout life and enable people to productively engage with changing times as thoughtful, active, responsive and committed local, national and global citizens.
>
> South Australian Curriculum Standards and Accountability Framework 2001

After reading those two sentences, what are your essential learnings about:

(i) education
(ii) children
(iii) the English language

Were you reminded of:

(i) Plato
(ii) Julia Gillard
(iii) no one at all

Name your essential learnings at birth. On a scale of 1–9, how would you rate as a global citizen the last teenager you met?

Now read these sentences:

> Students entering school demonstrating evidence of the Key Growth Points will develop these learnings through local and more immediate contexts. As learners progress through the Bands, they acquire and apply these outcomes in broader community contexts.
>
> An assessment logbook from Certificate IV in Education Support, a document of more than 100 pages, for Indigenous trainee assistant teachers in the Northern Territory

What outcome, if any, did you acquire from your reading? What outcomes have you ever acquired? What's the matter with you?

2009

Political Leadership

It is now all but universally agreed that the Australian Labor Party is a near-ruin, ruled – body and soul – by factional bosses and opinion pollsters. To the public the party presents the spectacle of governance either by faceless men, or by men with unappealing faces. These bosses decide Labor's leaders, Labor's candidates, Labor's policies and Labor's tactics. Finding they are mere spectators with no more influence on the direction of policy than unaligned Australian voters, unaligned is what hordes of party members have chosen to become.

As the bosses' grip grows tighter, the membership declines and branches fold. Recently, the stalwart Senator John Faulkner used the word 'anaemia' to describe his party's present condition. Leaping to his side, Kevin Rudd, who was deposed in a factional putsch last year, declared the factions were a 'cancer'. The former NSW Labor minister Rod Cavalier said they were 'killing' the party and that in much of Australia Labor was 'stone-cold dead'. The factional leaders deny all this, of course, but why are voters flocking elsewhere? Why, even when the party is standing for something (such as a mining tax or a carbon tax), is it perceived as standing for nothing, or for less than the Greens or GetUp! stand for, or unlikely to stand for it any longer than is politically expedient? Why was their last campaign derisory in almost every detail? Why does Bob Brown feel able to say the Greens will soon be the major party of reform?

It is possible, however, to agree in every detail with Faulkner's judgement and with the broad sweep of media opinion since he came forth with it, and yet suspect that while this is not the wrong tree, there is another one to bark up. The other one is that uncommon combination of sound and imaginative policy with articulate politicians of character – which, along with a lot of baloney, tends to go under the heading of 'leadership'. Indeed, for all its legends of grassroots organisation and democratic trail-blazing, the party's history is no less a story of leaders strong enough to drag a creaking and complaining Labor movement with them. In the modern era, think of Whitlam, Hawke and Keating; they led by force of personality and big ideas, and the factions either made themselves useful and followed willingly or were dragged along by the undertow. More recently, until the awful inner child took hold of him, they followed Kevin Rudd.

The point can be made by watching Julia Gillard in two television appearances: a Monday night ABC interview with Chris Uhlmann, which she managed expertly, and an address to the nation the day before, which was feckless and embarrassing. In the interview she was assured, unhesitating, in command of the policy detail and alert to the political traps. There were the sharply ordered intelligence and the equal instincts for advantage and danger of a serious political animal. But in her address she hinged her usual pedantry to confected inflections and a wildly veering tone: one moment defiant, the next didactic, the next ingratiating. It was like watching a bad method actor. No meaning could survive such a performance.

To be fair, Gillard is not the first Prime Minister to struggle in the first 12 months of office, and she has had more against her than any of the others. Less well known than Hawke, Keating, Howard and even Rudd were when they ascended, she has also had to contend with the facts of a hung parliament and being a woman in the role. Every day has been a struggle for legitimacy. All this, plus a hostile tabloid press and radio, and an outrageously unprincipled and unchecked opponent; her most bitter enemies have to concede she wants for nothing in resilience and steel.

Of course she has made some of her own problems and given the public reason to doubt her honesty. But there never was a successful politician who did not have avowals to live down and embarrassments to hide. Politics is a game played with two sticks of equal length – principle and pragmatism – and successful politicians are those who wield them well in combination: so well, in some outstanding cases, that folk give up trying to tell one from the other and roll over. What the German sociologist Max Weber called 'charismatic authority' is partly made of this. And it's what Julia Gillard so far lacks in spades. The problem is not a want of sincerity or conviction, but any means of exercising or displaying them.

Now, it might be that the Labor Party is beyond salvation by any leader. And just as possible that politics itself is too far gone to produce a leader capable of testing the proposition. To borrow something else from Weber, while passionate conviction and shrewd pragmatism are characteristics of great political leaders, what really distinguishes them is their detachment – not their proximity to the electorate but their distance from it. The natural posture for a politician has always been 'chief among equals'. But modern media does not allow this. Now it is at best 'equal among equals' and commonly last or least among them. Listen to talkback, watch *Q&A*, tune in to the internet and ask where the power and respect lies. Who lays strongest claim to the record, the knowledge and the authority, charismatic or otherwise? Not the leaders. Most of what used to be theirs is shared between the host and the audience, for whom pretty well any opinion is as good as another. The politicians scramble for the residue.

Every day they do what they used only to do in election campaigns. There is Tony Abbott, aspiring Prime Minister, in a hard hat or gauze one, staring down a mine, fiddling with a tractor, filleting a fish. The people are sovereign, he says. To hell with the sovereignty of scientific facts: popular opinion will determine if the Earth is warming and what to do about it – just as it determined the answer to polio and the movement of the planets. There was Prime Minister Rudd, tin-eared and ineffably graceless but a mind to be reckoned with – where else should we see him every day but surrounded by babies or hospital patients? And there is Julia Gillard, Prime Minister of the Commonwealth, daily risking her dignity in the nation's malls and school grounds, confessing her insecurities at the National Press Club, bringing herself close to tears as she asks to be understood, surrendering to the maw of magazine culture and afternoon television, and taking the office with her. The Oprahisation of Australian politics is now pretty well complete.

No generation of Labor leaders has been so devoted to opinion polls as this one, yet it is doubtful if any has been more inept at moving opinion when it needed to. Perhaps the organisation is too rancid to attract, or (vide Lindsay Tanner) retain, the talent from which leaders might be drawn. It could just as well be that such leaders as it has, though capable negotiators and effective scrappers, are victims of dodgy political fashions that in time will fade.

The other possibility is that the wretchedness of Gillard signifies a more general upheaval in the social and political setting. The clichés, the tortured and oppressive cadences are habits of the language she was raised in. Demotic it may be, but this language carries only the shallowest meaning. The phrases are not to inform or inspire the audience but merely to echo it and satisfy its narcissism. The spin the public loathes is made expressly for them.

So it is with contemporary politics: not enough formal culture remains to support a well-made argument over a fallacy or a speech over a slogan. The art is lost for want of belief in it. Which might be why, when called on to make the case for something as bold, complex and remote from immediate gratification as a carbon tax, an old codger such as John Hewson makes the case with twice the force of anyone in the Labor government.

The Monthly, August 2011

Riding High

Climb into a Toyota Hilux and at once you feel 'the commanding outlook'. It's just as the brochure says. Nissan Navara lacks very little in this regard, though Nissan calls it a 'commanding presence'. The Toyota is 'unbreakable', 'relentlessly tough and reliable', 'unstoppable'. The Nissan is 'tough as nails'; it 'looks tough, plays hard' – a bit like the Toyota which is 'ready for action when you want to play'. The Toyota has 'extra grunt'; the Nissan has a 'massive 170kw of power'. It 'will go as far as you dare drive it'. The Hilux is 'as rugged as they come'. To promote the Navara, Nissan are running something called a 'Power-up challenge'.

It's possible that some readers of *The Monthly* will not recognise either of these vehicles. Should they want to, they need only travel the arterials of our cities around 4 pm any weekday and keep an eye on the rear vision mirror: chances are the thing tail-gating you has 'striking road presence'; 'a big tough, powerful stance . . . an aggressive bonnet scoop . . . and large cat-like headlights . . . that show it means business'.

Four o'clock is the middle of 'tradie hour'. The tradies are going home in their unbreakable and unstoppable cars. Tough as they are, they are also cosily equipped – twin cabins, ten-speaker stereo, Bluetooth, cup holders, the works – because 'driving hard doesn't mean roughing it'. So when you drive 'Australia's most powerful tradie', you want for nothing compared to the jerk in the hatchback. And you've got a lot more horsepower.

They're horse surrogates really. Long ago the squire – or the squatter, or the trooper – enjoyed the same 'commanding outlook' from the saddle. It gave him an eye-line advantage and, should he be challenged by some pedestrian or donkey rider, the extra grunt he needed. 'Waltzing Matilda' is constructed on this social arrangement. The presence of his mounted superiors was so commanding the swagman could think of nothing better than drowning himself in a billabong.

The New World was different from the old in all manner of ways, but one of the more consequential was the supply of horses. Put a poor man on a fair horse and he was as good as a rich one. This was something Ned Kelly understood: you could put a lot of social disadvantage and indignity behind you just by getting on a horse. The rural workers who began joining trade unions around the time that Ned was galloping around spitting in the Establishment's eye were wont to go on foot or bicycles.

Horsepower is not always inimical to collective consciousness – think of the Light Horse – but historically it falls heavily on the side of brawny individualism. It plays to the idea of Australia as a land for the muscular and free-spirited, the practical over the ideological, the man of action over the ponce of abstraction.

In this sophisticated and mature capitalist democracy of ours, one might think that an aggressive bonnet scoop would not have much purchase on the public mind. But according to a recent report in the *Australian Financial Review* no other type of vehicle comes within cooee of the tradies' sales. In 2000, six passenger cars were sold for every utility. Last year it was four to one. In that decade passenger car sales increased by 7 per cent; utilities by 25 per cent – and twin-cabin tradies, the luxury end of the market costing around $50,000, by 137 per cent.

As the advertising for them makes clear, no less than any Holden or Mercedes, as much as they reflect need, these vehicles signify wealth, status, taste and belief. They go with the need to carry a wheelbarrow and to tow a trailer; and equally with the need to carry two trail bikes and tow a 10 metre cruiser.

They also go with the shift in national rates of remuneration which, presumably, goes with a shift in social values. According to the *AFR*, among all the categories of trade and profession, in the last two years only labourer and plant operators have enjoyed wage increases of more than 20 per cent. On average they now earn a good deal more than office managers, a great deal more than arts professionals and about the same as architects, auditors and accountants.

And they all go with the mining boom. To quote the *AFR* again, the editor of the local paper in Singleton earns less than a 25-year-old working at the mines – and very likely he goes on more expensive holidays and owns more property than she does. In Western Australia certain categories of welders earn more than the Prime Minister and a lot of labourers earn more than lawyers and treat Bali as a third home – the other two being a portable on the mine-site and a 40 square, twin garage, three bathroom $700,000 number in a nice development on a coast somewhere – anywhere, they can fly there – on the continent.

We should be glad to see such rich rewards for physical work (if not for certain kinds of it, such as those in the hotel and food industries), and the virtues of sturdy independence flourishing.

We might wish they wouldn't tailgate, yet be grateful for their spending power and in their twin-cabs the old strand of larrikin joie de vivre preserved. If only we all had their extra grunt.

Yet when I see their bull bars or their cat-like headlamps on my arse I confess to feeling a kind of existential threat. Not the kind I get from the kid in the old Commodore with his cap on back to front – he threatens nothing worse than death. But the tradie brings intimations of pointlessness. And when I hear our political leaders, I suspect at least a general trend and complete acquiescence in it, if not a full-blown conspiracy. What happened to Albert Schweitzer, Mozart and the CSIRO? Where is physics, anthropology or the simple promise of the Education Acts?

That editor in the Hunter Valley says none of the local young men want to work with their heads in a newspaper office when they can earn so much more with their hands. In Western Australia, the mayor of Mandurah acknowledges that only 29 per cent of the local kids finish high school and only 1.3 per cent go to university. Nor, we can be sure, do they want to take up farming.

It's all over in a matter of minutes of course, and no recourse is possible – not with that difference in horsepower. Missing your back bumper by inches, they veer off to their Foxtel-fitted pads in the new suburbs and leave the roads to the losers who totter along in their hatchbacks wondering if it is their fate to go on taking it, or if they should see what they can get on a trade-in.

The Monthly, September 2011

The Book Show and Ramona Koval

> To call up in oneself a feeling once experienced and, having called it up, to convey it by means of movements, lines, colours, sounds, images expressed in words, so that others experience the same feeling – in this consists the activity of art.
>
> Leo Tolstoy, *What is Art?*

For Tolstoy, art was not a place to look for pleasure, but for communion with each other. Art was one of the conditions of our existence, '. . . necessary for life and for the movement toward the good of the individual man and of mankind, uniting them in the same feelings'. It is not a definition that will satisfy everyone. Will any feeling do? A crass feeling? One crassly conveyed to a crass audience? The idea raises as many questions as it answers and Tolstoy surrounds it with a good bit of prescriptive moral nonsense.

Still, it might be apt enough for the ABC. What nobler ambitions does the national broadcaster have than uniting Australians in their feelings? The Corporation's charter talks about broadcasting 'programs that contribute to a sense of national identity and inform and entertain, and reflect the cultural diversity; and . . . programs of an educational nature'. Same thing; different dialect.

Of course, not every member of the board and management will agree with Tolstoy. When they think of art, some of them will think of pleasure, some of pain, some an enlarged sense of being, some enlarged boredom, and some of 'the network alignment process'. Alert readers among the last category will be alarmed by a definition which, on the face of it, treats both fiction and non-fiction as art. For Tolstoy, if a boy comes upon a wolf and later retells the tale and describes his feelings in such a way as to make his audience 'relive all that the narrator lived through – [this] is art'. By this definition Naipaul's novels and his travel writing are both art. Ditto, Chatwin and Twain. Ditto *Animal Farm* and *Homage to Catalonia*. Any prose work, in which the author infects readers with her experience, is art by this measure.

Whatever logic lies behind the 'network alignment process', it cannot allow this. Not if changes proposed for *The Book Show* are anything to go by. *The Book Show* has been running on Radio National every weekday at 10 am for six years: its predecessor, *Books and Writing*, ran weekly for a decade before that. The host and chief interviewer in both incarnations has been Ramona Koval. Such is the reputation for excellence Koval has gathered on the show, from all over the world the most exalted writers of all fiction and non-fiction genres submit themselves to her questioning, not only on the radio but at the Edinburgh, Cheltenham and other festivals.

Now it is true that most writers will knock each other over for a chance to talk to someone in public; but the record shows that even the shy ones believe Koval is as good as the chance gets. Her interviews have depth and intimacy, intelligence and wit. Much in the spirit of Tolstoy's longed for 'communion' with others, her disarmingly amiable seriousness very often yields more than her subjects might be expected to give and her listeners expect to receive. A talk with Les Murray or P. D. James will go well beyond the business of poetry or writing English crime fiction, and yet shed intense light on those two forms. Her regular chats with the American essayist and editor, Lewis Lapham, might range from Herodotus to Beethoven to Obama, and capture much of Lapham's disenchanted erudition, his irony and his insistence that nothing can be understood without historical understanding.

The Book Show covers plot and character, metre and metaphor, psychology, medicine, painting, crime, language, sex and animals – anything in books, in other words. What happens to books and what is happening to them now, are fit subjects. *The Book Show* is just that: a show about books. What sort of books, fiction or non-fiction, memoir or reflection, Arts or non-Arts, matters not, so long as they are good books.

Given this, and that there is no other book show on national radio, and that for all the present upheavals in the trade and the technology the book has an elemental place in civilisation, we have long assumed that the show would go on and on – for as long as, say, the *Science Show* has gone on, or *Singers of Renown* went on, which was as long as Robyn Williams and John Cargher were willing and able to go on.

But in accordance with the 'network alignment process', we learn that *The Book Show* will soon be no more. The show which used to be *The Book Show* will become *Books and Arts*. *Books and Arts* will leave out non-fiction and 'focus on fiction, memoirs, literary criticism and publishing news'. The manager of Radio National says, 'we do want to refocus the program on to fiction . . . [and] . . . reinvigorate the interest in fiction, so that the voices of fiction writers can be better heard'. This 'refocusing', which includes a proposal to 'enhance our Book Readings' by moving them out of *The Book Show* and filling the spare 15 minutes with 'key specialist arts stories or issues of the moment', means, the manager says, 'there will be no decrease in our commitment to books in the 10–11 am time slot'. Therefore, rejoice.

'Non-fiction content,' the manager says, 'is covered comprehensively on a range of programs across the network.' Koval's coverage, we must presume, was an excess. But non-fiction – that part of it at least which is not memoir, literary criticism or publishing news – will also be accommodated in a new Saturday night program, along with fiction, 'as well as publishing industry news as part of its [the program's] arts journalism focus'.

Next time a new translation of *War and Peace* appears, expect Fran Kelly to deal with the politics, Rachael Kohn the religion, Alan Saunders to do the philosophy, *Hindsight* the history, *Life Matters* to handle any implications for families, and *Bush Telegraph* the damage occasioned to crops by heavy artillery. Expect all of Coetzee's next novel or memoir on *Books and Arts*, but if he comes up with another *Diary of a Bad Year*, only part of it. It is fortunate, in these circumstances that W. G. Sebald will not be writing any more.

I began listening to the *Science Show* 30 years ago. I came to it through a recording of Dame Clara Butt singing 'Land of Hope and Glory' to an audience in Hyde Park soon after the end of World War I. I don't remember if Robyn Williams played it out of scientific interest in a voice that Thomas Beecham said could be heard across the English Channel, or for pleasure or communion, but I've been listening to the *Science Show* ever since: on and off, much as I've listened to *The Philosopher's Zone*, *Lingua Franca*, *Late Night Live* and *Singers of Renown*. The first time I heard Leonard Cohen was on *Singers of Renown* – there with Gigli and Schwarzkopf and Melba. The strength of these long-running shows is not only in the material and the quality of the discussion; it's because the presenters observe no categorical rules.

I don't know whether *The Philosopher's Zone* has ever dealt with management philosophy, but if it hasn't it should. It would be like putting Leonard Cohen among the stars of opera, except Cohen at least sings. The problem with much management philosophy is that it is less a way of thinking than a means to not thinking. It is ideology, as if its creators read Orwell and thought it described utopia. For an illustration of what I mean simply Google the ABC's strategic plan, or any other strategic plan. Or pay attention to the RN Manager's phrases.

Among the many things the ABC's strategic plan shares with other strategic plans is a commitment to the future. (This is natural: what sort of strategic plan would be committed to the past?) But must a plan for a broadcaster – as opposed to a car dealership – be *only* about the future? Not long ago I read a draft strategic plan for a Victorian university. Sure enough, it declared a commitment to the future, a 'passionate' commitment no less: from beginning to end it never let up on it. Nowhere in its many pages did the authors mention what some might think is a university's natural interest in preserving and passing on to students some knowledge of the past, or a sense of continuity or tradition. The plan gave no indication that our present reality comes from anywhere at all. There is only the moment in which fashion dictates we live; and, of course, the moments moving forward.

Until now this could not be said of Radio National. It has long lived in defiance of the fashion for strategic plans. Its programs on music, history, philosophy, language, science, religion and ideas are eccentric wonders of the broadcasting world. But then, these are good programs which fit happily in the ABC's Charter, and if not many young people listen to them, we can be sure that they will be older soon enough and some will come to them. (Besides, how many young people listen to any AM radio at all?) It makes sense to keep these programs on the radio, and it does a duty to the country.

So why does it not make sense and why is there no duty to keep a show (and a broadcaster) whose premise is the uncomplicated one that books are books, and that there is art in writing a good one?

The Monthly, October 2011

Palin Politics

Three or four years ago a monster storm swept across the centre of the United States and wrapped the land in a coat of ice. From an aeroplane a few days later, the country looked enamelled. Beneath the creamy porcelain the patterns of life in Oklahoma and Missouri revealed themselves in minimal relief: the grids of towns and suburbs, the linking roads, the gigantic satellite-directed circles of agricultural crops. In this immense stillness and silence, suggesting a nuclear winter or a new ice age, the lines etched in the rime took on exaggerated meaning, as if they might contain essential facts about a lost civilisation.

The fact of the Automobile for instance: and Big Oil which fuelled it; and the strip malls which made the car indispensable to commerce, including commerce in food, and agribusiness which made the greater part of US farming a state subsidised vertically integrated corporate industry and an alarmingly large number of US citizens obese. Those lines etched in the ice were the sinews of power and influence, though a great many of the people down in the ice would say that they were there by God's will. Either way, something in their design suggested that, for all the clamour and glory of its suburbs and satellites, poetry and bars, more than the will of the people and the tenets of the Constitution underlay American democracy.

Sarah Palin would doubtless be among those insisting that the lines were drawn by the hand of God. Campaigning for the construction of a gas pipeline in 2008, she implored students in an Assembly of God 'Masters Commission program'[3] to pray for it, 'to make sure God's will has to be done here'. She numbers herself emphatically among God's chosen and believes he made her Miss Wasilla 1986, John McCain's running mate in 2008 and everything in between, including Governor of Alaska. A lifelong member of the Assembly of God (and by its grace the Governor), she would say the lines made by pivot irrigators and highways were in truth made by God because she believes it. But an astounding mass of evidence suggests that she has never had to believe something to say it is so, if it suited her purposes. She would say those lines had been drawn by interplanetary aliens if it meant picking up the alien-abductee vote. And so long as God is the author of all things, including the things she says, once she's said it, it must be true.

Whatever persuaded Palin not to try for the Republican Presidential candidacy this time, the recent publication of two deeply unflattering books about her must have helped make up her mind.[4] Though different in approach and style, the books are strikingly alike in their gruesome assessments of the subject. The woman is a liar. Not just any old liar who bends the truth from time to time, or says things like, 'Watch my lips. No new taxes'; or like all political leaders and governments makes promises he cannot keep. Palin is an instinctive, incurable, possibly psychopathic, liar. She would lie even if she were not an outrageously ambitious politician, an ignoramus, a super-narcissist and a fundamentalist Christian, but because she is all those entangled things she is compelled to lie much more than she would if she had settled on just being a hockey mom.

Palin never had much hope of winning the nomination this time, and for now, outside a spot in the Fox News line-up, it is hard to imagine what she might make of herself. Still, it might be a mistake to write her off for good: not with those primordial instincts. She has been inventing herself since junior high school in Wasilla, and the last time she did it she became the Republican candidate for Vice President. Given a couple of relatively minor divine interventions, the Oval Office was hers. Those in whom she aroused the animal in 2008 will likely be just as susceptible eight years from now and, should the American heartland continue to decay, there will be plenty more where they came from. She could easily invent herself again, and with the bottomless inner resources of the victim she now believes she is, she could be even more potent than she was that day at the 2008 Republican Convention when she sent shivers down millions of American spines. Palin's a political lap dancer, to borrow a phrase from Joe McGinniss. It's not likely that she'll ever be President, but it was not likely that Richard Nixon would get back after 1961, or John Howard after a decade and a half of failing. Or that George W. Bush would be elected twice: and who is to say Palin would make a worse President?

Her hopes, like those of all populists, depend on the rot continuing. It's a reasonable hope to hold. Rank populists of the Palin kind live like a virus in the body politic, dormant for long periods, springing up at times of real or imaginary crisis. The country has always been a congenial home for tub-thumpers of various kinds, but in general the political system has found ways to limit or pacify the numbers of frightened, angry and alienated citizens they need for political traction. Now in the midst of the deepest economic and social crisis since the Great Depression, with fear abounding (terrorism, the national debt, foreclosure, unemployment, illness without insurance, bankruptcy – the Future) and mainstream politics in gridlock, the conditions are ideal for a mass hatching of demagogues.

Bizarre as some of her antics are, it was not Sarah Palin who said Social Security and Medicare are unconstitutional: it was the Texas Governor, Rick Perry. And it was Perry who in April this year officially proclaimed three 'Days of Prayer for Rain in the State of Texas'. Perry who said, *apropos* of the nation's problems, 'I think it's time for us to just hand it over to God, and say, 'God, You're going to have to fix this.' Perry who two years ago said Texas can leave the Union 'any time we want. So we're kind of thinking about that again.' If Palin lives in one fantasy world, Perry surely lives in another. And Michele Bachmann in another. And Newt Gingrich, for that matter, in another.

The difference between what is called populism and what is orthodox or mainstream is generally held to be the difference between the rational and the irrational. One confronts a complex reality with reasoned arguments and solutions; the other escapes it in a make-believe world of conspiracies, supernatural forces and flat taxes. In one, metaphors help to explain reality; in the other there is no distinction. A pipeline built by capital, labour, machinery and graft is a pipeline willed by God. A government that bailed out Wall Street is a government of socialists. A health system that affords insurance to the majority of citizens is a system of 'death panels'.

The striking thing about populist arguments is how they seem to gain force in proportion to their unreason. Enlightened self-interest, the country's watchword, becomes its opposite. Self-interested plantation owners persuaded the South's poor white trash that slavery was also in their interest and, as Ulysses S. Grant observed, on this fallacy the Rebel army safely depended for cannon fodder. The Tea Party – and the Republican Party – attracts hordes of poor citizens by vowing to abolish the government welfare on which they depend. The Tea Party states receive anything from twice to three times the government assistance received by New York or California.

To attend a Tea Party rally, or to listen to them talk, is truly to enter a parallel universe; one every bit as mad as, say, a gathering of university Maoists in Melbourne in 1970. But the Maoists were not in charge of one of the mainstream parties; they were not setting the terms of the national debate; they were not backed by the Koch brothers and given a free run on Fox News. And they were not feeding off the despair, poverty and ignorance to which great swathes of American society have been steadily reduced. The Tea Partiers are, and they have been for most of the last two years. If one of their heroes does become President, it will not be by putsch or civil war, but by popular election through orthodox political processes. A President Palin, Bachmann or Perry will be elected because her or his predecessors in office made it possible.

Let's imagine a President Palin. She maintains – or reinstates – the Bush tax cuts, slashes government welfare, cuts health care coverage, boosts defence spending, finds a foreign battlefield or two, leaves 30 million poor to fend for themselves, sacks the environment and drills baby drills, in the name of unfettered markets and rugged individualism faithfully serves the corporate interest and intensifies the concentration of wealth in even fewer hands. And all this before she gets to abortion, creationism, the war on drugs and ever more manic flag-waving activities. Has she no original ideas?

Mad as she and her fellow demagogues might seem, big as her lies might be, Palin steps directly from the last chapter of United States history, the one that begins with Ronald Reagan. So she is irrational: explain to us again, that one about how the wealth trickles down. Peggy Noonan reckons she's a nincompoop: but was it Palin or Reagan, Noonan's employer and hero, who made the world safe for trickledown economics and the neo-conservatives? Palin's a terrible liar of course, and a fantasist: then again she isn't the one who said it was morning again in America.

The Monthly, November 2011

focus

(v) To concentrate on. Not to be distracted. Purposefully attend to in the appropriate way: e.g. *focus* on the soufflé: cooking it; *focus* on the garden: weeding, fertilising, cultivating; *focus* on the children: feeding, comforting, educating, clothing, reading to, etc.

In business the *focus* is on *goals, core issues, key objectives, main game*, etc.

(n) That on which one *focuses* ('maintaining a strong *focus* on *core* business is the *key* to success' . . . etc.).

(adj) *Focused* – single-minded, resisting all distraction, switched-on, fired-up, pumped, come to play, etc. ('I was really *focused* today' – swimming, netball, high jumping, etc.)

> 'An *output* management *focus* by departments.'
>
> Victorian Department of Treasury and Finance

> 'Clear direction allows organisational *alignment*, and a *focus* on the *achievement* of *goals*.'
>
> Gracedale Private Nursing Home

> 'We must *focus* on our garden.'
>
> Voltaire

> '*Focus* on the lilies, how they grow.'

From *Weasel Words*

Phoney Education

With our Android phone at the drop of a hat we can see whether it rained in Auckland yesterday; what won the third at Bendigo and the winner's five-generation pedigree; the names of all those who served in the Dardenelles; a map of Nunawading or Cairo, and the time in each of those places; the words to 'Embraceable You'; Faye Dunaway's birthday; the right way to slaughter a pig; one's *own* five-generation pedigree. Some of these phones have spirit levels. Some warn the user if he or she is about to walk into a fire hydrant or under a tram. The modern phone combines all the qualities of a library, a university, and a Swiss army knife. It is nothing short of a miracle and a friend to humankind.

The best measure of the boon these phones have been is to recall the woe of life before them. Just 15 years ago on trams and trains people buried their heads in books, newspapers and periodicals, searching for the precious little information they contained, or stared out the windows at a world going past that without Wikipedia they could not begin to understand. People knew very little then. They were lonely in ways known only to those who knew the world before Facebook and texting; and who, to escape their loneliness, made eye contact with perfect strangers and even spoke to them.

Those who are too young to remember might get some idea of what this world was like by downloading Halldor Laxness's 1946 novel, *Independent People.* There are surely no characters in literature, those of Dickens included, whose lives are as bleak and impoverished as the Icelandic family of the novel's hero, Bjartur of Summerhouses. It is the decade before World War I. For six months of every year this crofter and his illiterate children are attended by ice and snow and darkness. Poverty, hunger and filth beset them for all 12. Should the world brighten for a day or two in spring, it is only as an overture to a fresh calamity. Salted fish and the rhymes of the old sagas are all they have to keep them going, along with Bjartur's obstinate will to remain 'independent' on his impossibly unproductive holding.

Then, deep in the cruellest winter, when Bjartur is away and the desolation and suffering of the children are becoming more than they or any reader can bear, a man staggers in from a snowstorm, and says that he has come to teach them.

At once the 'light of learning began to shine'. The teacher warms and animates them as nothing has before. For the first time their lives rise above those of their wretched sheep. He teaches them that 'the distinctive features of the world's civilisation are not simply and solely the giraffe and the city of Rome, as the children may perhaps have been led to imagine on the first evening, but also the elephant and the country of Denmark, besides many other things'. Every day he teaches them new animals, new countries, new kings and gods; how to add and subtract 'those tough little figures . . . with a life and value of their own'; and poetry 'which is greater than any country'.

For each of the three children the light of learning shines on something different; for one it is animals, for another countries, and the other is 'swept on the wings of poetry into those spheres which she had sensed . . .'

True, the world of *Independent People* being what it is, the teacher who brings the light turns out to be a reprobate and cad, and he takes the 15-year-old he has spellbound with poetry, gets her pregnant and breaks her heart. Now, no Android is going to do that. But then no Android can teach in the way that he does. This is a shortcoming we have to acknowledge: the best mobile phone in the world cannot do what a teacher can. It is dumb, like a mule, and no more the master of the information we download from it than a mule is master of the piano it carries on its back.

The children on the croft in Iceland wonder not only at the things they are taught, but also at a person who knows such things, who has been to such places and seen with his own eyes, who has 'the words which fit the locked compartments of the soul, like keys, and open them'. It is this 'personal contact with those who teach', Albert Einstein once said, 'that primarily constitutes and preserves culture'.

This theme of the teacher and child is as old as literature itself (as is the theme of the cad and child, of course). But we don't have to go to literature. Ask anyone from what they learned the most: an item of equipment, a school hall, or a teacher? With few exceptions it will be a teacher. It might not be the best teacher; just a teacher who for any number of reasons, including hormonal ones, for a term or two holds a student, if not actually in her spell, then at least in a realm of shy excitement wherein he learns something.

One might expect, then, that whenever education is talked about in the public sphere the words 'teacher' and 'teach' would practically be synonyms for it. But they seem to consciously avoid the words; any words in fact that predate 'enablers of quality learning and wellbeing outcomes for children'. And no regression tempts them. We hear we are in the midst of an 'education revolution' and the talk will be about more gymnasiums, halls and computers, and 'learnings' and better 'student outcomes'. The principal at a Victorian primary school last month told a meeting of 'Aspirant Principal Leaders' of his delight that 'staff' had made 'commendable efforts to improve student outcomes and learnings, setting high expectations for all. Leadership and School Climate are critical in driving the quality of student well-being hence student engagement,' he said. Let Einstein wrap his head around that.

Of course everywhere now education is 'outcomes-based'. Twenty or 30 years ago it was based on nothing, unless it was on teachers; which would explain why people who were educated at that time exhibit all the rank stupidity of Icelandic crofters from a century ago. No one cared about outcomes then. They only cared about teaching. Teacher-based education. So crazy.

Today in the Northern Territory there are remote communities where mobile phones are out of range and the people are determined to stay on their land, though it means they struggle to feed themselves sometimes and must endure in the wet season the kind of isolation the crofters of Iceland suffered in their winters. Territory education is as outcomes-based as the best of them, and they have an 'Impact Framework' to 'implement their strategy' and 'monitor the progress of the activity, the impact of that activity on the desired outcomes and continuous evaluation to determine whether effort is directed to the areas that will have the greatest impact'. With that sort of framework impacting on everything there is no getting round the need to send their teachers to Professional Development Days. Student outcomes depend on it – or are we going round in circles here?

This October, on the wall of a room in a sad hub-town where a Professional Development Day was in progress, the following three posters were pinned.

1. INTERSUBJECTIVITY
Sharing perceptions, conceptions, feelings and intentions IS a state of achievement. Scaffolding is one of the major processes whereby it is achieved.

2. SITUATION REDEFINITION
In the context of the established AL class where students have studied a number of texts then intersubjectivity happens when the teachers and students have shared control and explicit understandings of their INTENTIONALITY.

3. ZONE OF PROXIMAL DEVELOPMENT
. . . Development occurs through the interaction as the child is assisted to complete a task that they would not be able to achieve on their own.

If an Android could talk it might sound like this. Someone has mistaken the machine for the goods it carries, the library for the knowledge to be found in it. Maybe the scaffolding had a flaw, but after five years of outcomes-based professionally-developed teaching in one community school the children remain functionally illiterate and the teenagers cannot read

Where the Wild Things Are without referring to the pictures. Of course the school reports almost reverberate with 'achieved outcomes'. But the truth is there to see when you sit down with the children for ten minutes and pretend you are a teacher.

The Monthly, December 2011

From *Recollections of a Bleeding Heart*, Afterword, 10th Anniversary Edition

Paul Keating let me know what he thought about this book a few days before the launch: on the night itself in the Sydney Town Hall he let the audience know – not everything (some bits were reserved for me alone), but enough to leave them in no doubt about his loathing. The book was launched by Noel Pearson, who when he had read it told me he thought it was a 'love story'. I confess to wondering sometimes if therein lay a piece of the problem. A few years later Pearson wrote about the 'darkest and barely restrained dudgeon' of Keating's mood that night, and the 'variously erudite, humorous, vicious and thoroughly mesmerising black performance' with which I was 'surgically pinned to the wall'. I would take issue with 'surgically': it struck me as more a shillelagh than a knife.

After saying nothing more in public for the best part of a decade, last year Keating wrote an article in which, coopting to his case a remark alleged of Graham Freudenberg, he charged me with breaking 'the contract'. I knew what he meant by this 'contract' – it is the common understanding that political leaders own their speeches regardless of who writes them – but I could not see how I had broken it. I agree with the 'contract' and have affirmed it a hundred times on public platforms, including a couple shared with Freudenberg, the great Labor speechwriter and historian who also believes in it. Prime Ministers decide what they will say and what they won't, they bring their own judgement to whatever words we put before them; they fire the bullets or throw the streamers and bear the consequences. I don't recall Paul Keating ever uttering a word that he did not want to utter. Under the 'contract' all of them are his and he is welcome to them.

The occasion for his sudden assault last year was an article in *The Sydney Morning Herald* which reported comments I had made about the speech Keating delivered in Redfern Park in 1993. When the *Herald* reporter phoned, as usual I had told him that he should speak to Keating. But you wrote it, said the reporter. I was his speechwriter, I said, but it is Keating's speech. I *explained* the 'contract'. I have no recording of the conversation, but I am confident that I went on to say, as I say in this book, no other senior politician in the Labor Party would have delivered it – not as he did, without changing a word. No one else had the personal conviction and political courage in the same measure. My saying this, Keating said, was 'condescending'. To a certain kind of ego in certain circumstances it might be: to another kind, I'd venture it is no more than a statement of two discrete facts: that we thought the same way, and he had the mettle to say what he thought.

I spoke to Graham Freudenberg and he too was surprised that Paul Keating thought I had 'broken the contract'. Perhaps it was something in the way my remarks were reported, but from his article it seems he has come to believe that, because the speech was his under the 'contract', he had actually written it. Either that, or the matter of the speech was a surrogate for deeper grievances. Whatever the case, I cannot alter the fact that one dark night I wrote it. That was not to put words in his mouth, but to put them on a page: for him to use as he saw fit, as he would any other form of advice. In a political office a speech is advice formally composed. An offering. Whether he used all or some or none of it was entirely Keating's pigeon.

History devours millions, raises and lays on acolytes to so few. Why would any man who has enjoyed all the privilege and exhilaration of the highest office be so tormented by the thought it might go down in history that his words – no less than Kennedy's and Reagan's, Whitlam's and Hawke's – did not in every case scuttle from his own hand, or that from time to time he misread the signs or needed help to read them? Why *not* might be more the question. And if that is troubling, why not be agitated by a listing and imperfect monument like this one?

Paul Keating called *Recollections* the 'black box recorder' of his Prime Ministership. Though he meant to illustrate my failure, this remains the nicest thing he said about it and I have been tempted to infer that at least I did a fair job of getting down the last words of the government before it crashed in flames. The 'black box' was a good metaphor and useful for his caustic purposes, but it came from an outraged misreading of the book. A black box recorder records as God might: everything, with an omnipresent and objective ear. This I lack. The book was no black box for the only slightly less obvious reason that anyone writing history (or a speech) has to sift and select evidence, find a structure, a voice, a tone – the key in which the story's told. Anyone telling a story has first to decide what the story is going to be, and then how to tell it. All story-tellers worth their salt know that if you try to tell everything you will wind up telling nothing. They all know that the story you tell is determined by the angle from which you look at the events. The angle determines where the light falls. Change the angle and you change the story. Paul Keating will know this: he has a strong claim to being the greatest story-teller Australian politics has seen.

I prefer a different metaphorical machine: not a black box, but a hand-held camera. In this book the camera is focused on Keating in the main, but not to the exclusion of the people who worked for him; or to the contest of ideologies, the germination and defence of ideas, the moods, the psychology and the clamour of daily life of the PMO in which they were all engaged. It sees not only what was done, but what, for better or worse, was not done. What was started and not finished. What opportunities we grasped and what we missed. Who won the battles and who lamented. What was willed and what pure chance. The camera could not be everywhere, only where I took it; in and out of offices, cars, planes, hotels, and only when I remembered to switch it on; only when the words and images were clear enough. And then I added a voiceover, to create the context. I wasn't thinking of a camera at the time, but that's how I think of it now.

I don't have a single image of Paul Keating writing a speech. He delivered some *ad lib*, certainly; but the great majority were written for him. I have many images of him marking up drafts, at his desk and just as often in the car on the way to whatever was the occasion for the speech: deleting (sometimes with apologies and occasionally with belligerence), adding his own lines, instructing me in the realities of the case, drawing the big picture, checking with Don Russell or Allan Gyngell or any one of a dozen other people – taking ownership of the speeches. Not just of the words, but the ideas. Speechwriters do have ideas; at least they ought to, because they cannot write in any useful way without them. I saw Keating take intellectual and political possession of speeches, but one was as likely to see him pruning the wisteria in the Prime Minister's courtyard as to see him *writing* them. I wrote most, and Allan Gyngell, Ashton Calvert and John Edwards wrote the remainder: just as Graham Freudenberg wrote the majority of Whitlam's and many of Hawke's. And a long line of advisers 'wrote' other stories including the political one – as insiders always have, both for superior politicians like Keating and dismal ones like Billy McMahon.

But for good or bad, and regardless of whether he brought intellect and strength to the task or dullness and pusillanimity, whether he bravely led or followed bleating, the policies and the story belong to the Prime Minister. It is the way politics and government work in this country. They work in other ways as well, but this is the way I saw them work, and that, after long consideration, is what I chose to write about.

A sometime historian who made a living from freelance writing was bound to keep a diary, and I did – and made it known. When the government fell and everyone went off to new jobs, I went back to my old one. I had the makings of a book, but for three years I didn't have the will – or, as it happened, the wherewithal – to write it.

I began writing *Recollections* at the ANU's Humanities Research Centre in the summer of 1999. Canberra was the usual hell for agoraphobics: boundless sky and unfilled space; the nation's ghosts camped in mausoleums by an artificial billabong; the living, invisible shiny-bums in Parliament House, observing their protocols half-buried in a hill. The campus was a vacant field, except for the Pakistani scholars who gathered every day in the adjacent flat to watch the one-day cricket. Their voices and Richie Benaud's and the rest of Kerry Packer's scout troop mixed with the calls of the currawongs and mudlarks. No doubt the birds were hanging out around the flagpole over at Parliament House too: the birds and the sky and the weird seductive emptiness are the only things that place shares with the rest of Australia. 'It's all happening!' Bill Lawry shouted every hour or so.

But there was nothing happening in the nation's capital. Nothing you could see, at least. That's the way it is in Canberra: it all happens, but out of sight. With the shining light of the mighty bush outside, everything happens in that anaemic and unnatural glow inside. It's an unnatural city. And an insider's city, of course.

My problem was the voice. Who was speaking: a historian, an insider or both? The story of the insider was personal, close and unfinished. I was still living it. So was Paul Keating. In those days we often lived it together, on the phone mainly. The closeness of these events might be why I began writing from the magisterial position: to establish the distance necessary to lend the story the stature of magisterial history, and the insider the stature of a historian. The position demanded that the author hide the signs he had been in the vicinity when the events described occurred. Other insiders have written their accounts in this way and managed to satisfy more readers than the subject and his least demanding admirers. There are fine books by participants who, for the sake of seeming objectivity, have backed out of the room or taken up a position on the ceiling. Hagiographies, the subject's self-reverence projected through another's mouth, are not inevitable. But it remains that the elevated or omniscient third-person narrative demands an artificial logic for events that are often random and subjective: and when participants in those events do this, the most skilful and unflinching practitioners risk losing some of the truth – and the life – of the politics to which they were privy.

Whatever advantages an insider may gain from elevating his perspective, I could not find life among them. After trying for two months to translate first-person experience and perspective into a third-person narrative, I began to think that my efforts had a little in common with Graham Freudenberg's *A Certain Grandeur* and Stephen Mills' *The Hawke Years*, and even a little with Norman Mailer's *The Armies of the Night*, but much more with whatever it is that makes policemen address the media like zombies programmed by a malignant spirit. I wondered if an insider-cum-historian, with a collegiate story, threatened egos and precious reputations to protect, might become less of a witness to the subject than a proxy for it.

Just before I left the HRC I gave an afternoon seminar. Afterwards, the formidable Professor of History, F. B. Smith, approached and said, first, that watching him as Prime Minister he had often wondered if Paul Keating were depressed; then, that he doubted if he would read the book that I proposed to write. I do not recall his reasons with much clarity, but I think he felt that books written by political participants are invariably *parti pris* and, especially when they are written so soon after the events they purport to describe, should not be taken seriously. If he did not actually say it, I think he might also have found them dull and inconsequential. But had I thought of annotating and publishing the diary I had mentioned in the seminar, asked Professor Smith. He would not read the book I was proposing, he said, but a diary was a different matter. I had not thought of it, but I saw his point.

For a fortnight or so I took the idea seriously. A diary has qualities of immediacy and authenticity that secondary accounts cannot match, and it is an often alarming corrective and stimulus to memory. Yet useful as the diary was, both as a record of daily events and as a window on to my feelings about them, it was so far from being the whole story no amount of annotating could make up the difference. Some of it was of a purely private nature and some concerned matters that for reasons of legality or good faith could not be published: add to this the ephemera, repetitions, self-indulgence and baloney which would have to go and it would be as if instead of *Moby-Dick*, we had been left with Ishmael's day book. All odious comparisons aside, Barry Smith's radical suggestion led me to decide the book should be written much as the diary was: from where I had been, at that angle, on the deck of the *Pequod*, not halfway up the mast or trailing in a whaleboat.

I would not pretend to have had no role or point of view beyond that of silent witness or amanuensis. I did not decide this because I wanted to claim more for myself or anybody else, or to say that it was in the Prime Minister's Office that everything of significance was decided. It was to put what I knew – the Office – at the centre of the action. I had not been in Caucus or Cabinet or thousands of other meetings; I had had nothing to do with Keating as Treasurer. Not having experienced events in person is of course no barrier to conventional history; and had I not been in Keating's Office, that option would have been open to me, as it remains now for any other historian. But because I *had* been in the office, I felt no better equipped to attempt a conventional history of Paul Keating's Prime Ministership than Paul Keating himself was.

The veneer of a disinterested narrative might go some way to meeting the requirements of an unwritten clause in that unwritten contract of Paul Keating's, which in essence is one between the writer and the history he witnessed; but there is no such contract, and if there were, a self-respecting citizen invited to work in a political office would no more sign up to it than to one requiring that his tongue be drilled before returning to society. As much as they might stray towards believing it is their right and duty, history's great actors cannot lay down the terms of good history. They may prefer the elevated vantage point for the elevated authority and tone it grants the story of their lives, but elevation doesn't guarantee the quality of observation, the sympathy and curiosity of the reader, or the judgement of posterity.

Take William Manchester's decidedly magisterial two volume biography of Winston Churchill, one of Paul Keating's favourite books. There was Christopher Hitchens declaring on Slate.com the other day that Churchill 'probably has no more hagiographic chronicler than William Manchester'. And yet, as Hitchens wrote, on one matter (that of Churchill's attachment to Edward VIII) the hagiographer not only acknowledges a profound misjudgement on Churchill's part, but 'virtually gives up on his hero for an entire chapter'. The same Manchester found room within his paean to describe Churchill's heroic drinking habits, his chronic depression and his deeply eccentric personal behaviour which led colleagues and bystanders to declare him 'unstable'. If you can't trust your hagiographer with such things . . .? Except that Churchill is the more singular because of them; and more likely to see what others can't, and do what others quail from. The best political leaders are often made of unusual stuff, and the most rudimentary psychology tells us it is no accident.

Others have fair claim on the economic transformation of Australia, Bill Kelty, Bob Hawke and two or three Treasury officials among them; but Paul Keating's so-called 'big picture' vision, his political courage, the requisite luck and his gift for story-telling have earned him most of the credit. Certainly no one did more to bring about the successful economy we now enjoy – and inhabit. But history just will not behave. If this transformation not only brought economic growth and prosperity, but in some degree also laid the ground for the debasement of political debate to tin-eared sloganeering and second-hand managerialism, should he not share the credit for that as well?

To whose account shall we put it if the new 'competitive' economy spawned multitudes of competitive narcissists who crowd the verges of the lily pond, and Labor parties abandon not just their beliefs but their brains to satisfy their sovereign needs or vanities, and even frame their education policy for narcissists (*My* School)?

It is not such a long bow: just as Keating's political demise prompted a new generation of Labor politicians to discard big-picture politics for poll-driven caution, the subtle transition from society to economy did its bit to stifle the things from which he drew his strength, his inspiration and his language. A Labor movement of spirit and character, for instance: one with an idea and a story big enough to at least sometimes break the political culture's anaesthetising grip; one that might attract more individuals of character and independent mind, and fewer of the kind he recently labelled 'populist sickos'.

For as much as Paul Keating's career is inseparable from the economic revolution of the eighties and nineties, he also embodied its opposite. He was the poet and aesthete of the side. It was Keating who championed the new economy in animating and often irresistible metaphors. And, as Prime Minister, it was Keating who insisted that while the economy was the main game, it was not the only game. What made Keating rare in politics then, and would make him a genuine freak now, was his ear: I don't mean for music, but for language. He lived in the language, not as a pedant does, but in a visceral, intuitive way. Language – and music – kept alive in him the essential understanding now largely lost among our leaders that, as well as economics and politics and management and polling, there is a poetic key to human reality.

As in other things, in this he was old-fashioned, if not downright pre-industrial. He was all for the new – new economy, new money, new alliances, new eras, new republics – and he was also for the old: for Schinkel's architecture and Ormolu clocks. This was not simply a matter of taste; it was the Keating persona. It was who he was, and no one who knew him, much less who wrote about him, could ignore it. These traits did not always make for flawless politics or predictable behaviour (that is what we have now), but it did make him exceptional: the brilliance when it showed came as much from this temperament as it did from his political nous or his grasp of policy, and if ever there is a Keating legend it will come from the same sources. Not the political animal, the economic rationalist or the technocrat, but the contours and eruptions of his mind, his ego (his 'I') set him apart. All the others I could admire or learn from, but the last defined him, and, right or wrong, it defines him in this book.

If in *Recollections* there is too much of my 'I' and not enough of his; if the grand vision lacks definition; if I am too personal or too critical or wrong, there is always the autobiographical option.

Whitlam, Hawke and Howard have done it. So recently did Malcolm Fraser. And last year Blanche d'Alpuget added to

Bob Hawke's own take on his government her second biography of him. It is hard to say which is greater: the service such books do to the reputations of their subjects, or the degree of offence they give to their former colleagues. It's possible that in the broader sweep of things – broader, say, than sales in the first year – they do little of consequence to either category. The exercise cannot be other than self-serving to some degree, and transparently so. Yet, if anyone could transcend this obvious shortcoming it is Keating. Two large-scale biographical works, two or three smaller ones, David Love's *Unfinished Business*, a hit musical – the coverage of his life and career has been, as they say in Finance, non-trivial; and yet who would wonder if he thought it a bit slapdash, ambiguous, incomplete? I hope his autobiography is as big as *War and Peace* and at the end he is able to say what Tolstoy said when he finished: that his book 'is what the author wished, and was able, to express in the form in which it is expressed'.

Blanche d'Alpuget told me that there are people in the Labor Party who believe my book was an act of 'treachery'. D'Alpuget did not say if it was two or two hundred people but, whatever their number, in almost a decade only Paul Keating has expressed the sentiment to me. I have no doubt he expected a different kind of book and because, very near the publication date, someone who knows him as well as I once did urged me not to show him the manuscript, saying it would never be my book or the book it should be if I did, I know Paul felt I had deliberately deceived him. Though I wish he did not think this, I remain grateful for that mutual friend's advice.

Yet it has been painful to live with his accusation. If he feels betrayed, I have to concede the possibility that I betrayed him. In that case, I can only hope that one day he will realise the 'betrayal' had nothing to do with spite or neglect of his feelings, but with reasons concerning the business of writing that are no less compelling to a writer than reasons arising from politics are to a politician. It was not for want of admiration or loyalty or gratitude that I did not write a book that pleased him.

It comes down to the fact that everyone who sets out to write history must be free to decide how he will do it. It can't be any other way. I regret only a few things more deeply than Paul Keating's belief that he was betrayed by this book, but if I had written it according to his lights rather than mine, from any angle other than mine, I would have betrayed myself; and, for want of a more clinical term, history – the bit I saw at least – would have been betrayed as well.

2011

Draft for a Prime Minister's Address on the Occasion of Another Visit from the President of the United States

Mr President,
Thank you for making room in your busy schedule to see me while you are in Darwin. In the short time I have at your disposal, let me welcome you to our shores. I trust you have found your soldiers in good spirits and enjoying their vital role as guardians of our joint regional security. I hope they're putting on plenty of sunscreen, Mr President.

It is altogether fitting and proper, Mr President . . .

I wonder if you could turn your helicopter off for a moment. If not, I totally understand. I know they can be hard to get started again.

Mr President, our friendship is a mature one, a lasting one. It is a friendship set in cement. There is the love we share for Democracy – 'that sublime revelation of man's relation to man', as one of your predecessors so memorably put it. Our love of democracy is matched by a love of liberty and peace; for the sovereignty of the individual, the spirit of free enterprise and the dignity of men and women from the humblest to the most exalted.

You hold these things to be self-evident, Mr President, as we know.

[IF THEY CAN HEAR YOU, THIS MAY PROMPT APPLAUSE]

We have gone into battle together for these principles, Mr President, and we stand ready to go into battle again, whenever and wherever – after strenuous consultation – you decide we should.

Mr President, we can confer no greater honour on a friend than to call him 'mate'. And that is what our two countries are – mates, Mr President. *Mates* are us.

You have buddies in the United States, but I think I am right in saying that buddyship is not the core national value, as mateship is in Australia.

You have many other core values, of course. Core values that have made the United States a beacon of liberty to the whole world. And fondly do we hope, Mr President, fervently do we pray that those values and that beacon will continue to glow brightly going forward.

[APPLAUSE?]

It is far above my poor power, Mr President, to explain what we Australians mean by mateship. Yet that is a cardinal virtue of our creed: mates *don't need* to explain these things to each other. Real mates just *know* them.

Mateship is a quality of mute understanding, forged in the unsparing design of Providence to inflict droughts, bushfires, floods, weeds and vermin on all who dare to tame this continent. These are the things that made us us.

[POSSIBLE APPLAUSE FROM THE AUSTRALIANS IN THE AUDIENCE]

Indefinable, intangible things; elusive things, Mr President – but things just the same.

Mr President, a mate sticks by you when you find yourself in trouble, be it your own fault or someone else's. You can be a blithering idiot or a sociopath and a mate'll stick. You can make a complete animal of yourself, Mr President, and he'll stick all the stronger. That's us Aussies, Mr President – we stick.

Of course I don't mean to imply that the United States is in any sense a fount of humbug, or moronic, as your own H. L. Mencken insisted it was, or root and branch corrupt as Mark Twain and many others have said, or, beyond a few notorious examples, animal-like in any way.

[SOMEWHAT FORLORN PAUSE]

Mr President, mateship demands that one mate tell the other when someone's dogging him – that is, unless the one doing the dogging is also a mate. In such cases the proper thing is to hang out with a different set of mates till the thing blows over. This is one of those cases; and even if it were, we don't have any other mates in this part of the world to hang out with – none we feel really comfortable with, Mr President.

Mr President, not to mince words, these people are saying America's a wreck: the communitarian ethos by which it flourished in the great years has been replaced by outrageous greed and self-indulgence, the good society by the security state, the civilian economy by the military industrial complex. That's what they say, Mr President: not us – them. A kleptocracy sustained by unreasoning fear and ignorance, fantasies and brainless cults of materialism and celebrity. A hollow empire; rampant bully and quaking adolescent both; an eight-dollars-an-hour neo-feudal slum. Your republic is rotting at the core, Mr President. That's what they say.

Just the other day, in *Newsweek*, there was an investment banker with Lehman Brothers for 30 years – 'kissing ass and lying through his teeth' the whole time, by his account. He says the truth of modern America is the opposite of what Roosevelt and Kennedy inspired him to believe: corruption, he says, 'has settled like some all-enveloping excremental mist on the landscape of our hopes . . . and permeated every nook of any institution or being that has real influence on the way we live now'.

Mr President, feel free to have your military detain this 75-year-old indefinitely under the powers granted by the legislation you recently signed, we will understand. Let him learn that the rights of man derive from the generosity of the state, and not as some idealists have previously averred, from the hand of God.

[LIKELY APPLAUSE]

Mr President, according to the most recent statistics, on the battlefields of Iraq, 4487 American servicemen and women were killed and 32,226 were wounded. This does not include suicides, accidental deaths and Americans whose last full measure of devotion was made per medium of private contractors. The Pentagon also reports 229,106 cases of mild to severe traumatic brain injury among US soldiers in Iraq and Afghanistan. The RAND Corporation found 14 per cent of veterans suffered post-traumatic stress disorder and the same proportion suffered major depression. Fourteen per cent of 1.5 million is 210,000. Veterans of America estimates one in three – 500,000 – suffered PTSD, depression or brain trauma. For every soldier wounded in action more than four more were evacuated for other medical reasons. Chronic fatigue syndrome, migraine, memory loss, sleep disorders, malaria, hepatitis and tuberculosis were among many diseases suffered by returning soldiers. The Department of Veterans Affairs warns combat veterans that they may suffer lifetime debilitation from exposure to depleted uranium, toxic shrapnel, open-air burn pits and hazardous chemicals. Yet war is war, and as my mother used to say, it's no good getting upset at things you can't do anything about.

There have been 130,000 civilian deaths in Iraq, an unknown number injured, one and a half million refugees, at least as many internally displaced. Too terrible to think about, Mr President, and I'm sure that's why you never mention them.

Mr President, if the United States fails then the whole cause of freedom fails, John F. Kennedy said half a century ago. He meant it must lead by example.

Yet, Mr President, we could not help noticing that at the very same time as one bunch of Americans were paying any price and bearing any burden and meeting any hardship to assure the success of liberty, another bunch were behaving as if it were their equally solemn duty to make themselves obscenely rich. And I must say, as a mate, we did wonder why you rewarded them with bailouts and positions in your Cabinet, especially when to no one's surprise they put the great bulk of the money not to new lending, restructuring mortgages, stalling foreclosures or doing a single thing to help their country or their struggling fellow citizens, but to satisfying the same old scabrous greed.

But silence rules in these things, Mr President. It's not for us to ask why you saved the banks instead of the economy, not for us to ask.

'Man holds in his mortal hands the power to abolish all forms of human poverty and all forms of human life,' Kennedy said. Your military budget now totals 47 per cent of the whole world's. Are you mad? We don't care. Since Kennedy inspired you with a call to civic duty, you've increased the power to abolish life a thousand fold and 40 million of your people live in poverty. And they're getting poorer. We speak only of material impoverishment, Mr President. We haven't mentioned the culture.

You seem to have it arse-about, Mr President; but it's not the first time that's happened to a mate. We're here for you, now and forever. We'll always be here. Come back again soon.

[THE PRESIDENT IS DUE TO DEPART AROUND NOW. SHOULD HE DO SO, WAVE GAILY AND WITH DIGNITY. BUT DO NOT, I REPEAT DO NOT ATTEMPT TO FOLLOW HIM TO THE HELICOPTER, OR YOU WILL BE SHOT]

The Monthly, February 2012

Attack of the Clones

> They should just clone ministers, you know. So we're born at 55 with no past . . . and no genitals. Just a world of robots. It's like a futuristic film, and you'd enjoy that, wouldn't you? You'd be in your little space station surrounded by obedient androids . . .
>
> Hugh Abbot MP to Malcolm Tucker, Political Adviser, *The Thick of It*

People who watched the first series of *Yes Minister* might remember a fringe character called Frank Weisel, a young man of little apparent promise much loathed by Humphrey Appleby. For Humphrey, finding Frank in the Minister's office was like finding an ant in his whisky and soda. The worst thing anyone could say fairly about Frank was that he was gormless and dull; but he was lower middle class, and if, as seemed likely, he had a degree in Sociology or Communications or Media Studies or something of that nature from a red-brick university, in Humphrey's eyes this was all the more proof of his unfitness. A person of such rank deficiency could never appreciate the refinements of political power, and in his clumsy ignorance might very well trash them. It is likely that in the more ancient halls of Humphrey's Oxfordian civil-service mind, Frank lurked as a kind of Jacobite, an uncouth throwback who had somehow escaped the evolutionary axe, a menace to the beautiful and necessary order of things, and all the more dangerous for being as earnest as he was hare-brained.

With such an enemy Frank could not last long, and after just half-a-dozen episodes, he was done away with like an incontinent cat, and with a similar sense of relief.

The past, as they say, is another country and that includes the early 1980s. Certainly there were Frank Weisels nosing around the fabled corridors when *Yes Minister* was made 30 years ago, but the Humphreys had the real muscle, in Canberra as in Whitehall. There were Machiavels among them, cynics, careerists and the usual 24-hours-a-day arse-coverers: they were captive to timeworn conventions and saws, hostile to change very often, insufferably arrogant and remote from the mundane life of the country.

We can say what we like about them now because they are a broken tribe; not entirely gone, but with at least one leg stuffed in the dustbin of history. And the usurpers of their privileges and power have been, of all people, the immediate descendants of Frank Weisel. As politics and the media merged into one indivisible domain, the 'media-savvy' Weisels went forth and multiplied. Impervious to cliché and their own ignorance, they went armed with all the demotic tools: focus group research, polling, messaging and spin. Soon every office had one or two or even more. They colonised politics, made it their personal anthill, and soon enough they ran the show.

The triumph of Frank Weisel is most spectacularly made flesh in the British TV series *The Thick of It*, especially in the profane

Scottish genius of *realmediapolitik*, Malcolm Tucker – for which, we are advised, read Tony Blair's spin doctor, Alistair Campbell. Though we have never hesitated to do it with public servants of course, it is always perilous to generalise about any group of people. Not every senior servant is a Humphrey, and not all political advisers are like Malcolm. Humphrey and Malcolm are caricatures, wild exaggerations: no public servant is quite as lubricious as Humphrey and the modern political adviser – I mean the hard-nosed insider kind – is neither quite so base nor anywhere near as eloquent as Malcolm.

While it is reasonable to say that some political advisers have large and practical ideas for the country, it's unlikely that they have more than we would find among a similar cohort of farmers and school-teachers – or public servants. In fact, we might find fewer ideas among a profession that tends to attract the type of people who pride themselves less on any intellectual or imaginative capacity than on ruthless pragmatism and a willingness to kick heads.

Some advisers are articulate and informed by a wide variety of reading and experience. But you would find the same qualities in at least equal profusion among many of the professions – including public servants and their spouses and partners. Political advisers make hard decisions – or at least advise their masters to make them: and doctors and nurses and farmers also make them.

Malcolm Tucker's capacity for breathtakingly foul metaphors notwithstanding, the truth is modern political advisers are not a particularly articulate, imaginative, worldly, or even clever, category of person. Some are shallow and dull-witted, many are prolix, and more than a few haven't read a book in years. When they leave politics, if it is not into well-paid jobs with large corporations, including media corporations, it is often into consultancies that they go. But you would not necessarily consult them if you were looking for the path to enlightenment or grace. They do not harbour in their breasts more capacity for leadership – more good will or insight, or clarity of thought and expression, or empathy, or breadth and depth of vision – than the members of any other profession or trade, including the public service.

And yet their profession *is* leadership. They swarm round the seats of political power. And so thoroughly have they woven themselves into the fabric of politics they now define its character, its stripe.

When we think of politics these days we think of spin. When we think of spin we may as well think of our washing machine at the end of a wash, when the clothes are all stuck to the wall of the cylinder. We're the wall, and the clothes, twisted and tangled beyond recognition, are the truth after it has been processed by political experts. There's more to it than this of course, but not that much more.

Spin is the most obvious of the political advisers' contributions to our politics: it is also the most tiresome, corrosive and, as *The Thick of It* would have it, both the most outrageous and the most pathetic. Yet nothing in the fevered minds of that show's creators could match a recent grab from the rooms of the Federal Opposition. There was the Leader and his loyal lieutenants, Joe Hockey and Andrew Robb, sitting at a table like Malcolm's brushed aluminium androids and offering for the cameras their candid opinion of the government. This candid opinion was that the government was all spin – clichés and spin – and no substance. It was 'embarrassing', Andrew Robb said. And as each spoke, the others nodded as if they had just heard that Singapore had fallen again. All it needed was a laughter track.

The latter-day Weisels did not invent spin (it's hard to think of anything they invented), but they were the first to use it as a general anaesthetic. The basic art is older than politics, as old as language. Language and spin are cousins, surely. But it is one thing to seek advantage by putting the best or worst possible interpretation on events – it is a human trait and can be done with elegance: it is something else entirely to obey the axioms of the modern form – stay 'on message' and repeat 'key' words and phrases even if it makes you sound like a very bad actor or a school child or someone who may or may not be 'real'. And so long as you are hostage to these demands, even if you are engaged in a larger project, you cannot give the impression that you are, or that YOU WON'T at any moment throw it over for politics.

It is not altogether fair to blame the advisers. Our leaders decide what advice they will take and what they will reject, just as they choose their words. But then very often our leaders – both the Prime Minister [Julia Gillard] and Opposition Leader [Tony Abbott], for example – are former political advisers and it is no surprise that the familiar android forms appeal to them.

The political whizz, of course, is a very democratic personage, much more in touch with the people (including people of vast fortune and influence) than the notoriously Olympian public servant. Yet the record tends to elevate the public servant as a more effective and courageous agent of economic and social improvement. The big changes in Australia were made not by whizzes, but by policy-driven politicians in combination with like-minded public servants of equal conviction.

The political fixers have their uses, naturally. It is not their existence but their dominance that depletes our politics. If they can be kept away from policy and speeches (nothing will turn a speech into an embarrassment like a mauling from the party geniuses), two or three on each side of politics can be justified. Any more runs counter to the fact that the more they multiply the less likely it is that we will see the leaders of character, foresight and independence we wish for: or hear them speak to us in ways that are not maddening.

The Monthly, March 2012

Blessed Are the Wealth-Makers

> Entrepreneur – isn't that a lovely word? You know, entrepreneur – we want entrepreneurs.
>
> George W. Bush, 2004

In 1848 a drover named O'Shaughnessy, the son of a convict, came across a man living in a gunyah in the reed beds of the Lachlan River with a few cows. O'Shaughnessy faded quickly from history, but the man in the reeds, also the son of a convict, was James Tyson and before his life was over he had millions of cattle and sheep grazing on holdings that stretched from Gippsland to the Gulf of Carpentaria. 'Hungry' Tyson he was called, and he died very rich and very famous. Banjo Paterson managed to write a poem about him without using the word, but today we might call him an 'entrepreneur', even a 'wealth creator', and one of those who by their deeds prove that anyone prepared to work hard and live the dream can grow as rich as Rockefeller.

You have to love your entrepreneur. Really, you have to – it's a rule. Anything less might be interpreted as class war. Blessed are the wealth-makers. Bless them for their lively minds and optimistic spirit, their resolute and persevering character. They do create wealth and not all of it for themselves. Determined to improve their own circumstances, very often they improve ours as well. Think Andrew Carnegie's Bessemer converters and vertical integrations, Bill Gates' gadgetry, Lance Hill's Hoist. Think of the million and one amenities that their enterprise has brought the human race; the millions of jobs, the children raised in reasonable comfort on the wages their industry afforded. We also give thanks for the generosity which seems to be as much a part of the true entrepreneurial character as the get-up-and-go that defines them. Carnegie's and Gates' benefactions are proverbial. So in his day were Tyson's.

We are especially grateful for the relief they provide from the charmless moans of collectivism. A healthy human mind can stand only so many renditions of 'Scots Wha' Hae'. We prefer love songs, even if they're self-love songs. Entrepreneurs give expression to that bit of the human spirit which in most of us is never activated: the bit that tells us we should not die wondering. They pit themselves against Nature, extracting minerals and ores, smelting, refining, tinkering, inventing – and risking their own money very often. They triumph sometimes, but frequently suffer all manner of torture and defeat and go under. We like that too; for even then their lives, like their appetites, seem so much grander than our own.

Ever since Ronald Reagan and Margaret Thatcher set the neoliberal ball rolling, democratic governments have gone out of their way to praise and encourage the entrepreneurs, accommodate and step aside for them. In this they happily include everyone from Warren Buffett to Joe the Plumber or an enterprising busker. The British Prime Minister has declared the next decade will be nothing less than the 'most entrepreneurial' in his country's history. Think about that. In the United States, what was a pedestrian fact of capitalist life has become a full-blown ideology; reinforced, as ever, by Divine Providence and the internalised tycoons of the Old Testament. True, the Global Financial Crisis made a dent in the reputations of the financial market entrepreneurs, but not so big that they were made to pay much of a price. No gaol-time, no painful fines, not even a Japanese-style public apology, no begging forgiveness before the people's representatives. Not only were they too big to fail, the cult of the entrepreneur depended on them.

The British journalist George Monbiot recently reproduced some figures to show the effects of this cult on social equality. They pertain to the United States and the United Kingdom, but they are worth bearing in mind every time we hear a Clive Palmer or Gina Rinehart declaiming, or a politician doing it for them; or, on the other hand, a Federal Treasurer displaying a bit of entrepreneurial gumption of his own and giving them a poke in the eye. Between 1947 and 1979 US productivity rose by 119 per cent and the income of the bottom fifth rose by 122 per cent. Remember, these were years of strong trade unions, the GI Bill, big government investment in research (not least into developing what became the internet), infrastructure and social security. Over the next 30 years, the neoliberal years of 'small government' and declining trade-union power, productivity increased by 80 per cent, the income of the bottom fifth fell by 4 per cent and the income of the top 1 per cent rose by 270 per cent. No doubt there are people for whom these figures can be made to illustrate a great social improvement, or a situation that is better than it would have been had Reaganomics not prevailed: but for now Monbiot seems to have a case when he says they show that 'the wealth creators of neoliberal mythology are some of the most effective wealth destroyers the world has ever seen'.[5]

Other consequences of ungoverned entrepreneurial enterprise are not described in the figures. 'Hungry' Tyson was a self-effacing sort of tycoon who, according to his obituary, 'made his millions honestly, and at the expense of no one but Nature . . .' Nature is no longer such a minor expense, and the damage was not only to the physical environment, but to the people for whom Nature was the material and spiritual basis of existence. About two-thirds of his holdings were leased; that is to say (putting aside any notion of Aboriginal title to them) the expense was to lands that were not his but the Crown's – or, by its grace, ours. Tyson could no more repay these costs than Andrew Carnegie's massive benefactions in the United States could cure a dose of miner's lung.

Here then is the great conundrum. Had he been obliged to observe modern environmental standards, employee and animal welfare and the rules of racial equality, James Tyson would never have left his camp in the swamp. Yet without him, and without the pastoral industry, we would all be poorer, quite possibly – as the United States (and the UK) would have been without slavery.

As the doctrine of the entrepreneur has it, this just goes to show that governments should get out of the way and unleash the beast of self-interest. Any unfortunate effects will be corrected later by charitable bequests to medical research and conservation groups, with shortfalls made up by governments that know their place. Probably half of all political debate reduces to the conflict between this view and liberal notions of the collective good, and it is no less probable that half of the words on both sides have become unbearable platitudes and half of the time is wasted.

But every now and then an entrepreneur emerges from the field of enterprise to freshen up the battle and make the choices clearer. And what do we see in the embodiment of that to which we are urged to aspire? We see something that is not very bright or believable. We see little evidence that they have worked harder than anybody else or sacrificed more. Of course we are not seeing the truth about every entrepreneur, but nor are we seeing evidence that, even if all hard-working people could be as rich as Croesus (which plainly they can't), the entrepreneurial life is the highest form a human being can aim for. What we see are signs of monomania, self-interest pretending that whatever satisfies the reptilian instinct is good for all humanity, and very often a chronic inability to acknowledge that the accident of birth or any other good fortune played a part in their success. The fallacy of self-attribution is what we see.

James Baillieu was a contemporary of 'Hungry' Tyson's and had some of the same entrepreneurial fire in his belly. As a 17-year-old English midshipman, he jumped overboard into Port Phillip Bay and swam ashore at Queenscliff. He lived in a tent on the beach for a while, worked at several jobs, built a grand hotel and sired 13 healthy children of whom the most enterprising was William Lawrence Baillieu, miner, industrialist, speculator, politician and founder of the Baillieu dynasty. One of his descendants is Marshall Baillieu. Until last week M. Baillieu was dimly remembered as a Liberal member of the House of Representatives, but now he is much more deeply engraved on the public mind for raising his middle finger to a group of protesting nurses as he arrived at a family gathering. No one using the tradesmen's entrance could have done it with more eloquent contempt. That one photograph might have been enough to tell us that the man is a creep, but subsequent shots of him flapping his ears at the nurses seemed to confirm him as a creep of a particular, sneering Melbourne establishment kind.

But let us give thanks to Marshall Baillieu too. His gestures brought home to us another problem with entrepreneurs and the self-defeating logic of the cult surrounding them – one that, in hating all inherited wealth and privilege from the British monarchy to the meanest of dukedoms, Andrew Carnegie was on to – they have *children*.

We can only wonder if Gina Rinehart, having dragged herself up by her rhinoceros-horn bootstraps, wishes she had understood in time.

The Monthly, April 2012

A New Opium

Of all believers who might have debated Richard Dawkins on the ABC last month, Cardinal Pell was surely among the least suitable. There is no doubting the depth of the Archbishop's faith or sincerity, of course; there can be no doubt about Rupert Murdoch's faith in freedom of the press, either. That the Cardinal's public demeanour does not immediately bring to mind the author of the Beatitudes has nothing to do with the case: the poet Les Murray, to pluck a man of faith from nowhere, is certainly no less pugnacious and opinionated, but he would have been a much more formidable (and stimulating) opponent for Dawkins, even if our scientist had not been jet-lagged. The likes of the American novelist Marilynne Robinson would have been good too, albeit from a Protestant angle. Like Murray, Robinson is a believer who makes non-believers discreetly check their internal compasses; and neither of them, what's more, would have needed Pell's urgers in the audience imitating a Roman mob. Of course, it doesn't help that Cardinal Pell represents a church which currently has many charges against it, but since most churches have past charges against them, this hardly disqualified him.

What did make his presence unfortunate, not to say, by the end, excruciating, was his inability to mount a persuasive argument for the possibility of God without overlaying it with doctrinal baloney about the nature of such a God and its continuing powers, along with heaven, hell and a 'place of purification', presumably in between. *This* was what Marx likened to opium? It was not the Cardinal's persona or his church, but the barrenness of his argument and the patches of downright silliness: I don't know what believers made of his case, but those of us burdened with an absence of faith felt seriously short-changed.

Yet in the face of smug vapidity and braying, the stonkered Englishman's best arguments scarcely raised a welt, and at times he flailed around like a man trying to drive out the smell of incense with a hammer. It was a spectacle to remind us that scientists are most useful when quietly getting on with their business of discovering how the world works, curing disease and brightening the lives of multitudes, including the multitudes of intelligent people who believe there is Something beyond or within or without, which does not respond to scientific inquiry.

Whatever their intentions, militant atheists of the Dawkins kind nearly always look a bit like attention-seeking brats, or mirror images of meddling priests. And whatever they know of science, they do not seem to understand religion. Asking 'Why are we here?' is a silly question, Dawkins said, and was dismayed when the mob booed and Pell smirked. Well, it might be a silly question, but it comes with existence: the only people who have not at some time asked 'Why are we here?' are those who in one way or another are *not* here. Dawkins might have been less irritated by Pell's foetid old chestnut about communism (and Nazism, he said) being murderous because it was atheistic, if he considered the possibility that when he aims his boot at religion for good reason the threat is felt as an existential one.

The question turns out to be less one of why Pell was put up against Dawkins than why Dawkins was pitted against Pell. Better a fellow believer from a different branch – Protestant, liberal Catholic, Buddhist, Jew, Muslim, Kierkegaardian: not to restart the Thirty Years War, but rather because intellectual atheists can no more prove the non-existence of that in which believers refuse not to believe than your average professional wrestler can, and both have less hope than certain jolts of experience.

Take for instance the self-educated and much-loved memoirist, Albert Facey, in 1914 a near-perfect embodiment of the prototypical bushman-cum-digger. Bert Facey found his faith fading sometime between his first bayonet charge at Gallipoli and his 11th. Two of his brothers were killed in that campaign, and he suffered injuries from which he never recovered. His son was killed in the next war. By then Facey had decided 'there is no God, it is only a myth'. There was neither science nor theology to his conversion, unless 'the awful look on a man's face after he has been bayoneted' qualifies as one or the other; but his experience served better than Evolution to change what he called his 'outlook'. 'It's a terrible thing, a bayonet charge,' he wrote.

For Facey, as no doubt for many others, God died as Anzac was born. He was nothing less than a patriot and a proud soldier, but his feelings about the war were complex and contradictory. He had killed 'hundreds of men', and seen thousands die. He'd fought with countrymen he admired and some he didn't care for. He'd clout any larrikin who slung off at him for enlisting, and despised men who had stayed behind, he reckoned, to take advantage of the soldiers' wives and girlfriends; yet if he had known what the war was going to be like, he said, he would have stayed at home. Nowhere in his wonderful memoir, *A Fortunate Life*, does he say *why* he enlisted: if it was to keep Australia free or to preserve democracy, he did not think it important enough to say so. He didn't do it for mateship or any other 'value' as far as we can tell, unless it was for manly duty and imperial loyalty, Victorian creeds to which craggy Australian bush dwellers were very susceptible.

Myths, alas, do not accommodate such complexities. When old soldiers got together to remember and the nation murmured Lest We Forget, Anzac Day served a good purpose and retained a connection with the realities men like Bert Facey lived through and bore all their days. Late in his life Facey nominated Simpson, the stretcher bearer with the donkey, as his hero of the campaign, and it was the lesson of the saint-like Simpson, not the 'values' of mateship or identity, that generations of 20th-century children were taught. There were politicians, leader-writers and historians who could not resist editorialising about the 'meaning' of Gallipoli, but they never came up with much more than a handful of fairly harmless fantasies about the national character.

But Anzac has become something else now. The Prime Minister says it has grown 'organically'. 'That organic sense of growth has taken us to a new place on Anzac Day,' she said after delivering a very moving speech to the now-familiar overflow crowds at Gallipoli. By organic she seemed to mean that, unlike Australia Day, it had not been officially declared; it had grown of itself; 'the people' (or something) had taken it to this 'new place'. That she had just 'unofficially' declared the day a national one seems to have passed unnoticed. In any event, Anzac Day is now a day 'for all Australians' and represents 'the deepest of Australian values of mateship, good humour, endurance and bravery', she said. A VC winner, back from Afghanistan, concurred: Anzac Day, he said, is 'about the founding of our Australian values and our Aussie spirit'. Such strange produce from umpteen thousand bayonets in umpteen thousand gizzards!

From what the Prime Minister and her most recent antecedents say, you would swear we know better than the soldiers did what they were doing it for. Or from their graves have the legions of the dead somehow directed us to this new place? I mean we have never asked them, have we? Did their voices come to us on a bush track somewhere? Or does Peter Cosgrove double as their vicar?

Not for a moment would we say they are glorifying war: they are merely taking out the gore and all the other confusing bits and giving it a meaning that the dead could not come up with themselves. A much higher meaning. Dare we say a religious sort of meaning?

Not only do we have a new organic National Day (to be happily exploited by politicians, breweries and Peter Cosgrove alike) but we are also approaching the cusp of a default State religion. What does a religion do if not second guess the dead, turn them into an answer to that question – why are we here? Because they died for us. So we might enjoy our freedom, our way of life, our national identity, even our sense of humour. This is how the commentary now goes. They are our first cause. So well do we know them, an AFL football coach is reported to have told his players that they had betrayed the Anzacs by losing on Anzac Day.

Cardinal Pell has given the idea his blessing. He says it was a day of 'redemptive sacrifice'. In his view it may have been, but possibly not for Bert Facey when he learned that his brother had been bayoneted to death while on guard duty. Tell us again, Cardinal, who and what was redeemed by the Australian deaths at Lone Pine, or for that matter by the deaths of a couple of hundred thousand Turkish conscripts.

Who knows why, but Cardinal Pell says he doesn't 'think a country without deep Christian roots can make a national day out of a defeat'. It can, however, make an Anzac Day. It made one for the soldiers and the commemoration of the dead in secular memorials. It does not really matter what the Cardinal thinks. It is the non-believers and those of nondescript belief who in their bumbling ways are urging this leap of faith upon us.

The Monthly, May 2012

A New Dusk

In 1967, when La Trobe University was brand new and under-populated, John O'Brien, an Irish historian with a wild and feverish laugh, told us about the enemy within. It was not for anything the administration had done, or any of the horrid things that two years later Maoist students would bellow when they occupied their offices ('puppets of the ruling class', 'parasites', 'class traitors', etc.): it was for what he insisted was an administrator's natural tendency to unseat the academic staff and corrupt the principles of the university. Those Maoists, when they hatched, were mere heretics, and they'd grow out of it, but in the bureaucracy lay the seeds of treason.

It seemed odd: we students took our administrators for amiable co-venturers on the infant campus. But Dr O'Brien's judgement was severe: universities were places of teaching and research, of rigorous intellectual endeavour and inquiry. This was their glory, and it followed that those who did the teaching and research, who had the knowledge and valued it, should decide the course they took. Administrators, an inherently philistine self-perpetuating caste and fixated with power, should never be allowed to forget they were retained at the pleasure of the academy to perform such useful tasks as the life of the mind compelled. Let them think for a moment that the place was theirs to run and you could kiss goodnight to academic freedom and educational standards. It was in their nature to usurp.

Probably it was as much a streak of inner high Tory as liberal humanist speaking, but that hardly matters. Dr O'Brien had seen the future.

Of course it is one thing 'to cultivate learning in the broadest and deepest sense' in a tutorial or a laboratory, another thing to do it while satisfying the needs and prejudices of one's paymasters, whether they be church, state, business or fee-paying students. And it is another thing again to try to cultivate it as your province of a relatively privileged few becomes an essential highway for the masses. To be sure, John O'Brien had an idealised – the Maoists would say an 'ivory tower' – view of the university. But what is a university without ideals? Too easy: one with a mission statement.

The odd thing was that the academics didn't see it coming. Then again, the monks in that quaint little abbey on Lindisfarne didn't see the Vikings coming either – or did, and thought they wanted to be baptised. Maybe life had been too good. In the academy run by academics, useful and rewarding, sometimes brilliant and monumental, intellectual effort co-existed with a certain amount of equally well-paid Olympian lassitude. A year's sabbatical in every seven; a 30-week year; tenure with no obligation to publish; for some, little more than three or four hours of teaching a week; all conducted on campuses that were effectively closed for a third of the year: the model struggled to comply with basic measures of social utility, much less those laid down by the advancing neo-liberal hordes and their most brutal weapon – managerialism.

If, before John Dawkins was given the job of 'reforming' them, they had begun to reform themselves a little, they might have stood a chance. Run three semesters all year round, for instance; less tenure, more contracts; more reward for useful exertion, less for sloth; more signs of enterprise and palpable interest in the way the world outside was going, which was decisively away from the long lunch and towards competitive effort: had they done a bit more to look busy it might have been possible to save something from the rout.

It is 25 years since Dawkins became the Minister for Employment, Education and Training and set about remodelling the country's institutions of tertiary education into instruments of the dynamic new-fangled economic order. The new economy created a new frontier and, as on the old one, the heroic doctrines were pragmatic, utilitarian, impatient, tending to anti-intellectual. By these lights, the university run by academics and according to academic values was about as far from ideal as one could get. Much closer to the model was the modern corporation and the management principles they employed. Universities became massive revenue-chasing enterprises, academics became administrators, students became customers, managers became royalty – and management's share of revenue multiplied and multiplied.

From the current Prime Minister's box-ticking instrumentalist mantras it is safe to infer that, like her predecessors, she reckons the revolution was necessary, sage and wonderful, and all evidence to the contrary is, perforce, the pitiful griping of elitists and losers. If it is a bit of a shemozzle, or even a thorough catastrophe, it is also a cornerstone of free-market orthodoxy and an indispensable rhetorical thread; sceptics, therefore, must be sedated with a near-lethal concoction of various dogmas on the theme of opportunity and fairness – with our leader's own story as a sort of divine revelation or benchmarked proof of the pudding.

Yet, the protests from inside what the historian Jim Davidson calls the 'academic archipelago' speak of the follies conscientious scholars and teachers are required to perform: useless performance-measurement rituals; senseless strategic plans; bullying in the name of 'buy-in'; the culture of 'constant change', regardless of the consequences for the quality of education; the massive diversion of funds to managers and consultancies; the Orwellian language in which they are instructed – though, for all his formidable powers, Orwell could not have invented the language of HR, or even the idea of it.

Donald Meyers, a former science academic, has recently published a book in which he argues ferociously against the view – axiomatic post-Dawkins – that the old-style university administrations were inefficient.[6] On the contrary, he says they delivered a much better education for much less. Then academics were teachers and researchers with minimal administrative responsibilities: now they must combine their professional duties with mind-numbing administrative tasks straight from late-model management's most depressing handbooks. Much that was formerly done by a capable department secretary is now for all to do – if they can remember their 'FHUSS-specific parameters for the Workload Management System'.[7]

While you're wrestling with that, and trying to work out on your application form for research funding the difference between an 'output' and an 'outcome',[8] there might land on your desk a 'Behaviour Capability Framework' for which the university has paid a consultant umpteen thousands of dollars informing you that from now on you are required to demonstrate 'passion, energy and tenacity' in your work or be judged wanting in one or more of 'six behavioural clusters'; namely, 'Resilience, Connectedness, Commitment to Excellence, Innovation, Outcomes Focussed and Open Thinking'. Was any subject in the old ivory tower more arcane and of less use to humanity?

Each university has its own problems and, one assumes, advantages, but according to Meyers, 'pointless performance management is the default religion' at all of them – 'a policy, a plan and KPIs for everything and everyone'. So why should academics escape what every bank employee must endure?

Whether management is the cause or the symptom is less the point than what Meyers believes is the sickness itself – the dumbing down of university education.

The public need to know that the nation's ability to supply competent people, from tradies to neurosurgeons, is being compromised by the blind and persistent application of free-market ideology and soft options education theory. How much longer are we going to live with university management rhetoric that spruiks 'quality', 'excellence', 'innovation', 'world's best practice' and any other number of inanities to the would-be customer, when we know that the two-dollar-shop university degree is the order of the day?

Meyers is not alone in this view. Members of Science faculties speak (if discreetly and on condition of anonymity) of trying to teach young people who are simply not able to be taught, and of issuing degrees to people who could never be made capable of decently earning them. There are people in the Humanities and Social Sciences who would say the same. There are plenty who contend that the 'reforms' to tertiary education have corrupted it, defeated its most basic aims, including those of excellence, intellectual rigour and originality. To paraphrase Raimond Gaita: the universities have made 'mendicants' of philosophers and physicists and devalued their disciplines, while privileging the study of hospitality and gaming. Brendan Coventry, an Adelaide Professor of Surgery, declares the system has been placed under 'inexorable downward pressure' and is unsustainable.

The argument goes naturally to the primary and secondary systems that feed the universities. Meyers believes those systems are failing as calamitously as the universities are, and sheets much of the blame to the 'Educationalists' who have devised modern 'outcomes-based' pedagogy (he quotes some astonishing examples) and manage to persist in their follies by rationalising failure into (benchmarked) success.

Those 'Educationalists' will be among the many who disagree with Meyers. Others will include people who, diligent in their calling, can claim genuine success; and people of less accomplishment but equally deep investments in the present system, from politicians to bureaucrats to students. He can expect to be savaged for failing to produce evidence at every turn and neglecting to footnote. Coming from the authors and defenders of strategic plans and other malarkey, he need not take this badly. He has written a pamphlet, a whack at something atrocious and unforgivable. No intellectual tradition is longer or more honourable.

Let's imagine he is only half right, and the system is only half dysfunctional. That is still a mighty failure and, as Meyers says, 'a great wrong'. No doubt more important deliberations concern them, but if members of any of the 23 current inquiries, consultations and reviews were to ask why we have failed to provide high-quality education for all, they could do worse than read Meyers. Forget it. They're hardly going to admit to failure if it wrecks a thriving industry in calling it success.

The Monthly, August 2012

The Kings and I

The football ends, and the vanquished lie here and there on their backs, like blowflies after a spray of Mortein. It would make a telling coda to the season if the victors were allowed to go around stamping on them. Instead we are left this depressing spectacle and the cries of a triumphant army denied the right to rape or pillage. Allow the winning team to march away two or three players from their opponents' ranks; a trainer, their masseurs and massage oils; carry off their exercise bikes, their wives and girlfriends. For now, the final siren confirms the one thing which, for the sake of the industry, several million people have once more been persuaded to forget – that it's just a game.

And so the season turns to racing. The good horses come out, the not-so-good go to the spelling paddock, and the old and average look desperately for new careers in showjumping, or board a truck to the knackery. That's the difference between horseracing and all other legal sports: horseracing is for keeps. Racing is the meanest game, and not just because it's the only entertainment in which animals are whipped.

Of course the people who run the business pretend that glamour is the essence of it. You'll see the word 'glamour' every day until the Cup is run. At the Melbourne Spring Carnival the cameras will churn through celebrities and socialites who wouldn't know a racehorse from an anteater. Like sparklers on a birthday cake, it is not that they don't belong there, just that they are the least part of it.

Great though the variety is, from the most taciturn to the most ebullient and showy, the most urbane to the most frayed and rustic, racing types all carry the thorns and gravel of an earlier, harder age. They have not fallen for the idea that we are born equal and have an equal right to thrive, or even live. Their horses tell them that: a great and unbridgeable chasm separates the midweek country horse and the Saturday city horse; between an average city handicapper and a weight-for-age horse the void is just as wide; and between a good weight-for-age horse and Black Caviar or Tulloch there is one as wide again. And those differences do not describe why, when they all descend from a tiny gene pool, one horse is a tractable, brave and kindly animal, and another fractious and evil-tempered; why one is sound and another fragile; one stout-hearted, the other a squib; one bursts her boiler trying to be first, and the other is equally set on proving her inadequacy; why the heart of yours weighs ten pounds and the heart of Secretariat weighed 22 pounds.

Then there is the fact often remarked by struggling trainers that the good horse is ten times more likely to be struck by lightning or a wayward piece of an aeroplane's fuselage than a slow horse: that a horse which has excited connections with signs it is an athlete will find a way to break its leg while eating an apple in its stable, whereas if you tether a slow one to a railway line and leave it there for the night, the trains will go around it. Racing trainers – and owners and punters – must live with these brutal facts of Nature.

They also live with jockeys, the 50-kilogram men and women obliged to perch on the withers of these 500-kilogram animals and steer them in their 'arc of flight' at anything up to 70 kilometres per hour, balanced on ankles not much thicker than a Coke bottle. To make their living, jockeys surely take more physical risks than anyone else in sport, including bullfighters. They are killed. They break their necks, their arms, legs, ribs and vertebrae as often as footballers sprain their ankles. They are regularly concussed and in comas.

The difference between top jockeys and average ones (and good rides and bad) is very wide, though not as wide as the difference between horses. Great jockeys are as much marvels to behold as any gymnast or footballer and deserve to make a pile of money and get kissed by Gai Waterhouse and whole syndicates of owners and to meet the Queen. No less essential to the sport, the less great and the wholly down at heel (a category judged to include the many who have lost their nerve or never had it) get paid a couple of hundred dollars to take the same risks on horses that, while slower, are just as big and just as likely to suddenly shy, falter or drop dead.

Not only do jockeys ride these horses, they also carry with them the expectations, prejudices and wagers of trainers, owners and punters. Good rides are not proof against the rage of frustrated hopes: but 'butcher' the horse, and there must be times when having passed the winning post jockeys have wondered if they might clear the car-park fence and keep riding until sundown. With good reason it is alleged that sometimes they have also been known to carry the weight of intimidation, or something more than the standard fee, for finding a position in the field from which it is impossible to win, or riding a horse 'upside down', or dropping the whip, or by some means causing their mounts to hang in or out or race like hobbled ducks.

I have co-owned or co-leased a dozen or so racehorses, of which perhaps four deserved the name (and another untried one might have if it had not died of a heart attack while cantering). My co-lessees and I remain confident that a jockey whose career was fading once nicked (pulled, or did not allow to run on her merits) a plain, one-paced mare of ours at a meeting on a country course. Afterwards, in the cold drizzle he sat on a bench in his singlet; thin, pallid, smoking a cigarette (I've always had half a feeling he rode the race stoned on something) while we stood round, wanting to take his neck in a throttle hold or throw him up in a tree, and yet unable to utter the accusation outright.

Low as we were in racing's pecking order, he was lower. There had been an atrocity (and of course it remains possible that nothing more sinister than incompetence had caused it, or some kind of allergy or migraine or an invisible willy-willy or something had pocketed our horse for six and a half of the seven furlongs they ran), but the indelible sense of that moment was that he was the real poor bastard and we were just another lot of bullies in his life.

The basic relationships in horseracing are feudal. This is necessary to provide a thread of certainty in the most uncertain of callings. No doubt it also attracts the sheiks and tycoons who put up the big money for the best-bred horses and send them to the top trainers – hundreds of horses, hundreds of millions of dollars. Time was when Australian racing somehow balanced the innate hierarchy of the profession with a larrikin and democratic spirit; an equation which, among other things, fortified the language with marvellous drolleries and made Australian race-callers the unofficial poets laureate.

So long as the sport of kings was also the sport of the masses, trainers of modest means could still look to Tommy Woodcock or Vic Rail and think it not ridiculous to hope for a freak of nature among the tailings – like Reckless or Vo Rogue.

In the first big day of this year's spring racing, however, about three-quarters of the several million dollars up for grabs at Flemington and Randwick went the way of a casino owner and Gai Waterhouse, and a sheik and Dato Tan Chin Nam got a slab of the remainder. Increasingly, imported horses – imported, that is, by local heavyweights – win the main middle- and long-distance races, and even the country cups. Thus our little prospects narrow and the dreams grow more outlandish.

So why would anyone of modest means and average good sense invest so much as a cent of his own money in or on a racehorse, or spend a minute even thinking about the caper, much less making heroes of horses or jockeys, as I have since I turned five? It could be that in an age now dim, a horse or like animal was the totem of my ancestor; and the totem became in time a God; and like the totem, the God was, as Freud declared, a father-surrogate; and the jockey is me, shrunk by guilt and longing, flogging it, clinging to it 'horse and rider as one', and trying to outrun it at the same time.

It could be this. Or it could be that like Damon Runyon I thought all life was six to five against but, being a mug, assumed that meant for everyone.

The Monthly, November 2012

Prometheus and the Pen

You know the legend of Prometheus – there are several – but I mean the one in which Zeus binds him to a rock where each day his liver is eaten by an eagle. Were he an ordinary man, the agony would be brief, but Prometheus is an immortal: so his liver grows again, and the eagle comes to torture him each day.

The story has fed the human imagination since a century or two before Homer.

But here's another story. Scientists in Japan have created working human-liver tissue, not with embryonic stem cells, but with adult cells coaxed into pluripotency – a beautiful word meaning the ability to become a different kind of cell.

No more ethical concerns about building cells from embryos. No need to fool the immune system into accepting new cells, because the cells are the patient's own. It's the first step to building a complex human organ from scratch.

There's a little way to go, but it seems conceivable that all humans might quite soon end up with livers like Prometheus's – and, indeed, who's to say that in time they won't be able to grow all the other parts and, if Medicare will cover it, make us immortal like him.

We might think that growing a liver, not to say the prospect of immortality, would be worth a column inch or two on the front page of the Fairfax website, but no – this story, including a Renaissance picture of the Titan tormented on the rock, occupied barely a page in a recent edition of *The Economist*, which means that most people will come across it two or three years hence in the waiting room of their accountant or periodontist.

For my own part, while immortality is superficially appealing, I just know I haven't the necessary improvement in me to make it worthwhile. Who wants to be a writer of modest talent forever? Never to get within a bull's roar of Tolstoy or Dickens? That's the point of the myth, after all, isn't it? We'd each have our own eagles gnawing at us through the endless hereafter. I'd be very grateful if they could grow me a new neck for the time I have left to me, but immortality, no thanks.

To get back to the point – try to imagine the literary equivalent of this story. What book or play or poem in history comes close to this – *The Divine Comedy*? *Don Quixote*? The first performance of *Hamlet*? *The Owl and the Pussycat*? Is there anything a writer can do that compares to growing a new liver from bits of the old one's owner? I think not. Science dwarfs our imaginations, makes fools of us.

Some not so much, of course; which is why it took me 20 years or more to find the gall to say, 'I'm a writer,' when people ask me what I do. I still mumble it and say 'scribbler'. Tolstoy was a writer. George Eliot was a writer. Balzac and Kafka, Faulkner and Garcia Marquez are writers. Coetzee, Updike, Alice Munro, Margaret Atwood, Seamus Heaney, Les Murray, Naipaul – these are writers.

True, I used to be able to say I was an historian, but less because I wrote history and more because I taught it. Marc Bloch and Eric Hobsbawm are historians.

Then there's that humiliating term, 'public intellectual': it turned up on the sleeve of a US edition of a book of mine and caused me great embarrassment. A couple of American radio interviewers asked me what such a person was. I could smell the derision. I learned to say a public intellectual is a person with a platform and an opinion – like you, Homer, or you, Sean. Anyway, they liked the idea and shut up about it.

When I came back I found a poll had been conducted, ranking Australia's public intellectuals – one to 20. It left out journalists such as Ross Gittins, Paul Kelly and Les Carlyon, but included me. I don't know why.

The difference between thinking journalists and public intellectuals I do not understand. The difference between thinking journalists and thinking writers I don't understand. Was George Orwell a writer, an intellectual or a journalist? H. L. Mencken? Claud Cockburn?

I don't quite know what makes an intellectual, let alone a public one. Freud was one, I know that. And Einstein was. Keynes. Those Japanese scientists strike me as being intellectuals. And this list alone confirms that I am not.

This is not modesty – false, real or calculated. It's no more modest than recognising that one is not a gum tree or a polar bear. I'm not particularly modest: at least not so modest as to be immune to the idea that I am a better writer than some others who follow the vocation, that I find much writing by others tiresome and even pointless, believe it would be better for everyone if some of them just stopped. Survival in the profession depends on fighting off the thought, whatever the evidence for it, that I am one of them.

That there are writers like me and writers of a different order is something I must know if I want to call myself sane – which is more important to me than calling myself a writer. So I must know that I am not Mark Twain or Henry James either. Twain said he was 'drawn to writing of a low order'. I'd be happy to say that too – if it weren't that his low-order writing was of such a high order.

That's one reason for being a sort of reluctant writer: one's manifest inferiority to great writers, and the sense that, anyway, even the great writers are chaff in comparison to the people who discover DNA, see into deep space and grow livers.

It might have *something* to do with coming from among people for whom writing was a dubious profession – not a serious thing to be doing with one's life. A stupid sort of a thing to do with it, in fact. Maybe once subjected to that sort of conditioning, we never entirely escape its effects.

So, I don't know about the other writers here, but I am not comfortable with being a writer. I have more than once felt that my membership of the profession will soon expire: I will wake up one day and find I've been on a 30-year bender and don't know which side is up, and now must settle down and get a real job.

I am not even all that comfortable with the company of other writers, and surely that is true of most writers: we'd rather spend time with detectives, soldiers, sex workers, scientists – people we can write *about*. I mean, if you're a writer why knock about with other writers – even if you like them, you're not going to get much of a story out of them. I have travelled in the landscape with writers, and it was great fun, even if there was a lot of yawning. But I've also travelled with scientists and painters – and that was travel of a different order. *That* was marvellous. They're also better drivers.

My insecurity is not helped by the contemporary cult of writing, which requires the author – or *encourages* her – to be a performer, even a sort of celebrity. This applies in equal measure to very distinguished writers and writers of modest achievement. It's no bad thing of course, but it has little to do with writing – and sometimes not much to do with performing. I wonder if there are people who are choosing to become writers for the lifestyle it seems to offer, the chance to perform at writers' festivals, to have a more distinguished public persona than what is possible in the public service or on Facebook.

I am very grateful for having been able to make a living from writing for 30 years – and also amazed by it – and I take more pleasure from reading the works of other writers than I do from anything else, except racehorses. But when it comes to assembling writers in a room, even just a mental room, I have to be reminded that a writing community exists, with common interests and potentially common ambitions – with anything in common at all really.

And writers are so often wrong. I don't mean juvenile errors of judgement. I'm thinking of the bigger things they've been wrong about. There have been heroic writers of course, but in general their political judgement is terrible. In the 20th century so many of them were terribly – all but criminally – wrong.

How *could* anyone not actually in the pay of Stalin, or in fear of him, say upon visiting the Soviet Union when millions were starving in a government-sponsored famine – 'I've seen socialism and it works'? How did Manning Clark fall for it when he went there a quarter of a century later? George Orwell saw through it. Sartre didn't. Koestler saw through it. A lot of people with a lot less education and intellectual pretension saw the reality of Stalin before a lot of writers and intellectuals did. A whole generation of writers fell for it – and had I lived through the thirties I might have fallen too. Of course they wanted to believe: it is possible to understand *why* they did it, but surely a mistake to understand it so well that we can't judge them. To not judge them is unfair to the victims and to those with more sense and moral courage.

Three of the writers present at the beginning of the ASA were or had been pro-Soviet communists: Dymphna Cusack, Frank Hardy and Judah Waten. I remember meeting Judah Waten in the mid-seventies. A very charming, gentlemanly soul, sitting in front of a big poster of beautiful Lake Baikal. Not a corpse in sight. He told me how the US was on the way out, and the Soviet Union had the answers. I think Judah was one of the few to join – *re*join in fact – the CPA *after* the invasion of Hungary. He seemed to think they had proved their mettle there.

Fortunately for the ASA more practical enthusiasts prevailed: Walter Stone, Dal Stivens, Jill Hellyer, Nan Chauncy, Betty Roland. The thing took shape despite the political nuisances and the abstainers such as Patrick White who wrote to say writers should simply get agents; and Hal Porter who said it was not his 'nature or his inclination to belong to groups of any sort'. And groups of writers? Well, writers were 'a breed [he] held no brief for'.

I can sympathise with that. I don't think Proust would have joined the ASA either. But the truth is, however disenchanted with the profession, or insecure in it, and however sceptical about the promise of collective action one might be, there comes a time each year – and it is nearly always a dire time – when the cheque turns up from PLR, or ELR or CAL, and I give thanks to the ASA and with an image in my mind of Frank Moorhouse hovering over a martini in the Bayswater Brasserie, I send off my subscription and a small donation.

That is one thing I know I have in common with all other writers – the need to make a quid. And hard as it is now, it was much harder when the ASA was founded. It was harder 20 years ago, when you were lucky if you could get 40 cents a word from the newspapers.

But what else do we have in common, we writers? What other threads bind us?

I can think of only one, and that is language. The medium in which we work.

If you don't believe language is decaying, you haven't been following the election. Or much else. See if you can find in the swarm of messages, one concrete thing, one word or phrase to stimulate a thought or feeling.

It's not the politicians' fault entirely. They speak the language of the times.

Orwell saw it coming nearly 70 years ago, but he didn't see the whole dimension of it, or that decay would set so deeply in a democracy.

He didn't see the combination of managerialism, technology and new media that is annihilating not only formal English, but the vernacular. Orwell knew the power of verbs and how their absence betokened deceit or dullness of thought, but I doubt he ever imagined a public discourse conducted with so few of them; or how cliché would come to rule. Messaging, he certainly foresaw, and the mission statement, but not their pervasiveness – church schools now have mission statements written in the language of a corporation, aligning their core values with the person of Jesus Christ. And the Anglican Synod of Sydney, heir to the King James Bible and the Book of Common Prayer, is advised by a firm of consultants to substitute 'a culture of accountability for their culture of forgiveness'.

Orwell could not have foreseen the capitulation of the education departments and the universities.

But this he might have written – in his fiction. 'The Centrelink contact point for statistics, previously known as the Centrelink knowledge desk is now known as the Business Intelligence Frontdoor.' Or: 'A focus on planned, consistent customer experiences that embody the Centrelink brand and lead to optimum outcomes in terms of customer contentment, costs to Centrelink and Government, and improvements in customer circumstances (reflecting desired policy outcomes).'

If scientists can regenerate a liver, even grow one from scratch, can a society of authors regenerate a language, or even just defend it?

I doubt it. But, maybe, collectively we can demonstrate a care for it – its 'sacred quality', as Barry Lopez put it. I wonder if the ASA might propose that the language be granted protections under a heritage listing.

Writing is difficult, and the more one does it the more difficult it becomes. That is one of the reasons – perhaps the main one – why, in this information age, the language in which we express ourselves and think has been reduced so quickly to a conveyor belt for cliché and messages.

We writers have in common the knowledge that language is more than this, and with the knowledge comes some kind of duty to retain its glorious potential.

The truest thing about writing that I have ever read is this, by George Eliot:

> Examine your words well, and you will find that even when you have no motive to be false, it is very hard to say the exact truth, even about your own immediate feelings –

much harder than to say something fine about them which is *not* the exact truth.

That seems to me the thread that binds all writers together: not just the difficulty of the craft, but *recognising* the difficulty. And it could be that in this lies the seed of a common ambition.

Address on the 50th Anniversary of the Australian Society of Authors, 2013

Jan Senbergs

When Jan Senbergs was six years old, he fled Europe's horrors with his mother and little sister in a horse and cart. They left behind his father who had just been shot and killed at their home in the Latvian forest. From Riga, courtesy of folk we now revile as 'people smugglers', they took a boat in the night to a place behind the Allied lines in Germany. Then they walked. The next six years the Senbergs spent in various Displaced Persons camps. In 1950 they reached Melbourne.

Knowing this story, some of us see signs of it in Jan Senbergs' art: the monster machines, the ruins, the burned and broken bushlands, the contorted forests of habit and ambition, hubris and conformity, memory and invention, that he makes of cities. Starting from the same premise, his dark, malevolent seas; heroic ships; cars scuttling on sinuous roads; bleak, abandoned mining sites, even the chaos and squalor of human settlement in Antarctica, all seem like variations on a theme brutally imprinted in his childhood. Where human beings go there goes an element of the beast, more or less rampant depending on circumstances.

Senbergs deals in menacing shape and inexorable force: his cities cling to the coast and bend and warp as if caught in Earth's upheaving crust; his abandoned human sites are monuments to Time which is beyond our comprehension and the pathetically brief moment of humanity. His human beings are mocked both by Nature's grandeur and by the terrible instruments that their genius and flaws create. Their existence is implied by the technology with which they live, or the destruction they have wrought, but they are otherwise invisible. Those we do see occupy small corners, on meagre rations and furtive copulation.

Very likely Jan would reject all this as at least two-thirds tendentious hokum, and very likely he would be right. Even in the unlikely event that he thought it fair comment on his work, it misses the essential fact that grim and uncompromising as that work might be, he delights in the world he is depicting. God might be dead and the existential struggle hopeless, but there's glory to be had just the same. Senbergs meets indifferent Nature – including human nature – eye to eye, without sentimentality or pleading. He meets force with force. Paradox with paradox. Ambiguity with ambiguity. His dark signature line is his banner, sword and mind-bender.

Senbergs' paintings, prints and drawings can startle and incite something close to primal gloom and melancholy. Often enough they also chance upon a rare and original beauty, but never one he can be accused of seeking. That his work might ever be decorative, modish or gratuitously attractive, or didactic or moralising, heaven forfend! These are thoughts to haunt him. Irony he allows – indeed, thrives on – because irony is born of recognising our pitiful condition and is the natural means of managing it.

Senbergs does not tell the childhood story as if it were the thing that made him – his listeners retell it to themselves that way. To hear him tell it, one would think his life started when he got off the boat and, with barely a word of English, found a country congenial to his pagan taste. 'Towns are excrescences,' E. M. Forster said, 'grey fluxions, where men, hurrying to find one another, have lost themselves.' Not for Senbergs: a town was where he found himself, became a local and grew. The larrikin contrarieties of the landscape and its creatures; the rituals of football, horse racing, the punt, the pubs; the local insistence on not taking oneself or anyone else too seriously; the vernacular of Richmond and Fitzroy; the sun warming the democratic temper: he lapped them all up. A wog, a Balt or a reffo inevitably he was, but he was a very Australian one.

The streets of Melbourne and the bush beyond fed his imagination and his inquiring émigré's mind. So did reading, travelling, teaching, talking: there was the Melbourne art scene, the circle gathered round Rudy Koman, and he was also in time to angle his way into what remained of the old left bohemian push that gathered at Tattersalls Hotel. By the time I met him 25 years ago, in addition to his reputation as an outstanding artist he had acquired an impressive formal knowledge of art, an assured grip on the Australian art world and an intimate acquaintance with local characters and haunts.

How the 11-year-old Latvian refugee became this most generous, entertaining and obstreperous *bon vivant* might be called a miracle, were not these feats of creative adaptation proverbial among refugees when they are given any sort of chance. He was familiar with the paradoxical, overlapping worlds of Jorge Luis Borges *and* those of talkback radio. He read Calvino, Thomas Bernhard *and* the racing guide; listened to Schubert *and* the football; admired Max Beckmann, Soutine *and* William Barak; painted Antarctica and his studio and a kookaburra with equal bravura.

Many influences doubtless come together in his art, but minimalism is not one of them, or post-modernism. 'Isms' don't appeal to him; or if for a moment they do, he is quick to clear them from the decks before they get a hold. Students of his work see expressionism, surrealism and abstraction, but not to the extent that his name can ever be credibly linked to them. He is only comfortable as a maverick, an outsider, a dissenter like his Lutheran forebears. Originality is a faith with him, probably because he senses that to give it up will land him in banality; or worse, in fatal irrelevance: perhaps also because anything as prescriptive as a fashion or a 'movement' might dampen a mind tuned to adapting. Survival is a creative enterprise.

As figurative artists tend to, Senbergs takes his inspiration where he finds it: in travels within Australia and abroad; in writers he has come upon, such as the American novelist Donald Barthelme and the Scottish poet Edwin Muir, and in familiar scenes and fleeting experience. Barcelona has inspired him, but so has a ship on Port Phillip Bay, or the asbestos mines in Western Australia, or a dead sheep in Tuscany. His fantastic elevated views of Melbourne and Geelong, including the brilliant *Geelong Capriccio*, drew inspiration from the picture maps of pre-Renaissance cartographers which gave shape to his own longstanding fascination with geography and place.

The set for *Blade Runner* might just as well have played a part in some of his wilder city paintings, but I doubt he has seen the film. I'm not sure that he has ever come across E. M. Forster's remark either, but people who have might be put in mind of it by those same paintings.

And that is the nub: even if we could show that at that moment in the Latvian forests, or at any other in his lifetime, his imagination formed like an atoll in the sea, he still had to *make* these images, and go on making them. To make them he had to be Jan Senbergs, with Senbergs' indomitability, his acute and sympathetic eye, his curiosity, his joy and pessimism, his courage. If, as Simone Weil said, 'Nothing can have as its destination anything other than its origin,' then perhaps we are obliged to recognise that Jan Senbergs, artist, originated in his imagination and that's where he's been going all along.

Jan Senbergs Exhibition Catalogue, July 2013

On *Animal Farm*

Animal Farm is both a great political tract and a literary masterpiece. Read it a dozen times and Orwell's prose still beguiles, the story still grips, still leaves you wondering if you haven't just had your ears boxed.

When, in 1945, Orwell gave his savage little novel the subtitle 'A Fairy Story', he was being more than ironic. It *is* a fairy story: an enchantment with darkness at the core. Before *Animal Farm*, he had written novels and sterling works of reportage and reflection: indictments of capitalism and Stalinism, of the English class system, the deluded intelligentsia, the darkening age itself. These were books and essays of distinction and originality, the more forceful very often for being drawn from personal experience. In time they became classics. Yet for all their fine qualities they had less heft than *Animal Farm*, and far less inventiveness.

Orwell's experience of the communist forces in Spain where he fought on the same Republican side, but in an anarcho-syndicalist militia, confirmed his loathing for the Soviet regime and his belief that the Russian Revolution had degenerated into a monstrous farce. For minds willing to see, there was evidence amounting to proof. The first travesty, that of Stalin's regime, is the subject of *Animal Farm*; the second, that of European intellectuals and labour parties either in denial about the Soviet Union or supporting it, is the book's target. The point of the satire was to persuade liberals and socialists that the Soviet Union was not a socialist country and could never be a model for socialism. There could be no socialism without liberty.

Orwell was an austere, tubercular Etonian – 'a saintly repressed sadist' was Arthur Koestler's description – with a relentless eye for every kind of moral failure, deceit and delusionary bullshit. Like his published work, his wartime diaries reveal both the brilliance of his mind and the Englishness of his nature. Orwell's hens and vegetables interested him every bit as much as the collapse of civilisation or German bombs falling in the vicinity of his fowl house. He would always 'love the surface of the earth, and . . . take a pleasure in solid objects', he wrote very late in his short life. All that was plain, ordinary, clear and true, including prose, was good to him.

And, holding fast to 'democratic socialism', all that served liberty also was good to him. All that served totalitarianism, or apologised for it, was bad. This left a lot of people open to criticism, including the anti-Stalinist Koestler whom, despite their mutual admiration, he publicly savaged. Koestler, he said, had lost faith in communism but not in the prospect of an earthly paradise, the first premise of revolutionary ambitions. This folly stemmed from another one: the idea that the purpose of life was happiness. Koestler had also fallen for the nonsense that revolutionary creeds derived from 'neurotic impulses'. It was not the fairest criticism Orwell ever made, but it was typical of his impatience with abstract theorising, anything with even the faintest smell of pretension or blather.

In a 1941 broadcast, Orwell summed up the writer's dilemma. The realisation that civilisation's future was not assured had had the desirable effect of debunking the English aesthetes' belief in art for art's sake, in form over content, in art detached from social reality, in what Orwell called 'a worship of the meaningless'. The crisis also led a host of writers from pampered backgrounds where they knew nothing either of ordinary people or of terror and oppression into ideological camps where honesty was impossible and hypocrisy inevitable. Repelled by fascism and with not much love of democracy, intelligent people who should have known better had settled their sympathies – not to say their loyalties – on Stalin's Russia. For Orwell, James Joyce and Virginia Woolf would no longer do; but 'official Marxism' and Soviet fellow travellers would not do either.

So how was a writer to maintain his or her intellectual and artistic integrity? There is a sense in which *Animal Farm* is Orwell's answer to that question. Here for the first time the artist in Orwell spoke with a voice equal to his political purpose. He had never called on the power of his imagination or his deep well of humour to the same extent. Above all, the book is a satire, and it is hard to think of a more successful one. 'Whatever is funny is subversive . . .' Orwell said, and *Animal Farm* went a long way to proving the point. The book *is* funny: satire has to be or it won't work. Making the setting a sweetly familiar English farmyard and the characters farmyard animals is the central joke, as well as the device that makes the gathering treachery and violence so deadpan and convincing – and such a convincing echo of totalitarian violence.

Animal Farm was the product of Orwell's conscious attempt 'to fuse political purpose and artistic purpose'. That purpose, he said in another essay, was to expose totalitarianism and further the cause of democratic socialism. The result was a political work of art, an oxymoron when generally applied, but not in *Animal Farm* or in *1984*, which he wrote a few years later. In both books, far from compromising the art, the political message depends on it for resonance and clarity.

Anyone half familiar with the Russian Revolution and its rapid degeneration will recognise the store in *Animal Farm*: Napoleon the chief pig is Stalin; and around him henchmen and apparatchiks gather, along with the gullible cheering masses and even that most useful Stalinist creation, Boxer the Stakhanovite. Snowball, who believes in extending the revolution beyond the farm, is Trotsky, who wanted to extend it beyond Russia, and finds himself traduced, banished and under a death sentence, as Trotsky did. The show trials and purges are there, the secret police, the forced confessions, the cult of the individual, the corruption of the language, the Terror. Orwell creates an animal equivalent of the Kronstadt uprising of 1921, the Nazi-Soviet Pact and the 1943 Tehran Conference.

There is more to this than a marvel of compression. No one with a casual interest in modern history can read *Animal Farm* without wondering if the book is not a satire on *all* revolutions; if the people on whose behalf they are made did not get rid of their revolutionary leaders at the first opportunity.

Satire, Jonathan Swift said, 'is a sort of glass wherein beholders do generally discover everybody's face but their own'. This was what allowed them to enjoy it, he reckoned. But no one should think that in *Animal Farm* the satire apples only to those engaged in revolutions, those supporting them from afar and those contemplating joining a revolutionary militia. Look in Orwell's glass often enough and we begin to see other faces, including those in democracies who would despise Napoleon while performing Napoleonic tricks, or acquiescing in them. Read *Animal Farm* and be in no doubt – you are in it, even if only as a sheep.

Financial Review, 3 January 2014

Australia Day Address

My fellow Australians.

I have a resting heart rate of 35 bpm. To put this in perspective, a resting crocodile's is 30. Before I became Prime Minister, mine was 33. Malcolm Turnbull's is 76 on a good day. Even John Howard never clocked less than 70.

Some people might wonder how this is relevant to the national story that we celebrate today, but I believe the message will become clearer as I go on.

This low pulse I maintain with a program of regular frenetic exercise that pushes my heart to its limit. Bewitched by the hypnotic whirr of the wheels and the rhythmic gasp of my lungs, on my bicycle I have recorded rates in the region of 230, the human equivalent of an Etruscan shrew.

The more regularly one drives the pulse up through exercise, the lower it is likely to be at rest. And therein lies my problem. My pulse is so low that when reclining or seated, I am sometimes barely conscious. More than once, before rising to speak at important dinners, I have been consumed by a palpable sense that I was a python hibernating in a cave. Briefing papers, novels and newspaper articles have a similar effect on me. I rarely reach the second paragraph without either drifting into a near coma, or fighting off a manic urge to shadow box or put out a bushfire. To feel the smoke sear my lungs, to tear and pierce every fibre of my physical being, to break through the comforts of ordinary existence and enter the lowest deep of excruciating pain.

You see, it is only when I exercise that I feel truly alive: yet the more I exercise the less alive I feel when I am not.

Over the years I have developed certain ploys. Several years ago I was trying to laugh – I think it was one of Scott Morrison's jokes – when I felt a twinge in my glutes. That was when I discovered I could stretch them just by grinning. Constant repetition of the exercise during meetings, interviews, Question Time and while driving has not only kept me awake but free of soft-tissue injuries, though with the consequence that my grin has developed into something that frightens even me.

Today we celebrate Australia's remarkable progress from convict settlement to the wonderful country in which we live today. Surely no people on the planet have more reason to celebrate.

What a magnificent country this is and what a future lies before us. But only if we remain true to ourselves, steadfast in our principles and fearless as we confront the challenges ahead. Prince William is coming, *en famille,* in April and we must call on the best in ourselves and spare no effort to make them welcome. Let us now resolve to pay any price, bear any burden, meet any hardship, to make sure we can't think of anything else while they are here. I believe the Prince is a keen sportsman and adventurer and I have already invited him to join me in an Ironman contest and a few rounds in the ring. I cannot urge you too strongly to get involved: flock and fawn and hang out your flags up and down the land. Buy the souvenirs and mags.

Let them know that the sun will never set on your affection, that you would rather die than live without them, that you will never say goodbye.

Then, the future King and Queen having scarcely left our shores, we will begin the centenary of the outbreak of the First World War. And, as if that were not enough excitement for one year, nine months later we have the centenary of the landing at Gallipoli. What else can you say but 'Wow'.

Of course it should go without saying that these last two are solemn events. The commemoration of historical episodes that saw the deaths of millions must be conducted in a tone quite different to the unalloyed gaiety of Australia Day, which commemorates an event that caused the deaths of comparatively few. A few hundred thousand perhaps, if you count the disease and alcohol and so on, over several generations. Maybe half a million – tops.

That is a good many more than the 60,000 Australians killed in the First World War. I know. I can count. So what are we supposed to do – get out the armbands and bow our heads and fill our hearts with awe and sorrow every 26 January? And then what do we do on Anzac Day – dance and sing and fall down drunk?

Yes, there is a downside. In much of life there is a downside. It comes with the upside. That was what I was trying to show you by the example of my heart rate. Difficult things happen sometimes: and, frankly, if it means I can go on feeling the ocean surging in my swimmers, the very tissue of my lungs tearing apart, I will live with them.

Besides, the great majority of Aboriginal deaths were not deliberately inflicted: the worst we could say of most of them is that they were careless; incidental, as it were, to the colonial and national projects. Most of them were no one's fault really. And frankly, some of them were their *own* fault, partly, frankly. And unlike the Anzacs, they were defending no one's freedom or values, or the Australian way of life – unless you count their own. It's chalk and cheese, frankly – well, chalk anyway.

But let's not go into the micro-details of history, on a day like this. The important thing is not to politicise these commemorations. Under my government the rewriting of history will cease, once and for all. We will take it back and make an end of it.

Finally, I know all Australians would want me to extend on their behalf heartiest best wishes to our servicemen and women, who, as we soak up the lifestyle, are bravely defending the national interest in far-flung corners of the world. I include in this cohort those 'on water' who, even as I speak, patrol our northern seas ever ready to pounce on leaking boats laden with illegal refugees. No less deserving of our thanks the many dedicated people doing difficult work in trying conditions on Manus Island and Nauru. As these are operational matters, I can say no more, but I ask my fellow Australians to pause, reflect and raise their glasses – blessings be upon them, our protectors.

Good Weekend, 10 January 2014

From *The Bush*

He split wood under the pine tree out the back. We could hear the blows: hear the blue gum cleave if the grain was even, tear but not surrender if knotted, the next blow just hard enough to force it apart, but not so hard that the axe jammed in the block or sent the pieces flying further than he could retrieve by bending where he stood. Every move was practised: read the grain, use all necessary force but no more, so no energy is wasted or bones and tendons jolted. Leave nature minimally alarmed. Work with the grain of the wood, not against it; always work with the grain. Find the rhythm in it. As nature has rhythms, what is second nature to a man has rhythms. Don't force it. In getting a cow in bail, or drafting sheep in a pen, taking the harrows off the tractor or the horns off a cow, or saddling a horse, or grubbing a stump, there is a rhythm to be found. As nature finds the easiest way to do things, find the way of nature. He was a Zen sort of farmer.

With even steps across the hillside he sowed grass seed, each fluid arc of the arm the same, each dip of his hand into the hessian bag tied like an apron round his waist, the same. While his limbs kept such perfect time, he seemed to be in time with all around him, with every human being that ever sowed a hillside, as much a part of this scene as any peasant ever was of his. To calm the world, he whistled.

In the parable, the good soil speaks of a good heart. His heart was as good as he could make it: every wound of childhood sutured, every savage instinct denied satisfaction, but not always the indignation that thundered at the uncontained instincts of others, or signs of them in his children. As God and his conscience ruled him, he could not always resist their maledictions. The ungodly folk on whom he visited his judgements were those whose baser natures were not contained: sloth, drunkenness, profanity, foul mouths, lasciviousness, cruelty, troublemaking and bluster, he could not bear. He tried to love his neighbour but, as a righteous man regardeth his beast, who could love the neighbour who mistreated his animals, or the bully who raged at man and beast alike? Or the man who never cut his thistles or pulled his ragwort so the seeds blew across the boundary fence? 'The weeds are the people of the evil one, and the enemy who sows them is the devil.'

'Blessed are the peacemakers,' he always said, long after we were sick of it. He internalised his disgruntlements, rendered them to the same inner authority that kept everything else in check. And as he ruled himself he would rule this bit of land: with hard work and obedience to the commandments, with irony and without anger, envy or cruelty. He would make it in his own image. He would make it decent. Something fit for the Lord or any man to look upon with approval.

A man was permitted pride in his own work, if in little else except his family, and that in moderation. If it took him his whole life he would make this dirty farm clean. It was only 59 hectares, many of them not so far off the vertical, but he was no less a civilised man for that, and one on a civilising mission.

We had dairy cows, but he always preferred crops and sheep. Then he began buying yearling heifers from 'up north' where they were cheap as a rule, especially in dry seasons. They would arrive on the train, skinny and half mad, but our good grass reformed them. He'd calve them down, which is to say, get them in calf ('pregnant' was an impolite word that we did not use in any context), and once they were delivered of their offspring, he'd break them into the routines of the milking shed and sell them to the local dairy farmers as replacements for their herds. He also bought springers, heifers already in calf. Either way, the business involved a lot of bovine copulation, a lot of placenta and blood in the paddocks, a lot of bellowing and kicking and shitting in the cowshed, and on the way to the shed through the mud; a lot of dead calves, veterinary bills, ingeniously polite denial of the brutal reality of our enterprise, and a lot of guilt, loathing and confusion in me.

The bellows of cows separated from their bawling calves, the calf corpses hauled with ropes feet first from their exhausted prostrate mothers, the heifers madly following the tractor with their stillborn progeny dragged behind – from this daily puerperal spectacle he would return composed. Soon after the milking machines fell silent he would come walking through the grey drizzly murk of a winter's evening laced with chimney smoke, up from the cowshed to the back porch, past the doomed calves in the calf shed and the woodheap under the pine, as fixed and unfailing as the hens settling on their fowl-house roosts, the magpies in the cypresses. He washed for tea, put on a clean shirt if necessary and combed his hair; never let his standards slip, or the little rituals that maintained them.

Farming is like playing a piano: it is measured violence. It teaches a man willing to learn that there is a right way and a wrong way of doing everything. The farmer must meet every effort of nature with a calculated countervailing force: the thistle with the hoe or spray, the log with the axe or chainsaw, a disease with a drench, horns with a dehorner. Let things go for a moment and a week's work will become a month's, the month's a year's, and very soon the thistles are the size of saplings and the farmer is sitting defeated in his ant-eaten weatherboard and numbering his days by the level of the lavatory can. At least that was the impression from some road-gates. Some farmers never moved on to the spray or the chainsaw; they let their fences fall down, their dams silt up and their hedges shut out the light. They left the horns on their cows or took them off crudely with a tenon saw. Perhaps despair or regret, or poetry or nature, had crept into their souls. The difference between that kind of farmer and the other kind – our kind – was nothing more than a quirk of fate or character, but the world was divided on these lines.

The mental images have not faded. The subject cannot be separated from the settings in which he worked: the hills and the trees and the fences and wooden sheds and yards and the cattle and crops and the back porches with their boots and coats, the smell of mud and manure, and the rush of the westerly in the pines. In a dry spell he would tap the tank beside the kitchen window. He tapped the barometer just about every day of his life. In the evening the wind moaned in the Chinese cedars, the calves bawled, the bulls roared their lust. At night the possums rattled their throats in the trees, fighting for territory, discouraging owls and dogs. The dogs barked, howled sometimes. Magpies welcomed the mornings with a warble, the thrush with its thrill of a song.

The images are like photographs, except in most old photographs the subjects are gathered for a special occasion, a wedding or a dance or a picnic in some Arcadian spot, or just outside their poor huts. My subject labours on the unornamented earth: 'That huge and gross body of dust, stones etc. which supports our feet and affords us nourishment', as the family Dictionary of the Bible described it. When photographers followed their subjects to work they made them pose, on a reaper and binder, or beside a bullock team, on a plank with axe poised 10 metres up a mountain ash. We have to read what we can from the setting, from the looks in their eyes, the way they hold themselves. What happened when they moved we can only imagine.

Yet the way he moved is precisely what I remember about him. The images my mind retains are memorials to the force he exerted on the physical world – or at least the small patch of it on which he had made his home. So long as it was daylight, living and moving were the same things. Living and working were the same.

It stands to reason then that I remember him in the act of working, for in physical work he expressed his life's purpose and the grace this granted him. That is the puritan's creed, as well as his fate. Work was what he knew most deeply. With farmers of his generation and before, it was often all they knew, all they had time to know. At the same time as these images speak of abundant self-possession and power over their environments – and over their children – they also resound with what they did not know.

Striving to Stay in Existence

For Hindus, banyan trees are sacred. For Buddhists, bodhi trees; for the Arabs, certain date palms. To be stalwart in a 'tree-like' way was to approach goodness, according to Confucius. The Normans built chapels in the trunks of yew trees. Many other cultures attached religious significance to particular trees and groves and forests. Adonis was born of a tree. Daphne turned into one. George Washington confessed to cutting one down and the United States, as a result, was all but immaculately conceived. The tree is the symbol of the male organ and of the female body. The Hebrew kabbalah depicts Creation in the form of a tree. In Genesis, a tree holds the key to immortal life, and it is to the branches and fruit of an olive tree that God's people are likened in both the Old and New Testaments. To celebrate the birth of Christ his followers place trees in their sitting rooms and palm fronds, a symbol of victory, commemorate his entering Jerusalem. A child noted by Freud had fantasies of wounding a tree that represented his mother. The immortal swagman of Australia sat beneath a coolabah tree. In hundreds of Australian towns the war dead are honoured by avenues of trees.

The Judaeo-Christian God, however, did not suffer rivals. There would be no worship of the tree itself, no *Eucalyptus religiosa*. The faithful could set upon the most commanding and inscrutable gum with reasonable hope that the ring of their axes was music to His tremendous ear. The pagan, the sinful and the forbidden inhabit wildernesses, and people who go there are as if out of the sight of God. The sooner they clear the trees, the sooner God's sight can be restored and His kingdom on earth realised. No doubt there were settlers who went about the work of clearing scrub convinced that, as much their own work, they were doing God's too, and settlers for whom God's direction was not needed. Even John Shaw Neilson, whose 'terrible and thunder-blue' God gave way to one found in the gentleness and beauty of birds and light, and whose genius was to find the sublime in what had been all but vanquished by Man, went on cutting, grubbing and burning as he wrote.

Driving between the Victorian Mallee towns of Manangatang and Piangil in a heatwave in 1926, the Presbyterian Reverend Fraser Sutherland saw God in the mallee roots. While every other living thing was panting and distressed, the mallee trees were sending up new growth. 'Springbacks' the farmers called them, and cursed their defiance. As the roots were the trees' great unseen resource, and the source of their beauty and wonder, so was God to Reverend Sutherland in the struggle to establish His kingdom there. Encouraged by the psalmist who declared 'truth shall spring out of the earth', the reverend hoped that even as they slashed and bludgeoned them back into the ground his battling parishioners might find in these springbacks the faith to wait for a new heaven and a new earth.

Reverend Sutherland might have been onto something. The mallee lignotuber, universally known as a mallee root, is a storehouse of life and the vital instrument of reproduction. Each thing strives to retain its being, as Spinoza said: 'the power of nature is the divine power and virtue itself. Moreover, the divine power is the very essence of God.'

It is a common mistake of the ignorant, the philosopher said, to 'conceive of men in nature as a kingdom within a kingdom. They decree that the human mind is produced not by any natural causes, but is created immediately by God, and is so independent of other things that it has absolute power to determine itself and use reason correctly.' This is a fair description of settler mentality as well. In truth, according to Spinoza, human beings, like everything else, including mallee roots, 'are only a part of nature' and striving to exist. Whether we should think a man in nature armed with an axe or chainsaw or 380-horsepower tractor with a 5-metre blade, and a man contemplating a spotted pardalote are opposite states or one and the same and equally natural is not clear; nor is it clear if men wreak havoc on the natural world because it is in their nature to do so or because they imagine their existence depends on it. In any event, hope seems to rest on their willingness to look upon the other parts of nature with the same reverence that they look upon the part that is themselves.

Yet it seems possible, even likely, that trees retain some power in the human unconscious that a purely utilitarian perspective or a Calvinist one cannot entirely stifle. Romantic it might be, but whether it is held by a 19th-century poet or a 21st-century Green, human sympathy for trees is neither unnatural nor lacking respectable philosophical foundation. It merely lost the argument; like Spinoza, it was declared heretical.

I remember a couple of dozen or more eucalypts and blackwoods, their shape, juxtaposition, and exactly where they stood on our farm. Their imprint is at least as vivid as that left by half-a-dozen dogs or any other animal. Trees regularly appear in my dreams; the animals never do. One, a painfully slow-growing oak, is planted on the ashes of a maiden great-aunt. I am not sure if the pine tree under which I played and fantasised all my childhood and teenage years, and of which I dream repeatedly, is my father, my mother, the Church or the Allwise Disposer himself, but I've no doubt about the authority it exerted on me then, and I suspect still does.

Think of a tree as a tree and not as an impediment or a utility and its power quickly becomes apparent: the height, the mass, the form; the force, tenacity, grace or agelessness it expresses. The colour, light, movement and sound it generates; the vigour, strength, fecundity, the life force. The moods, the terror and the wonder it excites. Trees provoke the imagination and enliven the senses; they suggest mystery, remind us of freedom, lift our spirits, and carry us, if unconsciously and only for an instant, back to nature and in proportion to it. It was for this reason – to feed the human imagination (and serve as the lungs of the city) – that New York's Central Park was created. We plant trees for their many practical uses, but also to affirm life and commemorate birth and death. The power exerted by trees on our minds, and the strength of our relationship to them, may exist quite independently of their vast utility to our species.

We might best measure that utility by noting, as Colin Tudge has, that while we speak of the Stone Age, Bronze Age, Iron Age, and so on, every age, including that of half-a-million years ago when humans started using fire, has been a Wood Age. There could have been no bronze, iron or steam age without trees, or any human age if we hadn't lived in them for a long while. It was in trees that we developed our dexterity, and our brains developed in concert with our arms and hands, the hands providing the pay-off on our brains' abilities that assured our successful evolution. No trees, as Tudge says, no human beings: our debt to them is 'absolute'. And that's before we come to the part they play in keeping the earth cool enough for us to live on it.

The need to gather wood was something European Australians shared with Aborigines, but as was almost always the case, the Europeans needed to gather more of it. Mining depended on wood and consumed whole environments. The karri forests of south-west Western Australia went for railway sleepers and for mines in Australia, South Africa and Germany. The streets of Cape Town were paved with jarrah. The land immediately surrounding having been cleared of every sapling and twig, for 60 years the West Australian goldfields were serviced by a network of rail lines running out into the forests to the west. These were the woodlines. They consumed immense swathes of mallee, the gleaming copper gimlet (*E. salubris*) and the miraculous salmon gum with glimmering green leaves on flesh-pink limbs and trunk, and stigmata of blood-red sap. Employed by such enterprises as the West Australian Goldfields Firewood Supply Company, families lived for years among the trees, cutting, transporting and loading, moving as the wood ran out and leaving their iron and concrete and glass in the dust. Hard as the work was, the woodlines provided work and fellowship, and for many hundreds of people a start in a new country. A woman who had been part of a remarkable post-war community of Australian and European migrant workers in these baking woodlands said she and her family and friends loved life there. She confessed to a special affection for the gimlets: 'You'd think someone had been polishing them all day,' she said, which just might mean she would have preferred to leave them standing.

Had they been left, or at least large stands of them, the dust storms which have hit Kalgoorlie ever since would have been less frequent, and the salinity less rampant. A decade ago the CSIRO said salinity was threatening as much as 80 per cent of remnant native vegetation, and devouring the wheatbelt at the rate of one football oval an hour. But what becomes of the gold-mines if the trees are not felled and burned? Good human lives were lived where the forest had been, enterprise was rewarded, the fellowship of men and women flourished, history was recorded. The bush we know would not exist if we had not cut it down.

Our debt to trees continues to be absolute. We need them to bind and enrich the soil, to trap carbon, regulate the climate, lower the watertable, sustain biodiversity, and for the photosynthesis on which our survival depends. We need them for oxygen and for shade, and also because few other things on earth can tell us as much about the way life works. We need them for timber, food, drugs, fuel, chemicals, paper, and much else of a material kind, and we need them for what they give in the way of hope, beauty and inspiration. Long before tree huggers of the late 20th century, trees were credited with instructing us in the design of the Creator, and with feelings and intelligence. They were an essential element of the picturesque, which is to say, everything in nature that was held to be agreeable to the human senses. There was no perfection without them.

Given their profound importance to humanity – which is far greater than that of, say, sheep, cattle, dogs or horses – it might be that clearing them en masse is not without effect on the minds of those who do it. To fell, ringbark, poison, root out or in some other way bring about the death of trees may not be an act of genocide, but nor is it, surely, an act with no more implications than sweeping the veranda. It might be a little like war, brutalising or traumatising depending on the personality and the circumstances. Who knows what mental scars are left on the people who, for whatever reason, destroyed them. If the dead trees 'got on the nerves' of Rosa Praed, what did they do to less resilient minds? One man who spent his youth in the Strzelecki Ranges, where he 'helped destroy for farmland perhaps the best hardwood forest the world has ever seen', never got over the experience. His son, Lyle Courtney, wrote: 'The guilt of being a partner in that crime haunted him for the rest of his life, and instilled in him a deep repentant understanding and mateship with nature.'

2014

Introduction to Andrew Chapman's Book of Photographs, *Political Vision*

Politics is not the only human activity where envy and pride, love and ambition meet every day as a matter of course. They meet pretty well wherever people go. But only in politics do these base elements of human nature meet daily with self-sacrifice, ideology, dutiful public service, high principle and patriotism; along with bastardry, humbug and betrayal, and the more mundane motives of superannuation, travel allowances and free tickets. Sometimes politics can seem to be little more than blather, an elaborate disguise for nest-feathering, a cynical charade and, for that matter, a tiresome one. It's a game that attracts all types and sometimes the dullards and cynics are the winners. As consuming passions go, politics can be pretty ordinary. But in a good patch there's nothing like it: the most fun you can have standing up, folk used to say.

Ambition is inescapable and so powerful in the human breast, Machiavelli decided, because Nature has made it possible to desire everything but not to attain everything. Millions of corpses have wired us to fear ambition uncontained. The ambitious are wise to throttle down their inner drive, keep it commensurate with demonstrated abilities and usefulness, balanced by their altruism or anything that might pass for such a thing. Save the ambition for the savage moment of release, and then come forth sphinx-like and tell them you did it for the country, for democracy, for decency, for *them*.

Very often there's some noble truth in the midst of this dissembling, but that makes the business of politics no less savage. Politics is power: but what makes it different to power in, say, Hollywood films or the Old Testament, is that in politics power is denied. Richard Carleton's famous question to Bob Hawke on the night he deposed Bill Hayden riled Hawke so terribly because it went to the naked fact of the matter, the fact of power: 'How does it feel to have blood on your hands?' Carleton asked. How dare he suggest that power was involved, that blood was the inevitable consequence of ambition? Or take Sarah Ferguson's question to Joe Hockey on the night of his first Budget: 'Is it liberating for a politician to decide election promises don't matter?' Hockey's wounded grimace inverted the truth of the relationship; as if Ferguson were the powerful one and the Treasurer a mere servant of the people trying to do his best from a position of great disadvantage. So accustomed are we to this inversion, some of us almost felt sorry for him; and a fellow journalist commissioned to conduct an audit found insufficient respect had been shown the Treasurer and the interview had the potential to 'breach the ABC impartiality guidelines'. So we demand respect and impartiality for the powerful, but not the truth from them.

Enter the photographers clicking away, poking their lenses ever closer to the pollies' noses, as if deep secrets might be hidden in their pores. In general the subjects are of no more mystery, goodness or beauty than you or I; but they are politicians and they contain riddles which democratic duty demands that we unravel. Hundreds of reporters and commentators are employed to extract the meaning from the circus, and thus counter the hundreds more who are employed to bend it to particular advantage. Then we ourselves, when making what we can of politics from what we read, hear and see, re-bend it through our own partisan lenses.

If new media technology has reduced their once singular importance, political photographers continue to offer a penetrating light. In the still photograph, as opposed to the moving image, there is nothing to distract us from the face, wherein it is alleged the mind's construction can be seen. We might also see something of the mind in the way a politician walks, or waves his hands about, or tugs at his ear, or twitches under pressure – but you don't need a video to see them doing it. The very different swaggers of Keating and Abbott are plainest in still photographs. You can see Keating's ambition in his cuffs and in his shoulders, Abbott's in his bandy legs. A good still image will always tell us as much as a moving one will, maybe more for being nearer to a distilled essence.

Look at Andrew Chapman's photographs of the men who ran the Coalition of the late 1970s. They speak directly of power. They have desired everything and now think they have attained it. Their fate awaits them. We see them before they are undone. Those who were there will be reminded in an instant, not only of the men but of an era, and of a drama whose last act had yet to be played out. Those who weren't there, but who want to know what it was like, will find in those photographs a fertile place to start.

Look at the photos of the young R. J. L. Hawke and the young Keating and see the perfect self-possession the best politicians always seem to have, and the rest of us can only wonder at. But then look at John Howard, and wonder how someone who so plainly lacks this quality could end up serving as Prime Minister for longer than either of them, longer than anyone else bar Robert Menzies. Look a bit longer and we might begin to see behind the oversize spectacles and the uncertain smile a desire just as fierce as that which drove his rivals, which fed on theirs and on their vanity. Look longer at the rivals and we might see traces of doubt.

Andrew Chapman has been photographing Australian politics for 40 years. The record he has left is a marvel of acumen and perseverance. The acumen speaks through the effect of the photos on the viewer: whether his subjects are farmers in their blasted landscapes or politicians in theirs, his photographs testify at once to human ambition and what Susan Sontag called in a famous essay on photography 'time's relentless melt'. The perseverance is in what it takes to get a collection like these.

For all but a few players, politics is suffused with dreary repetition and inconsequentiality. Like life in the trenches, most of it is spent waiting. There are great dramatic moments and great characters; but some of Andrew Chapman's most telling photographs are surely the product of waiting through those political droughts described by John Button: 'when nothing much happens . . . people are constantly on edge, waiting for the first hint of a political development and terrified of missing it when it comes'. Somewhere in that tense stillness hides the true nature of the political game, and by pointing his lens at it for 40 years, Andrew Chapman has left us with a priceless insight into our modern history and ourselves.

March 2015

The New Normal

> 'Now look, your grace,' said Sancho, 'what you see over there aren't giants, but windmills, and what seems to be arms are just their sails, that go around in the wind and turn the millstone.'
>
> 'Obviously,' replied Don Quixote, 'you don't know much about adventures.'

It was a bit like Don Quixote, and a bit like being trapped in one of those old cinemas that played the news on hourly cycles, the news being in general about floods and fires, sport and other excuses for self-congratulation, lifesavers, the Queen and Prince Philip. It was also a bit like being trapped in a B-movie: the kind in which we watched our hero struggle with an insidious exotic menace when just looking at him told us half the problem was likely in his head. Like Cervantes', the plots were preposterous, but unnerving just the same. That's the thing about B-movies: often they stay with us long after we've forgotten the A ones.

And then suddenly we were out of this black-and-white world and in the sunlight. As it always does at such times, for a moment the real world felt stranger than the unreal one we had just departed, as if we'd left The Blob for Gigi. The country seemed bathed in a sort of furry Menzian radiance, and to be going backwards and forwards at the same time. As things came into focus, two venerable professors talked on ABC Radio about the new normal that Malcolm Turnbull had just ushered in, and assured us it was real. In the sunshine of that Sunday morning, to be alive was, if not exactly heaven, much more heavenly than it had been.

Odd to the last, the fallen leader saw out his last hours in Kirribilli House carousing with his old school chums. The sight of the former Prime Minister greeting the lads at the door might have been taken as yet another sign that the man had never left the boy behind. But it also spoke of the price he put on loyalty, and, by implication, his contempt for anyone who plied it at a discount. Here was the snake in Turnbull's Eden. Of course, the others cast out might also prove snaky, along with those who felt their faith betrayed or their judgement confounded. Then there were the potential snakes among those who simply loathed Malcolm Turnbull. As a veteran of the Rudd and Gillard ministries told me a fortnight before the overthrow, the Libs don't want Malcolm; they think he's their Kevin, and they're probably right. There is still time for that remark to prove prophetic, and on the chance that it might do so we should count egomania among the serpents Malcolm Turnbull must charm back into the basket.

Yes, there were snakes, but what is politics – or life on earth – without them? And who cares, when within minutes of the ballot there were such promising developments in vocabulary and sentence structure. In no time he was saying 'agile', and no doubt the word was music to managerial ears; for the rest of us it was a blessing that he sounded agile. You'd swear that he could speak and think at the same time, that he was an intelligent person who also could say intelligent things. Just five minutes of Turnbull's gentler, subtler cadences and Abbott's little era deliquesced like prickly pear before the cactoblastis moth. And the faint and eerie howl we heard, which was likely Andrew Bolt, did nothing to abate our hope.

That was the thing, hope. In the face of absurdity, hope sustains us, as Albert Camus said after a fashion. Politics throws up enough absurdities (and I'm not even thinking of George Brandis or Bronwyn Bishop) and needs no help in the matter.

Yet to the absurdity that is a natural condition of our existence the deposed Prime Minister always seemed determined to add more, and to make hope depend on our signing up to them. Under siege we were, from wind farms, refugees, climate science, budget emergencies, debt, deficit and a death cult. Only 'Team Australia' could save the citizenry. Everyone, including the national broadcaster and the Opposition, was to fall into line or risk the PM's boycott, or a silent unblinking stare, or something worse if necessary. And no questions about 'on water' matters. And so on.

Who knows if this bizarre, sub-Orwellian drama was an expression of the man's psychological need, or something he and his resident geniuses concocted for political advantage – or if the thing was both personal and political – but it did no one any good. He had imposed on us a regime of relentless slogans (or mantras, or messages, call them what you will) thought necessary for our education. 'Resonant phrases,' he says they were: as if 'debt and deficit', 'lifters not leaners' and 'stop the boats' deserved places in the Book of Common Prayer.

All this went to show how language fashions politics and the national mood. Belligerence begets belligerence, but also depression and resentment. Fearmongering begets fear, but also sullenness and disbelief. And slogans might as well be lies. They make politics as stupid and self-defeating as lies do. One can't debate in slogans. One can't hear in them. Nothing is explained by them. Slogans make a mockery of the 'conversations' that Joe Hockey so often called for, and of the democracy that all politicians reflexively extol.

Of course, better sentences can no more create jobs than a slogan can. Nor have they any purchase on the world's climate. They cannot be relied on to stop a slump in the housing market or head off a recession; will defeat neither ISIS nor Assad; will not create the economy we need in the 21st century, persuade a state government to act in anything but self-interest, or turn a bad policy in which you don't believe into a good one in which you do. They will not draw the teeth of the IPA, the radio hosts or the coal industry. Fine words will not of themselves win an election, create a republic or rout a prejudice, and too many of them at the one time are certain to produce antipathy. We wait to see how long the new Prime Minister can last before he gives up and utters his first slogan – if indeed the country can any longer be governed without them.

But for the time being, at least, Turnbull promises a language in which to think about the problems, confront ideology with argument and enlist the capacious centre. Already he has ministers – even Barnaby Joyce – talking with more intelligence about policies, even with a hint of changing them. He has them talking more about the future and less about the threats to it. If they keep it up, they might find that 'innovation' is more than a mantra to be uttered at every press conference, and that it starts right in their own portfolios.

All the snakes aside, the biggest risk for the Prime Minister is contained in that management word 'agile' and the example of Don Quixote: if through the enchantments of business he mistakes the country for a corporation and his new job for a CEO's, his own loquacity might mutate and strangle him, and the promise of a new politics with a modern glow will turn into the same old newsreel we've been watching for a decade.

The Monthly, November 2015

From *Worst Words*

matrix management structure

Structure for a university.

> 'ITS last year introduced the *matrix management structure* and the service owner *model* (i.e. portfolio-based) to provide clear management *accountabilities,* an agile response to *change* and *greater focus* on *delivering* superior service and *value* to the University. The decision taken will facilitate this by giving service owners *greater* ability to influence required *business outcomes,* noting that service owners are ultimately *accountable* for *ensuring delivery* of service *changes* to their respective *client* groups. This decision, along with many other *changes* we are going through in ITS, is vitally important if we are to keep pace with our changing business environment and *evolving customer* needs.'

In an email from the Executive Director IT and
Chief Information Officer at a Melbourne university,
April 2012

mentoring moment

One of these: '*A mentoring moment* is an intersubjective coming to know in *dialogue* that *engages* unitary humans in a *transformative process*, confirming beliefs and *values* in creatively imagining and launching projects . . . The human-to-human *engagement* in a *mentoring moment* is unpredictable and everchanging as *value* priorities shift with different experiences and new understandings' (Nursing Science Quarterly).

meritocracy

A social and organisational arrangement based on the idea that merit, rather than inheritance, nepotism, brute force or rat cunning should determine status, power and wealth. It is very much in favour among the relative few who have status, power and wealth, warmed as they must be by the sense that their status and influence (and every dollar of their handsome incomes) have been well-earned. The powerless must live with the sense that they too have earned their status, a stigma that feudalism did not confer on the poor.

Just why the meritocratic (and inevitably smug) elites would not 'harden into a new social class' (in the words of the inventor of the term) and consolidate their power through nepotism, cunning and various forms of inherited privilege is not very well explained.

> 'With the coming of the meritocracy, the now leader-less masses were partially disfranchised; as time has gone by, more and more of them have been disengaged, and disaffected to the extent of not even bothering to vote. They no longer have their own people to represent them.'
>
> Michael Young, author of *The Rise of the Meritocracy* (1958), *Guardian*, 29 June 2001

'It must be what Blair thinks. How else can he believe we can create a genuine *meritocracy* without nobbling private education – one of the main mechanisms by which the upper-middle classes retain their stranglehold on wealth and power? Blair's view must be that the current system is already not far off being *meritocratic* and that, generally speaking, the top positions are already populated by the most talented. The fact that these people invariably turn out to be privately educated upper-middle class folk is down to the fact that the lower orders are, generally speaking, congenitally less able.'

Stephen Law blog, 20 May 2008

'The American system works because we believe in merit. This isn't an aristocracy, it's a *meritocracy*. By and large, talent and hard work are rewarded, whatever one's background happens to be.'

Yash Gupta, Johns Hopkins Carey Business School

'We must find ways to mobilize employees around the firm's *vision*, to then *achieve alignment* with, and *commitment* to those central *values*. We must develop a leadership mind-set that embraces *meritocracy* as a vital force in how we improve our firms, and lives.'

Omni Consulting Group

'[Amazon] Employees say that the Bezos ideal, a *meritocracy* in which people and ideas compete and the best win, where co-workers challenge one another 'even when doing so is uncomfortable or exhausting', as the leadership principles note, has turned into a world of frequent combat.'

New York Times, 17 August 2015

'The Vanderbilts have asked us up for tea.
We'd go but they're not *meritocracy*.
No siree.'

2015

Looking Fear in the Eye, on the Phone

In every one of the 116 years since the nation was born Australia has been content to walk in the shadow of great and powerful friends: first as a branch office of the British Empire and steadfast representative of the white race in Asia, later as an equally stalwart ally of the United States. For decades, fear of communism and the menacing hordes to the north guaranteed Australia's fealty to Washington. The practical and ideological supports of the alliance merged happily in the cause of freedom.

Not anymore. The end of the Cold War did not end the alliance, but the case for it is no longer so easily made. The Domino Theory simplified the world: the War on Terror makes it murkier. And China, Australia's primal fear, is now vital to her future prosperity. Each year it grows harder to navigate a path for the alliance, and the words that once galvanised it no longer so readily apply.

For the comforting reassurance that comes with being Washington's dutiful deputy, Australia pays a price. Along with the blood and treasure expended on imperial battlefields, a degree of self-possession must be sacrificed. The security and convenience of walking in the shadow of the sheriff is accompanied by a debilitating sense of being America's 'long-time poodle-dog ally', to use Bill Maher's recent description. In such a relationship the weaker party is tempted to shore up its identity by exaggerating the influence it has, or by singing a descant to the anthems of the stronger partner, as if both countries were answering a 'call to greatness', or some other demand of destiny dreamed up by David Brooks.

As anyone who has worked in a political office knows, speaking to the powerful is a skill, and that speaking unwelcome *truth* to them is a skill of a very high order. This is only partly because many powerful people are insecure, ill-tempered and unreasonable, many have been corrupted by power, and for all their success in politics, not a few are stupid. It is also because the meaning and purpose of power is force. However enlightened or kindly power might be, force arises from it. Those subjected to force become something less than themselves: as Simone Weil said in her famous essay on this subject, very often they become corpses.

While we might never know exactly what was said when the Australian Prime Minister Malcolm Turnbull spoke with Donald Trump on the phone recently, we can be sure that the force was with Trump. With Turnbull lay the hope that he would come out of the conversation much as he went into it and not as a corpse or a poodle. But hope is not enough when you're presenting the President of the United States – *any* President – with an unpalatable fact.

The fact in question was a deal between Turnbull and Barack Obama signed five days after Donald Trump won the US election. Obama agreed that the US would take 1200 of the 2000 asylum seekers who have been languishing for years in camps administered by Australia on Nauru and Manus Island in Papua New Guinea. The people in these hellholes had been intercepted by Australian naval vessels as they tried to cross from transit camps in Indonesia to the northern coast of Australia in dilapidated fishing boats. Many hundreds on these desperate voyages had drowned. The island camps were set up when the Australian government declared that no one arriving in this unauthorised way would ever be settled in Australia, and directed the navy to turn back all boats. The boats promptly stopped, but the policy and the camps have poisoned Australian politics and, in some quarters, its reputation.

For Malcolm Turnbull the Obama deal was a chance to drain the abscess without looking like anything less than resolute on 'illegals' or 'queue jumpers'. Since coming to the Prime Ministership in the guise of a genuine liberal, Turnbull has been mauled by the right wing of the governing coalition, not least by the man he ousted as PM, Tony Abbott. An election Turnbull called last year to win more legitimacy left him with less of it – a one-seat majority in the House of Representatives, a Senate with a new cohort of xenophobes and Trump admirers under the banner of One Nation, and an ever more persistent need to satisfy Abbott's crew of sea-green reactionaries who have recently taken to calling themselves 'the deplorables'.

For a Prime Minister on the skids, the deal with Obama was a godsend. For Donald Trump, it was 'dumb', the 'worst deal ever'. He had a point. Just as he bans entry to people from seven predominantly Muslim countries, he learns that Obama has signed up to take 'thousands' of mainly Muslim asylum seekers, many of them from the same seven countries. Faced with the exquisite predicament of having to ask the world's most powerful human being to accept the world's worst deal, Turnbull tried to find common ground in the spirit of the alliance and the rules of business. (Before entering politics he made a fortune at Goldman Sachs.) A 'deal is a deal', we're told he ventured. But Trump didn't buy it.

Later, while Turnbull invoked old protocols and refused to disclose what was said in the call – except that as always in a friendship as 'mature' and 'robust' as ours, etc, it was 'frank and forthright' – the President's office let it be known that the conversation was the 'worst' the President had had and that it ended badly. The President followed up with a tweet: he would be looking hard at the deal, and should he decide to honour it, the detainees would be subjected to 'extreme vetting'. Then the White House referred to the Prime Minister as 'President' of Australia, and by the time the press secretary called him Mr Trumble and Mr Trunbull, and Bill Maher came up with the poodle, Malcolm Turnbull's humiliation was pretty well complete.

US commentators, politicians and the regiment of American satirists rounded on Trump for attacking a loyal and harmless friend, and the Australian press, as they often do, made the reaction in the US to something involving Australia their main story. But more intriguing by far was the effect the phone call seemed to have on Turnbull. Worsted in an unwinnable battle with the world's greatest bully he went into the parliament and bullied the Leader of the Opposition in a tirade described by some as 'withering' and by others as 'vile'. That the gist of the attack concerned his opponent's 'sycophantic' friendship with a billionaire seemed to offer a clue to his motives and to the psychological damage the phone call had done. 'I stand up to billionaires,' he later told the press. 'I look them in the eye and, when I need to, I take them on.' It seemed to prove that Malcolm Turnbull had indeed shrunk to something less than himself.

Since then Abbott has intensified his attack on him, and in a manoeuvre surely inspired by Donald Trump's belligerent example, Senator Cory Bernardi has defected from the government and formed a new 'Conservative Party'. Now trailing in the polls by a greater margin than his predecessor ever did, Malcolm Turnbull has taken to blaming journalists who focus too much attention on personalities. So far he has not used the term 'fake news'.

Arrangements are now being made for Turnbull and Trump to shake hands on the deck of a US battleship in New York harbour in the first week of May. The pretext for the photo opportunity is the 75th anniversary of the US Navy's success in the Battle of the Coral Sea, an action which Australians have long believed saved them from Japanese invasion. It is sure to be said that the handshake symbolises the importance and enduring strength of the alliance, and how straight talking is the hallmark of all great friendships – but the possibility remains that the President will break Turnbull's wrist, and that will symbolise something else entirely.

Maclean's magazine, Canada, February 2017

American Berserk

> It will be recognised with slavery and the Civil War. It will be recognised with World War One and the Great Depression. It will be recognised with World War Two. It will be recognised with the 1950s, and the red baiting and the witch hunting. It will be recognised with the tragedy of Vietnam, as a period of confusion and disaster.
>
> Paul Soglin, mayor of Madison, Wisconsin

The election of Donald Trump – even the *nomination* of Donald Trump – and events since his inauguration are like nothing that has ever happened in the United States. It unseats the habit of our minds to believe that whatever happens *had* to happen. To borrow a word from Philip Roth, it 'defatalizes' things. Donald Trump becomes President of the United States. As one commentator said, it sounds like the logline for a high-concept movie. One of the many reasons why he won is that millions of Americans could not take the concept seriously. Now they have to take the fact seriously.

And yet the uncanniest thing is the sense that Trump's election is a simulacrum for all manner of events imagined or foretold that hover in the back rows of our consciousness – way back from the daily flow of news, spin, messaging and commentary. A scam artist, an ignoramus, a professional liar, a colossal and malignant narcissist, a vulgarian, a casino operator, a serial bankrupt – a Roy Cohn–mentored billionaire with deep Mob connections – is in the White House. Has there ever been a more American presidency? What took them so long?

For devotees of H. L. Mencken, these are days of vindication. In a presidential election, he declared around 1920, 'all the odds were on the man who is, intrinsically, the most devious and mediocre'. It was the logic of democracy, he said, that the people would one day get their heart's desire and put a 'downright moron' in the White House. While understandable, the widespread belief that George W. Bush fulfilled Mencken's prophecy has proved premature. In the extent and depth of his deviousness and mediocrity – in the sheer grandeur of it – Donald Trump is to Dubya as Mighty Mouse is to Mickey. Dubya was just a shallow son of the political elite, one easily manipulated by tough guys like Dick Cheney and Donald Rumsfeld. (Though his manifest inadequacy did not stand in the way of re-election, let us never forget.) But Trump is the King Kong of shallowness: the only deep things about him are his roots in the American psyche. He brings forth not just the pout, the hair and the ties, but the greed, indulgence and psychotic menace of the 'indigenous American berserk' – to call on Roth again. The mistake of his opponents – including the satirists – has been to focus on his otherness: in truth he's dredged straight from the brute material of American culture.

No one ever went looking for George W. Bush in the high reaches of literature. But people are looking for Trump in these places, and finding him. 'Trump is Tom Buchanan farcically playing Gatsby,' Sidney Blumenthal wrote in a recent *London Review of Books*. (Blumenthal also found Trump – the old, real, wheeler-dealer Trump – satirised as the 'short-fingered vulgarian' in *Spy* magazine 25 years ago.) Others have gone to Sinclair Lewis' *It Can't Happen Here* for his literary likeness, or to films including *Batman, Who Framed Roger Rabbit, Bulworth, The Manchurian Candidate* and *Sweet Smell of Success*, or to the comic book *Judge Dredd*. When Roth was asked whether the Charles Lindbergh he presented in his 2004 novel *The Plot Against America* is Trump's forebear, he said that Lindbergh was too substantial a person to be compared with a mere 'con artist' like Trump. *The Plot Against America* is uncannily prescient just the same, and not only because in his inauguration speech Trump borrowed Lindbergh's 'America First' slogan, or because in the novel Lindbergh beats Franklin D. Roosevelt to the presidency by animating his personal brand, flying all over the heartland in the *Spirit of St Louis*, just as Trump beat Hillary Clinton descending from the heavens in his own Trump plane. The most intriguing parallel is the way Roth's counterfactual novel matches so precisely the sense we have that with Trump we are inhabiting a counterfactual world. No doubt the election has given *The Plot Against America* a second life in the bookshops. Herman Melville's final novel, *The Confidence-Man*, published 160 years ago, might also get a boost. Melville's con man sells get-rich schemes to passengers on a Mississippi riverboat. Like every good salesman he exploits the need of every mug for hope. Every mug on the boat, with the exception of the barber, takes his bait. Roth says he is Trump's most convincing precursor.

There's another difference with Bush Jr: nothing he did as president, including the massive expansion of homeland security and the surveillance system he established to spy on private citizens, made George Orwell's *Nineteen Eighty-Four* a number-one bestseller. But while Trump was sitting in his 5th Avenue tower, picking his cabinet of corporate moguls, tweeting away about anything he saw on Fox News or Breitbart (thus is Mencken's Morondom expanded) and issuing executive orders, that's what happened on Amazon.

With one sweep of the new president's right hand, he would cut federal funding to cities providing 'sanctuary' to undocumented migrants; with another sweep he would cut environmental regulations; with another, financial regulations; with another, funding for international organisations that perform abortions; and with another, block entry at American airports to people from seven selected Muslim-majority countries. This last move appeared to honour both his campaign promise of 'a total and complete shutdown of Muslims entering the United States' and his desire for continuing friendship with Saudi Arabia and other Middle Eastern nations in which he has business interests – but, to many observers, was as likely to please jihadists and Islamic State recruiters as much as it did the millions of American citizens (40 per cent or more) who fear a terrorist attack above all other threats to their country and themselves. And in case their worry was superseded by something more likely to actually happen, Kellyanne Conway, Trump's counsellor, aided by social media, Fox News and various radio hosts, reminded them of the great, though fictional, Bowling Green Massacre that terrorists had perpetrated. Equally fictional terrorist attacks, including a big one in Atlanta, were cited by the White House press secretary, Sean Spicer. Meanwhile, in a further sign of resistance from pre-Trumpian Americans, Hannah Arendt's 66-year-old, 600-page *The Origins of Totalitarianism* sold out on Amazon.

Mencken did not like democracy. Even late into the 1930s, when totalitarianism was at its atrocious peak, he did not like it. How could he like government by the people when he believed most people were stupid? The vote, the 'maudlin herding after rogues and mountebanks', gave to the citizen 'a sense of vast and mysterious power', 'a feeling . . . that he is genuinely running things' and 'a conviction that he is somehow wise', all of which was hopelessly wrong-headed, but satisfying to senators, archbishops 'and other such magnificoes' – and satisfying therefore to Donald Trump. Give him credit: when he spoke in the campaign it didn't matter what he'd said about Mexican judges or grabbing pussy; when he told them change was coming and that he was going to get even on their behalf for what had been done to them and the lies they'd been told, white American men and women (and not a few Latinos) felt something of that mysterious power. When Hillary Clinton spoke, they felt the power ebbing – or rather they felt their chronic powerlessness all the more acutely. When she spoke it was as if to shout – 'More of the same!'

For Mencken the entire worthwhile heritage of humanity depended upon the existence of an embattled minority that appreciated Beethoven and understood Nietzsche. On the knuckle-dragging fundamentalist mob outside the minority's cultural walls, Mencken showered hundreds of devastating epithets. For calling the white working class (including the non-working part of it) 'a basket of deplorables', Hillary Clinton must at least be given credit for originality. She could have borrowed from Mencken and called them 'morons', or 'immortal vermin'. But 'deplorables' it was. Consider – at a time when inequality is grotesque and worsening, a woman who demands a quarter of a million dollars for a 40-minute speech labels people who have not seen a wage rise in a quarter of a century 'deplorables'. The word will haunt her to the grave. It will outlive her. People will be quoting it in a hundred years' time, possibly as a marker of American decline.

Of course Hillary Clinton did not mean that the entire white working class was deplorable, but she must have known that the elements she didn't mean would be easily convinced that she did. It was a bit like calling Trump a misogynist – over and over. A lot of what goes down as outrageous misogyny among the cosmopolitan elites of Manhattan, where 88 per cent of people voted against Trump, is the natural (if not Godly) order of things in much of the American heartland, where 61 per cent of white working-class women voted for him, and 34 per cent for Clinton. Had she managed to get just 50 per cent of that vote, she would now be president. It was not identity but class that counted. Trump saw that and so did Bernie Sanders. Sanders would have taken Wisconsin and Michigan in a breeze.

Tired though it is after nearly two centuries of common usage, 'white trash' as Harriet Beecher Stowe defined it carries an essential truth that a 'basket of deplorables' does not: namely, that the 'trash' are defined by their loathing of federal authority and their fealty to the institutions that exploit and degrade them. The white trash of the old southern plantations would find this much in common with the Tea Partiers who began scaling the Capitol walls after Obama took the White House in 2008 and the hordes who have just voted for Trump in what the new President humbly declared 'the single greatest movement in the history of this country'. For the Tea Party, federal authorities are the great enemy – *remote* authority is their hook back to the Revolution – even though the federal authorities pay their welfare cheques, while Republican state governments screw their unions, attack their voting rights and keep wages pitifully low.

Inequality and unfairness do not upset Tea Partiers and Trump voters anything like as much as what they perceive to be attacks on their freedom. How dare Washington make laws for the nation at large: inflict a national health scheme on them (35 per cent of the population rank Obamacare among their worst fears); tax them and regulate them; secularise their schools; impose migrants, feminism, abortion and LGBT rights on them; tell them where they can graze their cattle; what words they can and cannot use to describe blacks and Latinos and women; lecture them and threaten to restrict the type and number of their guns. A recent national survey found that while guns killed 301,797 people in the US between 2005 and 2015 (and terrorist attacks killed 94), it wasn't guns but *restrictions* on guns and ammunition that was, equally with 'being a victim of terror', Americans' fourth-greatest fear.

The heartland is different, simple as that. The divide is as old as the nation itself, as old as Hamilton and Jefferson. It still threatens Lincoln's 'mystic chords of memory' and 'chorus of the union'. It was on that divide, greatly exacerbated as it is now by three decades of neoliberal impoverishment, that Trump built his success. John Feffer, a foreign policy commentator and author of a dystopian novel called *Splinterlands*, imagines Trump unshackling the states that gave him the presidency – 'America B' – from federal authority and creating by the beginning of his second term a United States 'in name only'.

That's one possibility out of many, and might be of a piece with Perry Miller's observation that Melville's *The Confidence-Man* was 'a long farewell to national greatness'. The other possibilities include impeachment (but probably not before Republicans get what they want out of him), voluntary retirement on grounds of ill health, and, building upon a successful job-creation program, the same eight years Ronald Reagan and Bush Jr got despite the early odds. There is also the possibility that Trump alone can inspire the kind of popular resistance that will bring the Democrats to their senses. There is the possibility of a mafia state, of rapidly accelerating national decline, and the possibility that, as it did with Richard Nixon and as it has always done, the Constitution will prevail.

The Monthly, March 2017

New Tricks

> He who gnaweth a cow's horn gnaweth in vain and shorteneth his life; for he grindeth away his teeth, yet his belly is empty.

So said an Indian prophet, we are told. Astute as his observation was, to be fair to inveterate gnawers the example of a dog will tell you how hard it is to give the thing up once you've started in on it. It's not for nutrition that dogs go on chewing a cow's horn long after the last flecks of blood and viscera have gone, but for the narcotic effect of the chewing. I have seen them: a dog with a cow's horn falls into a kind of stupor from which no amount of shouting, whistling or clod-throwing can release it. I have seen the same thing – we all have – among the power elites.

For three decades now, the politicians and their advisers, economists in both public and private spheres, many of the media wiseacres, and pretty well all our business leaders, including the most egregious rent-seekers, have had their jaws jammed round the idea that free markets are in every way beautiful, and that government, even of the most democratic kind, is the market's natural enemy and tends always to the horrid – even towards 'evil'. Call it what you will – economic rationalism, neoliberalism, trickle-down economics, monetarism, Friedmanism, Hayekism – this is the cow's horn of the political culture.

How else has the doctrine survived the madness performed in its name? Put aside the full-blown atrocities of the ideology in practice that Naomi Klein describes in *The Shock Doctrine*. Forget the criminal tragedy of Russia that gave the world Vladimir Putin. Forget the grotesque inequality that gave it Donald Trump. Forget the 2008 financial debacle. Leave out altogether, if you will, the example of the United States, where the doctrine evolved in partnership with the long campaign by corporations and 'libertarian' ideologues to reverse the New Deal and stamp out every other manifestation of Keynesian and liberal thinking. Forget the corporatisation and debasement of American democracy. As the American journalist Matt Taibbi said in a 2009 article about that 'great vampire squid wrapped around the face of humanity' Goldman Sachs, 'In a society governed passively by free markets and free elections, organized greed always defeats disorganized democracy.' But ignore this: pay no heed to recent indications that Goldman Sachs is already having as much influence in Trump's administration as it had in Obama's. And, leaving aside the fact that our Prime Minister is himself a Goldman Sachs man, think only of the local example.

How are your wages compared to ten years ago? How's your power bill looking? How are you getting on with the banks? Assured, are you, by their commitment to Corporate Social Responsibility and balancing the needs of customers and shareholders? Is life much better since all your services became 'contestable'? Not feeling a little gouged every time you walk through an airport or drive on a freeway or enrol in a course?

How's your debt going, keeping body and soul together? Any houses trickled down to you? Not feeling that despite regular smashed avocados you might be gently, almost imperceptibly, sinking into the realms of at least relative poverty? And politics: how's that looking? Dynamic, innovative, agile – or, in its pointless, inconsequential plots and bad acting, more like *Midsomer Murders* on 24/7 repeat?

Does anyone believe reducing the corporate tax rate from 30 per cent to 25 per cent over several years will yield all the 'competitiveness' of which the PM speaks, or the jobs, or that it will benefit anyone but their senior executives? Does anyone think cutting penalty rates will make the world a better place? Does anyone believe giveaways to business and takeaways from wage-earners will lead to Jobs and Growth? If we find it puzzling that so much of the daily political story is made up of matters that concern hardly anyone outside the hoary little legions who depend on them for nutriment, it might be because the economic debate has lost all inspiration and credibility. We are to be satisfied with a daily regimen of 'there are no quick fixes to the challenges we face', 'there are no overnight solutions' and 'it will take time to turn these issues around', and such occasional acts of less-than-electrifying dispatch as the government's recent instruction to the ACCC – to look into power prices and report back *in 15 months*. Whereupon the government – should it be the *same* government in 15 months – will consider what action, if any, should be taken 'to ensure markets are competitive and energy consumers . . . can have confidence in the reliability, security, pricing and terms and conditions of supply'.

Some of us recall the early days of economic rationalism, when it was a kind of religion, and converts spoke in economic tongues and apostates in whispers. To question the precepts of the new order was tantamount to confessing one's unworthiness. Parishioners and comrades who let it slip that they thought a political philosophy should draw on more fields of knowledge and experience than economics, and that not everything before the Great Economic Awakening lacked wisdom and intelligence, were self-evidently fossils of the ancien régime, counter-revolutionaries, infidels, Whitlamites. That is, until political necessity demanded some kind of compromise with doctrinal purity: a subsidy for the sugar industry to save a northern seat or two, something less than annihilation of the car industry to save them in Adelaide or Geelong. Here's a bit of drought relief; there's a bone for the environment.

The trouble with economic rationalists is not that they believe in free markets; rather, as fundamentalists, they cannot allow themselves to believe that anyone else does. In truth, pretty well everyone believes in them, but most folk also believe that societies, like life itself, are too complex, human needs too various and human nature too obnoxious to be left to private enterprise – commitments to the triple bottom line and Corporate Social Responsibility notwithstanding. As the examples of education and energy and employment go to show – along with child care, aged care, roads and roof insulation, to name a few of the responsibilities rendered corporate in recent years – some things just need regulation. Some, believe it or not, are better left in public hands. And to say that is not the same thing as saying you believe in a command economy – unless, that is, you think Bob Menzies ran a command economy.

It might be, rather, to say that the future belongs to the person or party who can offer up a compelling case for the *mixed* economy that in one form or another we have always had. To get things started, Labor could do worse than to announce in words no one can mistake that it is done with economic rationalism now and forever. Malcolm Turnbull's conditioned instincts will tell him to call it crude and outrageous populism – it's the econocrats' equivalent of what Stalinists called 'reactionary tendencies' – and he'll add that it betrays Labor's great achievements under Hawke and Keating. But they weren't pure and he's not either. He should take one last look at the US election and then offer Labor a unity ticket. Let them all note what happened when Trump and Bernie Sanders both recommended letting go of the neoliberal bone. Trump bowled over the candidate who had only pretended to let it go, and, according to a Fox News poll, right now Sanders is probably the most admired national politician in the United States. Fawning to popular prejudice, quailing before opinion polls, inciting fear, encouraging delusions and hysteria, abandoning your principles to save your political skin. Populism has all these unattractive faces, and one other – sometimes it's an expression of righteous anger, of resistance. Populists, like the people they appeal to, are capable of being right.

Quite apart from the prospect of pulling the debate back to what used to be called the main game, and offering the prospect of finding a new coherent narrative for the country, renouncing the doctrine, clearing it out from the debate and the language, would actually free politicians from the pointless, barely endurable hypocrisy and doublespeak that balancing corporate and democratic ideology requires.

Let us take as our models for the new order two old dogs from the existing one.

In late March this year, after the new ACTU leader, Sally McManus, declared her belief that the neoliberal 'experiment' had 'run its course', the chief political architect of that experiment, Paul Keating, said that she was right. In earlier days 'liberal' economics had dramatically lifted real wages and personal wealth, he said, but since 2008 it has 'run into a dead end and has had no answer to the contemporary malaise'.

A fortnight earlier, John Hewson, once the most zealous neoliberal in the country, wrote a column that in 1992 would have made the basis of a speech for Keating: the Keating who in that year made like a democratic socialist and with some justification painted Hewson as a heartless and unreasoning fanatic. Too often the makers of public policy forget that they 'are attempting to improve our society, not just our economy', Hewson wrote. 'Do we want to build a society where we consciously create an underclass . . . a group of people who cannot hope to share in the life, ambitions and achievements of the rest of our society?' Talk about a bleeding heart! Then he went after privatisation, the banks, the miners, monopolies, multinational tax dodging and unfair wages. In conclusion, Professor Hewson said he hadn't 'suddenly woken up a socialist' but was rather 'still basically an economist'. And one who believed in markets. 'But I want them to work for the greater benefit of our whole society, not just to benefit a few.'

Sorry, John, but judged by your old neoliberal canons you *have* woken up a socialist – or at least a social democrat, or someone in the very broad centre of Australian public opinion since Federation, and at all events a natural fit for a Labor Party where you might be usefully set to work writing a manifesto for the new order. *Fightback* would be a good title.

The Monthly, May 2017

There It Is Again: Or a Short History of Cant

> **Cant:** from Latin *cantare*, to sing.
> 3. A whining pretension to goodness, in formal and affected terms. 4. Barbarous jargon
>
> Samuel Johnson, *Dictionary*

> Once he had been dragged into the bush, the lion with its coarse tongue would lick off his skin, drink his blood, and then, leisurely, usually starting with his feet, eat him.
>
> Peter Beard, *The End of the Game*

Among all the ways to leave the world – ways not invented by humankind, that is, *natural* ways – to be eaten alive must be just about the worst. And imagine you're one of the poor blighters working for peanuts on a railway in southern Africa, lying out on the veldt at night, not knowing when the 'abominated jaws' might seize you. Did human ears ever hear a more terrible sound than the ravening lions' roar?

Neuroimaging carried out on animals early this century showed that fear activated the midbrain – the para hippocampus, the thalamus and so on – while *de*activating much of the frontal cortex, the hypothalamus and other regions. Among the parts activated by fear were those which are also switched on by dire need for air and water, the primordial parts: the parts *de*activated were in general the parts that make reasoning possible. Anger, naturally enough seeing that it's a primordial emotion, showed up in a pattern very like that of fear.

Sixty years ago when unlit towns spread no light into the landscape and country nights were darker, the westerly ripped up the valley and battered the old weatherboards of our house on the hill. At other times the air was still and the drizzle drifted down in silence. Thalamus glowing, frontal cortex kaput, I lay in the perfect blackness of my bedroom and listened for man-eaters.

The critical moment, the one that might decide our fate, is that which falls between the first sign and the second: the first tells us something may be there, the second tells us that probably it *is* there – which leaves us to decide *what* it is and what to do about it. For excellent reasons of survival, fear reaches a rat's amygdala in 12 milliseconds, and I doubt it took longer with me. How is one to judge in an instant what is commonplace and what not, what harmless and what deadly? How to be prudent but not timid; brave but not stupid? Of such deliberations my childhood was made. And so, possibly, were *homo sapiens*.

Of course that footfall I heard outside my window was not a lion come to eat me alive. Nor was it the Demon of the Abyss, or some rival clan planning to kill me and kidnap my sister. But it might have been a couple of demented escapees from the prison on French Island 20 miles away, or town delinquents on a killing spree. That voice in the whistling wind and the creaking branches of the cedars was likely just the bull bellowing his desire, unless it was God calling me to be his evangelist – not calling, *demanding* with menaces. If none of those parties, probably it was some repulsive thing just arrived from space and eating people whole.

We need fear. It's necessary for our survival, and therefore an engine of our evolution. Before stepping into a thicket the more sensible early humans imagined a man-eater lurking there, and thus survived. Before they lit a fire in a cave, and round it gave birth to a greatly enlarged frontal cortex and civilisation, some of them must have imagined how nice it would be to sit and warm their hands and talk. But when the fire had died, they must have imagined – as I did when ours had – the enemies that prowled outside. Fear and imagination are of a piece. The stuff of nightmares is the same stuff that keeps us alive and gives us a taste of both wisdom and baloney.

The solution – though fallible and often dependent on negotiations with the gods (another offspring of fear, surely) – was to identify patterns. (It so happens, at least according to Freud, that our first fear is that of being born, and it is heralded by a pattern of contractions.) Our hearing, vision and sense of smell were feeble to those of predatory animals. We were slower, weaker; pathetically inferior in tooth and claw, as we were in climbing and burrowing. But we had a brain with which to learn the habits of our enemies and prey. We learned to distinguish the sound of a lion padding about at the cave's entrance from that of a passing ibex or angel. In the same manner we could separate familiar voices and friendly footfalls from threatening ones, and the screech of a curlew from an enemy imitating it to disguise a message to his colleagues. We learned to read the signs. A sign being 'something by knowing which we know something more', we stood a chance of getting to know how to overcome our woeful inferiority and exercise dominion over all the fangs of Nature.

Before exercising my own dominion over them, I learned to cope with fear by silently reciting *The Owl and the Pussycat;* and if that didn't work, the *Apostles' Creed*. As if to a drumbeat I would chant my way through Kipling's *If,* a framed copy of which gathered dust on the dressing table, or the words of *Galway Bay,* all of which I find I still know. It was another tactic to tell myself a story in which I was the hero, a person of exemplary courage and flair, and not the trepid child quaking between the blankets. To make myself a worthy member of the human race, I made myself up. Thus I discovered the usefulness of cant.

It must have been the same in the cave. To drive out fear they sang, or chanted as people do in cathedrals and the animals do in *Animal Farm*. The art of song was born. And at day's end they told stories. From what happened on the hunt, the things they saw, the frights they got and the fear they conquered, they made what Yuval Noah Harari calls the 'narrating self' – a delusional and dreadfully destructive animal, and the only one to believe in things that do not exist outside its imagination. We are ourselves a kind of invention, a primitive form of artificial intelligence soon to be replaced by a more sophisticated form. For Harari says the great journey of *homo sapiens* (lasting about ten seconds on the evolutionary clock) is about to end, and the era of robots about to begin. It is a telling reminder of our true nature and of our origins, that this kind of information, like that relating to global warming or the prospect of nuclear war, activates scarcely a thalamus while a bump in the night still lights them up everywhere.

As usual we can only wait and see if those with the finest frontal cortexes, including the many who design the things that point to our annihilation, will be smart enough (or *inclined* enough) to save us. But as we wait for the end, if the end it is to be, some people may be tempted to look away from their smartphones for long enough to ponder their beginning. While the study of palaeontology will help, there is another way. Much as scientists can 'hear an echo' of the Big Bang of 14 billion years ago and through giant telescopes see its faint glow in microwave background radiation, we might hear echoes of humankind's beginnings in language.

Listen to the affectations and numberless deceits of politics, commerce and the media; the dumb certitudes, the posturing, the simpering apologias, the cant that 'stops up the mouth of enquiry'. We might wonder if the daily flood of self-narration – the 'narcotic narcissism', in Toni Morrison's words – does not faintly reverberate with the ancient effort to keep fear at bay. Stay listening, and in your mind's eye (your primary visual cortex) you might see dimly the ancestral bully who first turned the lion outside into his own instrument of terror, and still rules us with it when he can.

In Chekhov's short story, *Ward No. 6*, Ivan Gromov finds the familiar, banal and crushing patterns of daily life suddenly becoming signs of imminent persecution and imprisonment. The story goes to show how fine the line is between the common interpretation of things and the heretical or mad; and, seeing that Gromov ends up in the living death of a lunatic asylum, how much is at stake. Anyone who tries to write about society or politics can profit from this example. One at least starts from the premise that the truth is only sometimes in appearances. There are patterns beneath the patterns, and that's where we'll find the best story and possibly the real one, if not the evolutionary design itself. But remembering that one is part of the same design, and as much as every human being and the birds that sing in the morning, as prone to cant, we should leave some room for laughing.

September 2017

Endnotes

1 In this context a report that Mr Ashcroft's advance staff asked Dutch officials in The Hague to make sure that when the Attorney General visited there were no tabby (US = *calico*) cats in the region of his rooms is interesting. Tabby cats are believed by some Christian fundamentalists to be satanic agents. Ashcroft's people insist there is no truth in the report, but once you've seen him singing nothing will reassure you.

2 www.cnn.com/video/us/2002/02/25/ashcroft.sings.wbtv.med.html

3 In which 18-to-25-year-olds are instructed in 'deference to authority, Biblical memorization, prophesy and miracle healing'. Three years; no dating in the first year.

4 Geoffrey Dunn, *The Lies of Sarah Palin: The Untold Story Behind Her Relentless Quest for Power*, St Martin's Press, New York, 2011. Joe McGinniss, *The Rogue: Searching for the Real Sarah Palin*, Crown, New York, 2011.

5 *Guardian*, 8 November 2011.

6 *Australian Universities: A Portrait of Decline* (www.australianuniversities.id.au). When I say published, it is an ebook. Dr Meyers was unable to find a willing conventional publisher.

7 'The parameters listed in this document were amended directly from the global parameters circulated in late 2011 from the University's central WMS project team,' it seems.

8 It was a frustrated senior CSIRO scientist who showed me one of these forms.

Acknowledgements

Acknowledgements

For aid of all kinds over the past two decades I owe thanks to more people than I can name, foremost among them my acute and generous publisher (encourager, fixer and friend) at Random, Meredith Curnow.

Also, her incomparable predecessor, Jane Palfreyman. My editor on this and other Random House projects, Patrick Mangan. Helen Smith, as always. Morry Schwartz, Chris Feik, Nick Feik, John van Tiggelen, Ben Naparstek and Sally Warhaft and the rest of the team at *The Monthly*, past and present. My agents, Jo Butler, Sophie Hamley, Sadie Chrestman, Jane Cameron and the late, unforgettable, Rose Creswell.

Don Watson's writing has won many awards, including *The Age* Book of the Year (twice), the NSW Premier's, a Walkley, an Indie and the National Biography Award.